THE RITES OF WAR

THE RITES OF WAR

An Analysis of Institutionalized Warfare

Sue Mansfield

BELLEW PUBLISHING · London

Timor chant from HEAD HUNTING IN TIMOR AND ITS HISTORICAL IMPLICATIONS, by P. Middelkoop, Oceania Linguistic Monograph #8, 1963. Reprinted by permission of The University of Sydney, Australia.

Papago warrior chant from SINGING FOR POWER: The Song Magic of the Papago Indians of Southern Arizona by R. M. Underhill. Copyright © 1938 by the Regents of the University of California. Reprinted by permission of the University of California Press.

Mesopotamian penitential psalm from THE TREASURES OF THE DARKNESS: A History of Mesopotamian Religion, by T. Jacobsen, 1976. Reprinted by permission of Yale University Press, New Haven, Conn.

Quotes from THE SONG OF ROLAND, translated and edited by Dorothy L. Sayers, 1957. Reprinted by permission of Penguin Books, Harmondsworth, England.

Lines from THE COMEDY OF DANTE ALIGHIERI: PARADISE, translated by Dorothy L. Sayers and B. Reynolds, 1975. Reprinted by permission of Penguin Books, Aylesbury.

WAR REQUIEM music by Benjamin Britten. Copyright © 1962 by Boosey & Hawkes Music Publishers Ltd. Reprinted by permission.

WAR REQUIEM lyrics: The poems of Wilfrid Owen are reprinted by permission of New Directions Publishers, New York, N.Y.

"The Promised Land" © 1978 Bruce Springsteen. Used by permission.

"Sail Away" © 1972 WB MUSIC CORP. & RANDY NEWMAN. All Rights Reserved. Used by Permission.

TUMBLEWEEDS by Tom K. Ryan. © 1981 Field Enterprises, Inc. Courtesy of Field Newspaper Syndicate.

This edition first published in Great Britain in 1991 by
Bellew Publishing Company Limited
7 Southampton Place, London WC1A 2DR

Copyright © 1982 Sue Mansfield
New Preface and Chapter 14
copyright © 1991 Sue Mansfield

Sue Mansfield is hereby identified as the author of this work in accordance with section 77 of the Copyright, Designs and Patents Act 1988

All rights reserved. No part of this publication may be reproduced, stored in a retrieval system or transmitted, in any form or by any means, electronic, mechanical, photocopying, recording or otherwise without the prior permission of the publisher.

ISBN 0 947792 82 1

Printed and bound in Great Britain by Billing & Sons Ltd

For Jon Hart Olson,
priest and friend

love, wit, and courage

Contents

Acknowledgments / *ix*
Preface to the Second Edition / *xiii*
1. War and Human Nature / *1*
2. The Rites of War / *20*
3. The Neolithic Revenge / *41*
4. The Destruction of Chaos / *55*
5. Cultures of Greed / *70*
6. The Satisfaction of Guilt / *89*
7. Honor and Glory / *106*
8. Harrowing Hell / *127*
9. The Cadence of Time / *144*
10. The Danger of Fear / *167*
11. The Rage of Impotence / *188*
12. The Mega-Tantrum / *208*
13. Boundaries of Power / *232*
14. Of Machines, Bureaucrats and Outlaws / *243*

Source Notes / *261*
Bibliography / *273*
Index / *285*

Acknowledgments

The germ of the idea for this book first surfaced in 1971, when the attempt to teach a course on the history of women led me out of the narrow confines of my professional work as a military historian and introduced me to anthropological studies. From this sprang the intuition that there was a connection between the position of women in a society and the way that society made war. A sabbatical semester spent investigating psychological and sociological theories of aggression convinced me that gestalt psychology could provide a useful tool for exploring the connection. All of my free time since then has been dedicated to tracking down and giving concreteness (as well as an unexpected shape) to that hunch. This book is the result.

My hunt would have been impossible without the support of friends and colleagues. I am particularly grateful to John Rodman, Paul Shepard, June Shepard, Robert Albert, and Werner Warmbrunn, who were, in their different ways, part of the original stimulus. James Rogers also read part of the draft and contributed from his own special knowledge of intellectual history, while Allison Heisch and Joan Hartmann gave me valuable critical support. J. Glenn Gray, through his book *The Warriors,* also provided an inspiration and insight that has continuously informed and directed my own thinking. We met only once and corresponded sporadically, but one of the sorrows of the last few years stems from the fact that his untimely death means I will never be able to thank him again.

In a different vein, Allen Darbonne, my gestalt therapist from 1972 to 1975, helped me to self-awareness and whatever clarity of vision and good contact I have been able to achieve. It would have been impossible to tackle a work of this sort without the understanding and freedom I gained by working with him, while his own interested response to the whole range of human emotions has been a model for my own efforts. I must make it clear, however, that the explication of gestalt theory propounded in this book is my work and my responsibility, not his.

I also owe a special debt to the students who took experimental courses in The Ecology of Aggression and Women, Violence, and Self-Defense and argued briskly and creatively with me (and each other) every step of the way. David Carruthers, Sebastian Graeber, Lincoln Gardner, Cynthia Stead, Lark Loveday, Maggie Paul, Ella Pennington, and Carolyn Lyon, in particular stand out in my memory as involved and independent thinkers who helped make those semesters a truly communal learning experience.

Finally, the book simply could not have been written without the help of Pat Padilla and Polly Baker, who have typed and retyped this text innumerable times. It is testimony to their courage and grace that they were always cheerful, infinitely patient, and incredibly fast. They had also the sense to rebel when my search for perfection became simply silly.

Working with such potentially disturbing material (which had to be felt through in my guts, as well as thought through in my head) would have been terrifying in the absence of emotional help and comfort. David Brewer gave me love, companionship, and private space. Eleanor Anderson, Agnes Jackson, Tess Henry, Lucille Busby, and Michael Butler gave me unstinting friendship, while Jean Walton provided a sustaining model of courage and integrity. I am also particularly grateful that my mother, Fay M. Mansfield, and my uncle, Percia E. Miller, were determined to foster my independence and ability to stand on my own two feet, at the same time that they were living examples of the satisfaction provided by lives formed around humane principles and values, in which the need to get and spend had little priority or power. It is hard to imagine a more valuable heritage.

The dedication of this book already indicates the special role that Jon Olson, my priest and friend for the last fifteen years, has played in my life. He has also been intellectual godfather to this book. Our weekly, after-mass breakfasts have been a constant source of delight and learning as we ranged over every imaginable topic and the whole emotional spectrum. In particular, he generously acted as a widely read and unfrightened sounding board against which this book has been tested each step of the way. There was nothing I could not say to him—and nothing that might not be tossed back at me. The hope I have that life can indeed be integrated, creative, and joyful is sustained by the memory of our dialogues as a model of Being.

Preface to the Second Edition

It is just ten years since the first edition of this work left my hands. In the intervening decade, the world and my own perspectives have changed.

The collapse of the Cold War in the late 1980s, following as it did on both an arms race and growing peace, environmentalist and anti-nuclear movements, produced for most of us a sense of quiet euphoria and hope. It seemed for a time as if the desire for material plenty and "progress" could move entrenched bureaucracies onto peaceful and liberating paths. As even Ronald Reagan was forced to abandon his "evil empire" rhetoric, it seemed possible that the world might turn from sterile pursuits of violence to address the very real economic and social plights endured by much of the earth's population. There might, indeed, be a "peace dividend."

The haste, however, with which the world then declared war on a demonized Saddam Hussein has been both depressing and instructive. The underlying motivation for the Gulf Crisis, for example, was still anxiety: the long-standing Anglo-American fear that loss of control over, or access to, that oil-rich region would threaten Western "security needs." But that fear was no longer connected to the threat posed by a super-power like the Axis or the Communist bloc. It was created, instead, by a small, under-developed Third World nation whose leader had rejected his country's earlier role as a client-state and was seeking independent power. Resentment as well as fear fueled the violence. The ghosts of Anthony Eden and Nasser, old-fashioned colonialism and Arab nationalism hovered around the Thatcher-Bush confrontation with Saddam Hussein. The Northern versus Southern hemisphere, industrialized versus under-developed, "have" versus "have-not" nature of the actual conflict was only thinly disguised by the, normally ignored, resolutions of the United Nations.

Leaders of First World nations, moreover, found it difficult initially to provide an acceptable, emotional justification for the looming conflict. (The internal "have-nots," in particular, exhibited a deep suspicion about the value of exchanging "blood for oil.") Hence, Bush's desperate scramble for an acceptable public explanation of his policy. Unfortunately, the eventual and widespread Western acceptance of, and jubilation over, the Gulf War demonstrated that the human liking for war, as a ritual for resolving psychic dissonances and imposing symbolic order on the chaos of existence, had not abated.

Instead, as Saddam Hussein's forces crushed rebellious Shi'ites and Kurds under the very eyes of the troops who thought they had destroyed the "new Hitler," Bush and other world leaders found themselves under public pressure to "do something," to intervene again. Since the alternative to tolerating "the evil one," appeared to be either long-term involvement in a civil war (like earlier ones in Vietnam, Algeria or Afghanistan?) or substantially increased power for an equally "suspect" Iran, they have so far declined to act. Thus, the war may have been "glorious," but the peace is likely to be messy.

We have been faced again with the fact that (in the words of George F. Will, a very conservative American columnist) "wars sow disorders that last 20 times longer than the wars do...[while] their therapeutic value — making people [and leaders] 'feel good' — is evanescent."[1] Hence, I think, the renewed interest in the psychological theories I posited in 1981-82.

In the intervening decade, my own interests have shifted to a form of warfare closely connected to the underlying tensions present in the Gulf crisis: guerrilla warfare. My earlier avoidance of the topic was occasioned primarily by a theoretical constraint. Guerrilla wars do not conform to the framework I developed for analyzing more conventional and clearly institutionalized forms of warfare. Since they have occurred in a variety of historical settings, they cannot be explained by the shifts in family and socialization structures occasioned by shifts in economic practice. As a result, I have moved away from Gestalt psychology as a tool of analysis. A new, final chapter now discusses the different historical and psychological processes which precipitate guerrilla wars, as well as the mythic meaning of this form of violence.

Some of my original suggestions as to how humans could escape their addiction to war — such as incorporating women in the armed forces — now seem naive. Though the creation of greater international social and political justice seems increasingly important, the intervening years have not led me to more concrete proposals for institutionalizing peace. Margaret Atwood, in her poem "The Loneliness of the Military Historian," speaks for me when she says:

> But it's no use asking me for a final statement.
> As I say, I deal in tactics.
> Also statistics:
> for every year of peace there have been four hundred years of war.[2]

I can only hope that others will find my work useful in understanding, and therefore devising effective means of addressing, humanity's destructive addiction to the rite of war.

I would be remiss if I did not acknowledge my special debt to three women: Nancy Van Itallie was my wise, demanding first editor; Marie Denise Shelton was my best critic, chiding me gently but firmly about my avoidance of "revolutionary wars;" Mary Bowen Hall lured me into co-authoring texts on war and peace for children and teenagers. She also held my hand as I worked through my first analysis of guerrilla warfare. Good friends are a special blessing.

Sue Mansfield
Claremont, California
April 1991

1
War and Human Nature

> Any society selects some segment of the arc of possible human behavior.... This fact is always interpreted ... as being due to the fact that their particular institutions reflect an ultimate and universal sanity.
> —*Ruth Benedict*[1]

It has been fashionable since World War II to argue (on the basis of ethology in particular) that not only are human beings naturally aggressive and that therefore war is inevitable, but that war making is somehow an innate human propensity or instinct. When one attempts to analyze such arguments in a critical fashion, the first difficulty one runs into is that of terminology, the use of words in such a loose and unspecified fashion that any kind of meaningful precision is hopelessly lost. The first problem, then, is one of defining terms in such a way as to preserve the distinctions observable in reality.

In this book the term "war" refers to organized, premeditated, socially approved action involving groups of men[2] in relatively complex operations of aggression and defense, and pursued in a rational fashion in order to accomplish certain goals. This is not to say that mistakes are not made in warfare as in any other human venture. But the trend is certainly to wage war in a rational/functional fashion so as to maximize the chances of achieving its goal. The rationality of the goals is another question and an unanswerable one, since what seems "rational" or "common sense" to one society may not to another.

The general social approval that has traditionally surrounded warfare is a historical fact to which our American experience of the divisiveness of the Vietnam war should not blind us. Aside from historical truthfulness, the socially approved nature of war is important because the emotive overtone surrounding war is one of the factors that leads to confusion concerning what is or is not war. Thus President Johnson in calling his domestic program a "war on poverty" was not literally describing the program as a "war" but was instead counting on the approval surrounding war to gain support for a politically and socially controversial plan. Conversely, when an ecologist speaks of mankind's "war against nature" or a black orator denounces the white society's racist war, both clearly hope to evoke the disapproval attached to the idea of inappropriate action. Warfare is supposed to be directed against an enemy, not against a friendly environment or part of one's own society. Interestingly, it was often just those groups most opposed to the war in Vietnam that also approved Johnson's domestic policy and showed no substantial unease about the phrase "war on poverty." And, of course, black "militants" are willing to fight in defense of their own people.

The ambiguity of popular usage is further illustrated by the tendency for fights between street gangs to be referred to as "gang wars." For the subcultures involved the term may be appropriate, and indeed their tendency to refer to themselves as "war lords" undoubtedly reflects their perception or belief that they are engaged in actions approved by their particular social groups. (A certain amount of self-deception is involved in this view, however, since such gangs are neither emotionally nor economically independent of the society that surrounds them, nor do they possess the generational span that is characteristic of true societies.) For the larger society of which the street gangs are a part, the very words involved in the phrase "gang war" seem inappropriate and unacceptable; hence its use helps reinforce the desire to eliminate such activity. But this emotive use of the term "war," while it is instructive about social attitudes, should not be allowed to encourage or validate misuse of the term in rational discourse.

Though war involves violence, aggression, and homicide, it is not simply equatable with any of these. Specifically, there is violence, homicide, and aggression that is not war; for example, there is murder that may be individual, unorganized, unpremeditated, or socially disapproved. Nor is homicide a necessary goal of war (though aggression is always involved). In fact, to speak as some have done of war as "mass homicide" is to miss an essential point. It is possible to wage war with a minimum of killing (as was done by the condottieri of Renaissance Italy or the dynastic armies of eighteenth-century Europe) because the goal of "civilized" war is simply the imposition of one's will upon another group, not killing per se. Even when homicide is the goal of war, as it is with certain forms of primitive warfare, it is usually minimized by the "rules of the game."

Concerning the question of the "inevitability" of war, further problems of terminology emerge. The first difficulty here is that the term "innate" is extremely vague and is generally used in a normative fashion. Thus on investigation the statement "reason is innate to man" usually turns out to mean that the writer is delimiting an ideal human type regardless of the fact that the definition excludes large numbers of human beings (youths, the insane, idiots, barbarians, women, etc.). In fact, the exclusionary results may be just the point of the definition. Those who are not reasonable, or who are not warriors or warlike, can be dismissed as infantile or less than fully human. Thus Frederick the Great could defend the elitist class structure of the Prussian state by his belief that only the aristocracy were "innately" brave and therefore good warriors.

"Instincts" is a seemingly more precise and simply descriptive term, carrying with it the aura of scientific authority and respectability. Konrad Lorenz, an eminent ethologist, has popularized the belief that there is an "aggressive instinct" ("urge" or "drive") that humans, in common with other animals, have inherited from their evolutionary past. Such a drive is, Lorenz asserts, "spontaneous," constantly seeking release or discharge, and includes specifically what he calls "militant enthusiasm." This is "man's most powerfully motivating instinct [which] makes him go to war."[3]

If, as Lorenz claims, war making were a human drive or physiological urge, one would expect it to be a common, nearly universal human experience, like eating or orgasm. In fact, however, though the majority of cultures in historic times have engaged in war, the majority of human beings have not been participants (i.e., soldiers or civilians actively involved, as compared to observers or sufferers) in war. One must be very careful about exaggerating the commonness or universality of war, lest one read back into history our twentieth-century experience of democratic war. (Even here one is being selective. What percentage of men have been soldiers since 1945? For the world as a whole, maybe 1 percent at a maximum. At least one generation of Europeans has lived without being warriors and may die in the same condition.)

Indeed, the historical record suggests that warfare has usually been a minority experience. From the rise of peasant-agrarian civilizations in 5000 B.C. until the middle of the nineteenth century, in one geographical area after another warfare has tended to become increasingly the province of professionals, for the very good reason that professionals are generally more successful than amateurs. To support a class of men who are not producing material necessities is costly, however, and agrarian societies cannot support very large numbers of nonproductive members, be they artists, priests, or soldiers. (Even in industrialized societies, putting 10 to 15 percent of the population in arms, as was done in World War I and II, involved a tremendous strain on the economy.) As a result, in peasant societies it was very rare for more than 1 to 2 percent of the male population to be actually engaged in soldiering. When one adds to this the fact that active soldiering is usually confined to men in their late teens and twenties, plus the fact that in any decade probably 40 percent of the earth's population has been at peace, it is extremely likely that the majority of men living in historic times (to say nothing of women) have never been soldiers and the vast majority have never participated in a battle. An experience confined to, at the most, 20 percent of the male population seems hardly to qualify as an instinctive drive or basic human need.

Nor can nonparticipation in war, if war is an instinct or urge, be explained merely as the result of social repression. Physiological drives are not so easily repressed, and a society that did not allow at least minimal satisfaction to most of its members would soon be overthrown. Thus some humans may be persuaded to repress sexual drives all of the time and most may be persuaded to repress them some of the time, but the overwhelming majority of people have in fact found ways to satisfy the drive most of the time. By contrast, the vast bulk of men have been satisfied never to experience being warriors and, indeed, have been likely to complain about being forced to join the army except for "good cause." For example, even though as an aristocracy they were presumably socialized to think of themselves as warriors or knights, by the seventeenth century the Prussian Junkers were loath to serve in the Elector's army, preferring to attend to their families' farming interests. It took almost a century and a series of determined rulers, using both coercion and seduction, to overcome this reluctance and make military service seem "natural." Indeed, men have rebelled because they were not getting enough to eat or were being forcibly drafted, but not because they were being denied their right or need to be a warrior.

One could possibly argue that the nonparticipant satisfies his (or her) instinct or need for war vicariously, by identifying with the participants or by viewing battle or listening to battle stories. But in a preindustrial society the vast bulk of rural inhabitants (and over 95 percent of such a population was rural) might well not know until the war was over that it had occurred. The famous story of the English gentleman farmer who stumbled upon King Charles's army on his way to hunt and learned, almost a year after it had begun, that a civil war was being fought suggests how little identification and therefore satisfaction was likely to be available to nonparticipants before the days of mass communication. Moreover, in a very hierarchical society where wars were the province of rulers and aristocracy, the interest of peasants in the war, unless the army actually passed through their territory, was likely to be small. If an army intruded on their land, then they might become actively involved (either in trying to make money from the army or to defend the community against loot and pillage), and this without much concern for whose side the army represented. In neither case would they feel much identification with the military.

As for the visual or aural appeal of battles, before television only an infinitesimal part of any state would observe a battle, while the experience of Vietnam television reporting certainly throws doubt upon the satisfactions provided by merely watching. In addition, one must ask what kind of an instinct it is that can be satisfied simply by words or pictures. While it may be debatable, for example, whether pornography encourages men and women to engage in sexual activity, it has never even been suggested that it provides or could provide a substitute for the orgasmic drive for the majority of mankind. It is possible, however, that war stories may teach appropriate behavior and indirectly satisfy humanity's liking for excitement, community, transcendence, beauty—even aggression.

But aggression is a different thing from war and is not even the same thing as anger, though much writing about the subject tends to use the three terms interchangeably. History and personal experience make it clear that although anger, hatred, and aggression often overlap, they are distinguishable experiences. Anger is an emotion that has physiological effects on the body, and that can be typified by the jealous husband confronting his wife and her lover. Depending upon the degree to which violent behavior has been sanctioned or inhibited by socialization, either physical or verbal expression of the anger may follow, in which case the anger has led to aggression. However, not all aggression necessarily involves anger: thus the lion pursuing an antelope or a hungry human devouring a steak are being aggressive, but are not usually angry.

The distinction is important because war need not always involve anger. In fact, at least at the command level, the really angry man (like the really frightened one) is not a good soldier because his anger may lead him into inappropriate, rash, or irrational action. Both the charge of the Light Brigade and the Duke of Cumberland's ill-fated charge at Fontenoy are examples of the unfortunate results of uncontrolled temper. It is important to note, moreover, that in both cases the frustration-produced anger was triggered by the actions of compatriots rather than those of the enemy.

Although anger may flare up under the frustrations that accompany battle, the mood of soldiers at the beginning of battle is likely to be a combination of excitement, fear, and determination—not anger. Whatever may be the emotions of stickleback fish or howler monkeys as they defend their territory, the mood of human beings before battle is likely to be a complex blending of emotions. This is especially true of professional or mercenary soldiers fighting for a dynastic or nonideological cause, but it is also typical of conscripts in a patriotic, ideological army. Thus on the night before his first combat experience in World War II, Captain Charles MacDonald of the United States Army remembers having the following conversation:

> "This is it! This is it!" my brain kept repeating madly, over and over. "I must not appear afraid. I must give these men confidence in me, despite the fact that they know I'm inexperienced. . . ."
> "Scared, Captain?" Sergeant Savage [a veteran of combat] asked.
> "A little," I admitted. I took a long, slow drag on my cigarette.
> "We all are," Savage said. "We always are."[4]

But several months later, as his troops waited through an artillery and air bombardment that preceded their attack, the mood had shifted.

> I was ecstatic with an elation born of excitement. The men around me were laughing and patting one another on the back. This preparation was something for the book, and the unexpected appearance of the planes had added the finishing touch.
> I looked at my watch. Four minutes to go before the barrage would lift. The men in the two assault platoons knew that the time was near and stood in half-crouches like animals waiting for the moment to spring. The smiles were gone from their faces, and in their places had come expressions of determination. It seemed impossible that any human being could survive the pasting which Ellershausen had taken and was taking, but the Germans always came out again when they were not supposed to come out.[5]

Indeed, during the carnage of World War I enemy troops felt such minimal hostility that the supreme command on both sides had to prohibit fraternization (including Christmas parties) in the barren wastes of No Man's Land.

Of course, the decision to declare war (as contrasted with actually fighting it) often involves anger, but it need not. Instead it may be made in a mood of cold rationality (as when Frederick the Great decided to occupy Silesia in 1740) or of unhappy regret (as when Czar Nicholas ordered total mobilization in 1914), though a posture of anger is then often adopted publicly (as in Frederick the Great's ghost-written diatribe about the injustices done his house by Austria). Indeed, it is possible that the evocation of anger as a justification for declaring war tells more about human attitudes toward violence (which is perceived as more understandable and therefore excusable if provoked by anger) than it does about the nature of war itself. Thus as social approval of war wanes or as the need for general public support of war increases, individuals and governments have every inducement to elicit anger (via propaganda, as in both world wars) as a means of breaking down inhibitions against homicide.

Nor need the justificatory quality of anger be confined to civilians. Another incident recorded by Captain MacDonald is illustrative in this respect. One of the few cases in which he reports feeling intense anger during eight months of active combat occurred right after the battle whose beginning was quoted above.

> The fifth house was a mass of flame.... A grey-haired German farmer stood with his arm around his aged wife and stared at the burning house, tears streaming down both their faces.
> "Alles ist kaput! Alles ist kaput!" they sobbed hysterically as we passed.
> I was not impressed; instead, I was suddenly angry at them and surprised at my own anger. What right had they to stand there sobbing and blaming us for this terror? What right did they and their kind have to any emotions at all?
> "Thank Adolf!" I shouted. "Thank Hitler!" I pointed to the burning house and said, "Der Führer!" and laughed.[6]

The psychologically defensive character of this anger as a protection against his own, in this context dysfunctional, feelings of compassion and sorrow seems quite clear. In fact, it is possible that men are angry because they are engaged in battle as often as or more often than they fight because they are angry. Moreover, this justificatory, defensive nature of anger may help explain the common twentieth-century phenomenon that anger and hostility diminish the closer one moves to the battlefield. The soldier actually in danger of being killed can understand and justify his own aggressive actions in more direct terms of simple self-defense: "Kill or be killed."

War does always involve aggression, however, though not all aggression involves war. Understood in its broadest terms (and only the broadest and least normative terms are at all useful for the historian concerned with warfare), aggression is a response that destructures or attempts to destructure one's self, another organism, object, or ideas in order to satisfy some need or desire of the aggressor. While it can be charged with hostility and anger (as in the desire to harm the body or undermine the intent of a sexual competitor), it can also be purely instrumental (as when artists chisel a block of marble in order to give physical embodiment to their vision of beauty). It can be direct and active, as in the Algerian rebellion against France, or it can be passive and indirect, as in Gandhi's campaign to get the British out of India. Moreover, as these examples make clear and as military leaders have always known, aggression can be carried out by emotional and intellectual means and aim at purely intellectual or emotional results. Thus the historian attacking a theory in order to create a more satisfying one out of its remains is being aggressive (as well as creative). What all of these acts have in common, though, is that they are attempts to destructure existing reality in order to make it more conformable to one's desires.

Such aggressive action is never simply spontaneous in the sense, for example, that hunger or sexual desires are. In the case of hunger, when the cells use up blood sugar, certain centers of the brain are stimulated, which in turn produce contractions in the stomach, and one is ready to and indeed desirous of eating (a process that will restore blood sugar to the cells). Despite intensive physiological research in this area since the 1920s, no such cyclical buildup of tension has been found to precede aggressive actions. Instead, aggression (like anger) seems to be reactive behavior, a response to cue-specific stimuli (including the stimuli provided by hunger or sexual tensions). For this reason it is most accurate to define aggression (as Fritz Perls and other gestalt therapists have done) as a physiological and psychological capacity—a combination of energy mobilization with motoric, intellectual, and emotional capabilities—that is available for satisfying externally or internally defined needs of the organism.

In many animals the release of certain aggressive energy is closely and almost rigidly connected, in a "key-in-lock" manner, with specific cue stimuli. The manner of response is also specifically patterned. Such specific motor responses occur without reference to, or in the absence of, learning and seem built into the genetic code. The by now famous aggressiveness of the stickleback fish is an example of such cue-specific, manner-specific aggressive action. Similarly some animals seem genetically coded so that other specific cue signals (such as the wolf baring its neck to another wolf) act as inhibitors, limiting certain forms of aggressive behavior.

In the human animal, however, there is little evidence of any such fixed, invariant patterns of behavior. Only in the earliest years do humans seem to act according to specific, genetically coded patterns (as in smiling, head turning, crying, or walking). Only three of these early, genetically coded behavior patterns are clearly potentially aggressive (sucking, grasping, and biting), and all are susceptible to wide changes as the animal matures. Beyond that, the most current biological thought believes that human beings are genetically coded primarily to create, transmit, and learn "culture." At most there may be a "genetic predisposition toward learning some form of communal aggression,"[7] but the predisposition can be either ignored or channeled into activities other than war. Indeed, the learned stimuli that will provoke aggressive action in human beings and the form that aggression will take are susceptible to enormous variations, both as to range and intensity. Thus while the capacity for aggression is present in all animals, the amount, form, and direction of human aggression is determined by culturally defined and learned patterns of behavior.

No animal could continue to exist as an individual or a species without the capacity for aggression, since at a minimum such a capacity is necessary for securing food, sex, and defense. Like their primate ancestors, humans' aggression originally was primarily oral and manual: grabbing and biting food and sexual partners or defending the self against other animals in a similar fashion. With time, however, human beings learned to destructure plants and rocks in order to form tools, just as they also learned to use their brain to destructure the mass of undifferentiated sense data in order to create symbols and conceptual patterns. Both developments extended humans' capacity for aggression as well as for creativity and cohesion. Thus while human beings are not the most physically aggressive animals (an accolade that must be reserved for ants, hyenas, lions, langur monkeys, and hamadryas baboons), it is certainly true that humans have developed the widest variety of ways in which to employ their aggressive capacity.

Certainly no one would wish to eliminate mankind's aggressive capabilities, without which humans would never have been able to build cathedrals, fight disease, or devise scientific theories. But the ways in which humans have used that capacity to get what they want, and the ways in which they have defined what they need, are certainly open to question. Thus the same aggressive capacity that allows dentists to drill our teeth in order to eliminate physical infection has also allowed inquisitors to break bones and burn people at the stake in order to eliminate moral sickness. Both groups, moreover, have acted for the good of their "patients" and with the social approval of their respective societies. Similarly, the same aggressive energy that can build a canal or a dam can also be used to create a cannon or wage a war.

But the channeling of aggressive energy into warfare and killing is usually not an easy achievement, as military leaders have always known. Hence the tremendous concern in any army with the proper training and discipline of troops. Human beings are not ants. They know they can die and they have usually been socialized to believe murder is wrong; therefore aggressive capacity in battle is always at war with fear and with social (and perhaps biological) inhibitions against killing. Thus Brigadier General S. L. A. Marshall points out in *Men Against Fire* that the average soldier "will have less resistance to firing on a house or a tree than upon a human being," while Medical Corps psychiatrists in World War II "found that fear of killing, rather than fear of being killed, was the most common cause of battle failure."[8] Even among troops who were veteran fighters with good morale and the capacity to overcome fear and move forward, in World War II it was rare for the number of American front-line soldiers who actually fired their guns *once* during a battle to rise above 25 percent, and 15 percent was the more common figure. During the Korean war, mainly as a result of new training procedures suggested by Marshall that involved teaching men to fire on command and to aim "against whatever target may be designated —the embankment of a river, the bases of the forward trees in a line of woods or the crest of a hill" (i.e., nonhuman targets), the number firing was raised to 50 percent.[9]

We have no comparable data about earlier wars, though Colonel Ardant du Picq's nineteenth-century *Battle Studies* suggest a similar conclusion. Moreover, there is nothing in American history or homicide statistics to suggest that the inhibition against killing is more highly developed in the United States than in any other civilization. It seems fair, then, to conclude that, if to be a warrior or warlike is to be a "killer ape," only a minority of the minority of men who are soldiers possess this capacity or desire. We are potentially aggressive, but we are not inherently warriors. In fact, war (like aggression on the individual level) is not a need but a capacity, an institution for satisfying needs that are socially defined. Like other social institutions (the state, religious organizations, the stock market), it is a complex instrument human societies have created. The important question then is why human beings have developed this particular institution? What needs does this special form of communal aggression satisfy? Why, especially in a postatomic world when its potential costs would seem to outweigh any of its benefits, has it proved to be so difficult to eliminate?

For the student of warfare, most theoretical discussions of the nature of aggression suffer from two basic flaws. Either they are so vague and all-embracing that (like Freud's theory of Thanatos or the death-instinct) they are impossible to apply to an individual case except as a *deus ex machina,* or they are so narrow in their definition of aggression that they are useless in dealing with the various types of aggression involved in war. Gestalt psychology, however, particularly as developed by Fritz Perls and others from a merger of the work of German academic psychologists, Freudian psychiatry, and the body work of Wilhelm Reich, offers a tool of analysis that suffers from neither of these limitations.[10]

At the core of gestalt theory is a conception of "the need-fulfillment pattern in the individual as a process of gestalt [figure/background] formation and destruction." Gestaltists hypothesize that as needs arise in an organism, they form a figure or gestalt (sense of hunger, thirst, etc.) that comes to dominate the emotional and perceptual experience of the individual. (The rest of the environment, including other attributes of the body, becomes in the process merely background.) The perceptual capacities of the organism then sharpen the figure (images of a spring or a faucet, an antelope or a piece of cake will form in the mind), while the motoric capacities of the body are energized and directed toward activities that will satisfy the need. After satisfaction, the no-longer thirsty mouth or hungry stomach recedes into the background (i.e., the figure is destroyed) and a new gestalt emerges out of a new situation. The process is a never-ending one whereby the animal organizes its needs according to their intrinsic importance (placing the need for air before the need for safety, for example) and marshals the energy and skills necessary to secure those needs from the environment.

In a healthy organism aggression is obviously one of the essential tools for bringing the gestalt formation and destruction process to a successful conclusion. Thus the hungry lioness takes initiative in stalking and running after food and uses the destructive capacity of claws and teeth to attack and destructure (by biting and grinding) her prey in order to facilitate its assimilation as food. Such aggression in the service of physiological needs is self-limiting. When hunger has been satisfied, the gestalt and therefore the motivation for aggression disappears. The healthy organism, in fact, strives for completion of its needs, not for the perpetuation of an emotion or action.

If obstacles interrupt the process, anger may arise to overcome the frustration. If the frustrator is belligerent and dangerous, however, then a new gestalt (the desire to eliminate the danger) may replace the original figure and the frustrated predator will try to annihilate it either by running away or attacking. If it is impossible either to overcome the obstacle or to remove the danger, an animal will usually respond by employing emergency methods: numbness, paralysis, fainting. In a less extreme situation (for example, if the desire to hit another is accompanied by the perception that such an action might be too dangerous), the motoric impulse of aggression (the movement of the arm to strike out) will be "held back" by muscular processes. "There are contractions in the jaws; there are tensions in the arm that prevent, for example, shaking the fist."[11] Similarly, a child who perceives abuse as a constant possibility is always watching for the danger, ready to run or throw up his or her arms in defense.

If the external frustration or danger continues, then the emergency methods of "blotting out" also become chronic. For example, faced with continuous low-level frustration, the animal will attempt to avoid experiencing the desire. The aggressive energy retroflected against the self and thereby the repression of the desire to act in a "dangerous way" will become habitual and almost unnoticed muscular contractions. Thus behavior that was originally a creative and healthy response to a painful or dangerous situation becomes a static stance of the individual: process becomes structure. Muscular patterns are persisted in long after they have lost any relation to the actual existence of potential frustration or danger. But the resulting muscular rigidity involves a lessening of contact with reality (diminished perception of one's internal needs and/or distorted perceptions of the external environment), a deflection of energy (which is engaged in the repressive contractions), and a loss of motoric capacities for manipulating external reality.

These muscular distortions then become part of the bodily given, affecting the manner in which other needs are handled: The inhibited biters, for example, will be unable to "get their teeth" into either sexual or intellectual concerns. To the extent that some of the natural facilities of the organism are eliminated by being repressed, satisfaction of all needs are likely to be that much less complete. Since the need is not eliminated, but merely its expression and even its recognition, the number of unfinished gestalts and unsatisfied desires carried around by the individual grows. As a result there is compulsive repetitiveness in a necessarily unsuccessful (because weak and unrealistic) attempt to bring desires and gestalts to completion.

In human beings (and possibly in other animals as well), certain changes in consciousness usually accompany motoric repressions. Most obvious, since it is most similar to motoric action, is "retroflection." The emotion originally directed against the external world is retroflected against oneself. Thus the child who distrusts his or her parents but is afraid to express or act on that distrust may retroflect it against him- or herself. As an adult he or she will still distrust his or her own body. Accompanying this shift in energy often goes an identification with the external inhibitor. For example, the punitive mother or father is "introjected" as part of the child's own personality. In this way the defeat imposed by external forces is turned literally into a "self-conquest" that is then maintained and even prized as part of one's own "character." (Such introjection differs from a healthy learning process in which one "chews" over an idea and finally assimilates it as one's own. Introjections, by contrast, are swallowed whole and never really digested.)

Just as introjection involves identifying oneself with an alien impulse, so motoric repression is often accompanied by alienation of parts of one's own identity. In particular, since repressed desire is not eliminated, consciousness of the existence of such an impulse sporadically disturbs inhibitors. Since they cannot or will not identify it as their own and yet are aware of its existence, they "project" it onto another object or being. Such projection is particularly "antisocial" since, unlike introjection and retroflection, which primarily distort internal reality, it involves a distortion of *external* reality. Moreover, since it is the disapproved parts of oneself that are projected, aggressive action against the projection often follows.

Though little research has been done by ethologists on the exact mechanisms involved, there can be no doubt that animals other than humans engage in both emergency and neurotic behavior. Thus C. R. Carpenter's studies of rhesus monkeys make it clear that under conditions of stress (being transported in close contact with unfamiliar monkeys in the hold of a ship), whole groups of primates can adopt emergency modes of adjustment.[12] In Carpenter's unwitting experiment, the stress did not continue long enough for neurotic (i.e., structured) character to develop. When returned to unstressful conditions, the monkeys abandoned the stress-based aggressiveness. But what if, for the individual or the group, the stress had remained chronic?

A number of laboratory experiments by H. Harlow and his colleagues have indicated that when infant monkeys are raised in isolation from their natural mothers, the product is a "neurotic" adult.[13] Such monkeys are seemingly incapable of close affectional or sexual contact with other monkeys and their behavior is abnormally aggressive and hostile. From the perspective of gestalt psychology, what such animals have learned from infancy is that if they remain in contact with their desire for bodily warmth, petting, and so forth, they will subject themselves to the continuous pain of frustration. As a result they inhibit their own desires: They make stereotyped movements, rock back and forth for hours, and bite themselves. Their seemingly objectless and repetitive aggression in later life parallels that of similarly deprived human beings and may be subject to the same explanation:

> The combative man [and monkey] strikes one as a man [or monkey] with appetite who initiates an approach and then frustrates himself because he feels inadequate, disapproved, or so on; his anger flares against the frustrator; and he projects the "obstacle" into any likely or unlikely object; such a man [or monkey] clearly wants to be beaten.[14]

Among animals in a "state of nature," such behavior would be self-limiting because, to the extent that its normal aggressive capacities are weakened or deflected, the animal's chance to survive or reproduce is drastically diminished. But human animals (at least temporarily) seem to have avoided, through their tool-making and society-building propensities, the consequences of weakened or misdirected aggression. Thus the knife means that humans can survive, even though their capacity to bite has been inhibited. Social cohesiveness and specialization means that even the cripple, the person who cannot or will not see, can live and reproduce, passing on (either genetically or socially) his or her incapacity to future generations. Indeed, it is possible that some of mankind's most basic technological or social advances were originally creative adjustments to internal rigidities and neurotic motoric blocks. At a minimum, "progress" has been a means of alleviating some of the usual biological consequences of neurotic bodily and personality structures.

The process, moreover, has clearly been a two-way street, since many technological changes have required deliberate inhibition of physiological aggressiveness. Thus instead of running for food like the hunters they originally were, historic humans must regularly constrain themselves to walk behind a plow or sit behind a desk. Similarly, social structures require repression of physiological responses: Thus the children of a serf or a slave must be taught to retroflect their desire to defend themselves against the abusive anger of the aristocrat or slaveowner. Whether "progress" is the result or the cause of neurotic repression, the two clearly go together in human history. Advances in security (so important to neurotics, since their very rigidity makes the prospect of confronting the unexpected or novel frightening) have usually been achieved at the cost of decreased spontaneity and increased repression.

Because of its impact on the totality of the body, emotions, and thought processes in general, such culturally required self-conquest is never limited or self-contained. For the society (as for the individual), retroflection is also accompanied by projections in the form of myths and theories (the angry dead, the judgmental God, the struggle for survival) and by repetitive aggressiveness directed against both nature and other humans in an attempt to complete unconscious and unfulfilled gestalts. Indeed, for human beings self-conquest and the ability and need to dominate and control the external world have gone hand in hand.

Anthropologists have generally distinguished five basic human cultural structures, defined by their basic modes of food production and social organization: hunting and gathering, horticultural, and pastoral tribes; peasant-based civilizations; and technological societies. Military writers, on the other hand, have been aware of the existence of four basic modes of warfare: "primitive," heroic or feudal, civilized or regimented, and mechanized war. It has also been perfectly clear since the time of Clausewitz that there was a close and necessary connection between the technological capacities, the political structure and goals of any particular society, and the extent and manner of its military activities. However, the analysis of the relation between war and society has generally been allowed to remain at a fairly superficial level. Only the most visible and public social structures have been perceived as controlling the nature of war, while official pronouncements and propaganda have been taken at face value as explanations and evidence of motivations. Where these proved inadequate to explain the actual nature of warfare, analysis has been replaced by lazy excuses: "human stupidity," "inadequate understanding," and "the fog of war."

What such an approach avoids seeing is that the function of war cannot be encompassed simply by political goals; indeed, war is often waged by societies properly characterized as prepolitical. Moreover, while stupidity may be an adequate explanation of the course of individual battles and wars, it can never be applied justifiably to a pattern of action adopted by widely dispersed peoples over long periods of time. But if one accepts that the goal of war need not be purely political or even economic, and that the intelligence quotient of all human groups is roughly similar, then it becomes necessary to look behind the formal explanations of battle for the assumptions and unconscious motivations on which the institution rests.

In this book the strategy and tactics of war making itself are taken seriously as indications of its goals, while the ritual and mythic elements associated with it are used as clues to the unaware intentionality and emotional forces that created and supported the phenomenon. Such an approach allows one to probe further into the connection among war, more "hidden" social structures (such as the family, child-rearing practices, basic economic patterns), and the common psychic structures (revealed by dream/myths) shared by all individuals in a society.

In the chapters that follow, this method is applied to four basic cultures of war: the ritual warfare of horticultural people (chapters 2–4); the political wars of peasant-based empires (chapters 5 and 6); the heroic wars of "feudal" elites (chapters 7 and 8); and the total warfare of democratic/industrial societies (chapters 9–12). In the first three cases the process by which war was created or transformed is lost in the dim reaches of prehistory. As a result, the discussion is basically static: The institution is described and investigated as it has existed with little attention to its evolutionary aspects. The transition to modern warfare, however, is well documented and accessible to investigation; hence chapter 9 addresses the process by which Europe moved in approximately six centuries from a feudal mode of military operations to the unprecedented form of technological war that has characterized our century.

Each section begins by focusing on the actual strategy and

tactics of war, on the assumption that our bodily language is our most honest and true statement of intent. (In the case of modern warfare, this is also extended to demonstrate the close ties between modes of war, visual aesthetics, and musical developments.) The analysis then moves forward to explore both the conscious psychic and unconscious mythic meaning of such actions.

The basic result of this investigation is a description of war as a human institution that satisfies deep-seated psychic needs (the infantile desire for revenge on powerful parents, the anxiety-based insatiability for goods and power, a paranoid sense of powerlessness, etc.) and as a ritual attempt to force nature and the divine (the environment) to conform to human will. Unfortunately, it is clear that in each case war (like any neurotic pattern of behavior) is incapable of ultimately satisfying the needs that produced it. Ritual does not control reality nor does war produce intergenerational reconciliation, security, or a centered sense of power. Thus human societies have seemingly been condemned to an unending and ultimately boring compulsiveness.

2
The Rites of War

> The transfer of unsolved problems to ideal and artistic spheres in accord with the principle of sublimation keys the civilization to the society around, against which it arises.
> —*Don Martindale*[1]
>
> All men wish to control nature in order that they may live.
> —*Arthur Hocart*[2]

Any serious attempt to understand the origins and meaning of war as a social institution must begin with the recognition that the institution emerged in a particular period of human development and in a particular ecological setting. Though humans have unquestionably possessed the capacity to kill each other with some ease since, in the early Middle Pleistocene (200,000 years ago), they invented hunting tools such as hand axes and clubs, and though they have possessed the capacity to kill other humans with some safety and ease since, during the later stages of the Upper Pleistocene (about 35,000 years ago), they invented the bow and arrow and stone-tipped throwing spears, there is no clear evidence that they began manufacturing weapons deliberately (i.e., artifacts designed specifically for use against other human beings) as opposed to hunting tools until the Neolithic period (about 13,000 years ago). In other words, hunters have possessed for at least 190,000 years the technical capacity to create shock weapons and for 26,000 years the capacity to create missile weapons of outstanding effectiveness. But though they may sporadically and in anger have used hunting tools to kill one another, apparently the species did not deliberately make weapons in order to wage war during these long, early years of human evolution.

The implication of this lack of specialized war-making weapons before the Neolithic period is reinforced by the fact that, while those artifacts, myths, and paintings that have survived from the Paleolithic period tell a great deal about how man hunted and even about human religious or ritual life, they give no indication that men engaged in battle. Anthropologists who have specialized in the study of contemporary societies based on an economy of hunting and gathering disagree, however, as to whether they are warlike or not.[3] Certainly in all such societies men may fight with and even kill each other, especially over women or for revenge. Beyond this the clans of some tribes will defend their territory against the encroachment of other clans, while in other tribes clans happily share resources. All will fight, and fight effectively, against the encroachment of agriculturists in defense of food sources and way of life. What is impressive, however, is that even among groups that consistently defend their territory, or that will fight for access to water or food, such warlike action remains loosely tied to current physiological needs. It has not led among the surviving hunters and gatherers to the development of special weapons, training, rituals, or the glorification of warriors and battle. This means that though such societies may fight sporadically, they do not institutionalize warfare.

Rather, as far as archaeological and anthropological evidence can tell us, the institutionalization of war began during the Neolithic period, when some humans abandoned hunting and gathering as a way of life and had turned to gardening and farming. The first clearly identifiable weapons appear in the middle layers of sites used by societies engaged in a mixed economy of some hunting and some agriculture whose techniques of farming required periodic abandonment of overworked soil (i.e., "slash-and-burn" farming). The first clearly defensive fortification of villages, indicating the existence of substantial war making, appears shortly after the emergence of settled agricultural communities but well before the use of bronze, the stratification of society, and the emergence of urban centers and writing. In effect, then, war emerges before civilization and coincidentally with farming. Unfortunately, what the archaeological evidence by its very nature cannot tell us is how or why these farmers waged war; it can show the existence of weapons but can throw no light on motives or objectives.

Though the origins of war cannot be tackled through the medium of direct evidence on which history normally depends, it can be approached via circumstantial evidence. Down through historic times and into the present day, societies have survived that have remained at the Neolithic or horticultural level of technology. They are spread throughout all of the continents except Australia and they share, besides a common horticultural economy, generally similar social and intellectual styles. They are organized around clan or tribal formations based on blood lineage and involving little or no formal authority structures, while their intellectual life is dominated by a mythologic, ritual-oriented approach to reality. More important, almost all of these societies wage war. Recent ecologically influenced anthropological studies of such cultures have demonstrated, moreover, that their warfare tends to operate in a fairly effective fashion to maintain a stable balance between population and food (especially protein) resources.[4] Such studies help explain how these people have combined war and survival, but unfortunately they do not explain why the tribes developed this particular method for coping with their environment. The studies describe the result but not the motivation.

The difficulty most modern writers have faced in dealing with such primitive warfare is that, though it exhibits enough of the characteristics of modern warfare to be clearly recognizable as a similar institution, it also differs enormously, especially in its strategy and objectives, from the kind of war waged by civilizations. One senses the frustration this "similarity-with-a-difference" creates most clearly with military scholars. While they can dismiss the revenge party or formal duels of hunting and gathering peoples, they do recognize that warfare exists among Neolithic peoples. Such fighting is clearly a social institution to which a great deal of time and resources, as well as societal organization, are devoted; true weapons exist; the raiding parties, formal battles, and early-dawn ambushes of such wars involve at least elements of strategic and tactical expertise.

Yet while the skill, courage, and cleverness of such fighters again and again attracts military scholars' respect and sense of identification, the simultaneous lack of centralized command, the apparent failure of strategic thought, the unexpected cowardice or indiscipline repels and confuses them. In the end they say with Tacitus that these are warriors, not soldiers; they engage in battle but do not wage war. Or, as does H. H. Turney-High in his classic study of primitive warfare, they differentiate true war from its primitive ancestor, explaining that the Neolithic warrior has not yet reached the "military horizon" of "adequate teamwork, organization and command working along certain simple principles."[5]

This lack of structure is at least partly explicable in simple sociological terms. Most horticultural societies do not possess either the political or economic structures that would make possible unified, hierarchical command, compulsory enlistment, enforced discipline, and sustained logistical support. More difficult to explain or even understand, however, is the fact that "The bulk of nonliterate mankind failed to establish certain simple rules and strategy. This is what kept non-literate man a warrior instead of a soldier, despite the fact that he ordinarily valued war and the warrior far more than does civilized man."[6] This is a special problem since Neolithic man's failure to observe the principles of strategy is clearly not the result of lack of training or concern. Typically men (but not women) were trained from childhood in the manual arts of warfare; much of the lore shared by all adult males concerned past battles and proper procedures for fighting. The static quality of weaponry and the limited field of operations meant that the basic strategic problems remained constant and therefore subject to review and experimentation over generations. Moreover, any conclusions or lessons were perfectly easily transmitted by oral tradition.

Nor is it the result of stupidity or an inability to conceive of the proper strategic solutions to basic problems; such warriors often exhibit great strategic precocity, even if they do not always carry such solutions to their expected conclusion. Thus Turney-High reports, but cannot explain, this fairly typical example of Neolithic warfare involving Plains Indians (who were seminomadic pastoralists at the time, but whose warfare, like much of their ritual life, had its roots in their farming past):

> A small Ojibway party organized to harass the Sioux near St. Paul. The leader deployed warriors in a line behind adequate cover near a road the Sioux must travel. He ordered them to hold their fire until the proper moment. But he allowed the main body of the entrapped Sioux merrily to pass by so that they could murder one man who had straggled behind. This feat enabled one Ojibway to wear fancy clothes [i.e., to wear the regalia appropriate to a brave who has killed a man].[7]

What makes this exploit seemingly inexplicable to Turney-High is that the Ojibway commander, like many another primitive fighter, seems to have understood all the elements of effective strategical disposition. (Indeed his ploy is in its essence similar to one that in 1708 helped make the military reputation of the great Duke of Marlborough.) And yet the Ojibway's strategical expertise seemingly produced no appropriate result.

> He exercised all necessary knowledge of surprise, use of terrain, and commanded his fire fighters to form the all important line. Adequate cover was taken and a beautiful trap laid. He had every opportunity of dealing his enemy an effective blow. . . . The principle of concerted effort was easy for him, but he threw it away. . . .[8]

The only explanation possible is the one Turney-High actually gives, though he fails to grasp its significance or take it seriously. The Ojibway leader intended "to indulge in ceremonial murder . . . for the benefit of one of his coup-counters." In effect, his objective was different from that of the commander of a civilized army. What Turney-High has forgotten is the truth aphorized by Clausewitz in the early nineteenth century: Good strategy is subordinate to, and dependent upon, a correctly understood objective. But as soon as one begins reflecting upon the connection between strategy and objective, it becomes apparent immediately that, on the whole, tribal warriors fight for different objectives than does a civilized state. Indeed, using categories drawn from civilized warfare, it has proved to be very difficult to discover just what is the objective of primitive warfare.

It is clearly not political. Most of these Neolithic societies do not possess any political structure at all, much less one that could be imposed upon conquered groups of human beings. It is generally not economic. While a raid may produce some booty, this is usually incidental and not a strategic objective; land seldom changes hands or is intended to do so as a result of a victorious battle. Crops are likely to be destroyed rather than garnered. Captured women and children are either killed or adopted into the tribe; they do not become slaves (unless under the impact of contact with civilization such societies turn to slave raids and slave trade, as certain African tribes did). Even the horses gathered with such assiduity by the Plains Indians during the historic period were an economic drain rather than a source of sustenance; moreover, horse-stealing raids were explicitly distinguished by most North American tribes from war per se, and in war any economic gain was purely accidental.

Even wife stealing, which is often put forward as a justification for such war, is as much a result as a cause, since it occurs most regularly and indeed is only a necessity among those tribes (like the Yanomamo) whose addiction to warlike and therefore masculine values leads them to practice excessive female infanticide. In other words, such tribes need to steal wives because they wage war; they do not wage war because they need to steal wives. Moreover, such tribal people engage in many raids and battles that cannot, either in their objectives or their strategy, be explained by a desire to accumulate women.

The question of wife stealing, however, points to a more general difficulty that attaches to some of the explanations that have been offered for "primitive warfare." Though they may explain why individual men fight once a society has institutionalized war, they do not explain why the society institutionalized it to begin with, nor what the societal objective of such a war could be. This is particularly true of prestige as an explanation or objective of "primitive" war.[9] Certainly the prestige that attaches to success may be an objective for an individual warrior and a device whereby society induces individuals to go to war. (It also hints at the underlying reluctance that must be overcome if an individual is to do so.) But it leaves unanswered the question of why the society should value war making so highly or what it hopes to gain from it. Prestige, like shame, is a device for controlling social relations; it is not the objective of the control.

Similarly, though less obviously, the argument that war is the product of frustration and boredom is circular and inadequate. Certainly once a society has institutionalized war, socialized and trained men to be warriors since boyhood and given them a taste for the excitement of battle, the men may become bored and even frustrated in times of peace. But such frustration and boredom are socially induced moods, not causes or objectives of war. They offer no explanation, for example, as to why civilized men, living in peasant societies where life for the ordinary person is much more monotonous, backbreaking, and encircled with rules and discipline than it is in a Neolithic society, should nonetheless be so much more peaceful and unwarlike. Certainly the relief of frustration and boredom is not an objective of war, which may require of its practitioners long periods of both if it is to be successful.

As the answer to the riddle of strategy and objectives cannot be found in categories drawn from the experience of more "civilized" societies, the explanation must be sought in the actions of the societies themselves, that is, in the actual practices that surround such warfare. A widespread pattern common to almost all tribal people is apparent almost immediately.

Once war has been decided upon and the warriors have been gathered, and before any act of violence is undertaken, there is a ceremony that, in different proportions and importance, includes the assumption of special decorations by the warriors, a series of traditionally prescribed dances with accompanying songs, and ritual interaction with a sacred object (fighting stones, war bundles, etc.). At this point special taboos on food and interaction with other members of the tribe go into effect, and sexual intercourse is likely to be prohibited; the women of the tribe also come under special obligations as to what they cannot or must do. The warriors then go forth to battle, usually led by the sacred object (or the man who has charge of it).

The actual fighting consists of either an ambush-type raid or a face-to-face battle to which the enemy has been invited. Once the raiders have killed one of the enemy (regardless of sex or age) or lost a member of their own party, they will hurry home. Looting or wife stealing will be attempted only in those rare cases where there is little chance of being pursued. If a formal battle is fought, it will be continued until a man is killed or until sundown; it may, therefore, continue for several days, and will usually be surrounded by all kinds of rules that effectively limit the number who are actually killed. In the case of either raid or frontal battle, the conflict generally ends once one or more human beings have been killed.

The tribe that suffers a death will devote itself to the traditional mourning rites and to plans for a return engagement. The tribe that manages to inflict a death will hold a celebration ceremony in which "gloating" over the dead body may include cannibalism and/or turning the skull, head, or scalp into a ritual object. The same ceremony will usually serve to lift the taboos established by the opening ritual. The warriors who have personally been involved in inflicting death, however, will be subject to a period of seclusion, heavy taboos, and an eventual purification ceremony.

The foregoing is the description of a rite, a religious ritual. Moreover, it is a single rite, rather than a collection of rites intended to insure success in, or offer celebration for, the functional, secular act of war. Instead, battle is one element, a particular step, in a ritual enactment under the leadership and protection of sacred forces, which is held together by a consistent pattern of symbolic acts and powerful taboos. It is, in addition, a ritual that can ideally be completed only if its central step (to fight a battle in such a way as to kill one of the "enemy" without yourself suffering a death) is successfully carried out. Once this is appreciated, once war is seen as part of a rite, then much that seems militarily curious about it becomes understandable. For example, obviously no coercion can be placed upon individual warriors to participate; reluctance may well mean that they are in disfavor with the spiritual forces or at least out of touch with them, and therefore potentially dangerous to the ritual activity. More important, the strategic thinking of Neolithic warriors appears much less primitive once one recognizes that their objective is the successful completion of the ritual.

From this perspective it is clear that Neolithic warriors are generally quite efficient soldiers, employing the basic principles of strategy effectively in pursuit of a clearly prescribed aim. Thus the Ojibway leader discussed earlier, instead of exhibiting an unexplainable mosaic of highly intelligent and incredibly stupid actions, emerges as a war leader of consistently high caliber. Like the Duke of Marlborough in a different context, he employed concerted effort in a simple offensive plan, using secret intelligence to achieve surprise with security, while utilizing the terrain effectively in order to obtain his objective: a single death. Moreover, by attacking only the last straggler and then retreating, he achieved the most meaningful form of victory available to him, since he avoided any loss of life in his own war party.

Such an understanding of Neolithic warfare leaves us with a picture of the "primitive" warrior that has at least basic psychological unity. Additionally, it relieves one from having to argue that societies that have for generations devoted a great deal of time and attention to the pursuit of war, and whose general intelligence and functional capabilities are unquestionable, were nonetheless, for some strange reason, incapable of grasping what all its modern practitioners admit are the simple truths of the art of war.

Once one accepts that ritual warfare is just that, a rite in the most basic sense of the word, then the question arises as to the meaning of the rite itself. And here both the content of the ritual and the mythology identified with it are fairly explicit. The content, like the rite itself, is almost universal and older than the accompanying mythology. Indeed, it is at least possible that the rite, along with the cultivation of crops, was one of the cultural elements diffused throughout the world in the late Mesolithic period; if so, one need not rely upon the common properties of the human mind to explain its widespread dispersal.

Two themes are universally present in the ritual: death and fertility. Death dominates the initial and central steps; fertility is a subtheme that emerges to dominate the conclusion. Thus the rite is usually initiated by a death (a recent homicide, a "natural" but resented death) that needs to be avenged. The other common, effective cause is a dream in which a supernatural spirit prescribes war and the manner in which it is to be pursued. Thus among the Crow only a warrior who had been inspired by a supernatural vision that specified exactly where the raiders were to go and what the result would be would dare to lead a war party or would be granted absolute control over the actions of his followers. A similar, though less common, origin of a war party involves the incorporation into a warrior of the spirit of a dead but war-desiring ancestral spirit. Among the Jivaro of South America, for example, the desire to engage in warfare begins with the acquisition of an *arutam* soul, which is the soul of an unknown ancestor. Such a soul is highly desired since it bestows upon the living warrior great power, forcefulness, and immunity from death, but it also fills him with the need and desire to kill so that he will shortly join or initiate a raiding party.

Once the decision for war is made, the ancestors of the tribe are invoked through song, dance, or the handling of sacred objects and asked to identify themselves with, and to insure success to, the ritual and its participants. So important is this procedure that, even under the more functionally oriented and despotic leadership of Shaka in the late 19th century, no Zulu warrior would have dared to engage in battle without first returning home to stand in his cattle kraal and invoke the blessings of his ancestors. Indeed, Shaka himself performed sacrifices to his own ancestors and to former Zulu kings to insure their involvement.[10] A good example of such an invocation (addressed in this case to the *le'u*, or sacred object, identified with the ancestral hero figures) is this Timor chant, sung before a head hunting raid:

> I am going oh, Thou hidden Lord, and Thou, Lord, who
>   comes to life again!
> Guard me and keep watch over me; protect me and
>   overshadow me.
> Don't let me fall and my blood be shed . . .
> Thou are the Hiding One and the Overshadowing One . . .
> But go Thou ahead to guide me and lead me by the hand . . .
>   that I may overpower and kill him, may get hold of him
>   and take him up.
> But when I come home, I hang him up on Thee, and make
>   him hanging down from Thee.

> So that it is Thou who tread upon him and took him up in
>   Thy sphere,
> So that, when I go, Thou are the Leading One and the
>   Guiding One, that Thou mayest conquer in such a way
>   and be victorious in such a way,
> So that Thy kraal and the shelter of Thy pasture may be full
>   and choked up—[11]

In the form of the sacred object, the dead ancestors are accepted as the leaders or principals in the actions to follow.

Simultaneously, the participants identify themselves (through decoration of their bodies, special language, and/or taboos) with the spirits of the dead ancestors or even with death itself. The ritual dance of the Yanomamo warriors on the night before a raid is particularly instructive in this respect. Three times each warrior individually identifies himself with a carrion-eating animal or insect and proclaims his desire for meat. At the conclusion of the dance the warriors retire to their huts and simulate vomiting.[12]

At the same time sex (the spirit of life and fertility with which women are especially identified) tends to be completely prohibited, so as to intensify the identification with death. Thus among the Maring of New Guinea, once men have been brought into contact with the "sacred fighting stones" of the tribe and painted with ritually acquired ashes, they may not have intercourse with women, touch a woman, or eat food that has been cooked by or even roasted at a fire tended by women.[13] Among the Kiwai of the South Pacific (and the Hebrews) not only was intercourse proscribed, but the husband of a pregnant woman had to stay home lest he endanger his companions.[14]

The warriors then go forth and, if successful in battle, *act as if they were death*. They kill a human being without being destroyed themselves. In the act the warriors are felt to acquire tremendous, if primarily spiritual, power. In particular, the actual manslayers are viewed as potentially dangerous to themselves and others and must be ritually secluded and purified before they can resume normal forms of social intercourse. Thus among the Orokaiva of Papua, the killer must not drink pure water or stewed taro root or engage in sexual intercourse for several days, at the end of which time he must be thoroughly and ritually bitten by a certain kind of ant and then fed the steaming stew *(suma)* that is also used to end the initiatory seclusion.[15] Indeed, the purification rites that killers must observe are almost inevitably similar to those that their society imposes upon menstruating women, those undergoing initiation, and the successful hunter of big game: that is, upon individuals who have come into contact with and become channels for tremendous and nonhuman power.

The structure of these purificatory rites is perhaps most clearly illustrated by the traditions of the Papago Indians of the American Southwest. There the scalp-taker immediately blackens his face and stands apart, unable to participate any further in the expedition. From then until the end of his purification, he will be under the guardianship of an older, experienced killer; he will fast rigorously and will not touch his body with his hands. As soon as he reaches his own village, both he and his wife will go into separate quarantine; they and every relative will have daily ritual baths; and the slayer will remain motionless, seeking through a vision the supernatural magic song that will forever make available to him and his people the power he has acquired by killing a human being.[16]

For the society as a whole, however, the rite is concluded with ceremonies whereby two things are accomplished. First, the ancestors are repaid for their aid and the taboos and emblems that have identified the warriors with death are removed, so that they may be reintegrated into the community and into life. Thus the Maring establish a truce in their fighting by first sacrificing, at the house of the ancestors, pigs to the spirits of both the high and the low ground, thanking them for their aid; this is followed the next day by a ritual feast during which the war taboos are removed and a special *rumbim* tree is planted.[17]

Second, the power the warriors have acquired is channeled into increased prosperity and fertility for the tribe. For the Maring this involves having all the males of the tribe touch the *rumbim* tree as the earth is tamped about its roots (an action that insures that their sexual intercourse will produce strong and healthy children), and then planting the *amame* tree for the women, while asking the spirits of the low ground to insure that the women, pigs, and gardens continue to be fertile. On the other hand, the Jivaro, who are headhunters, conclude a raid with a ceremony in which the shrunken heads are bestowed by the killers upon the women of their family in the belief that the power of the *muisak* (the avenging soul that is incorporated in the head) will thus be filtered harmlessly to the women, making it possible for them to work harder and have more success in raising crops and domesticated animals.[18] Similar results are clearly intended when the women of the Plains Indians carry the fresh scalps in a celebration dance or the Dani women of New Guinea dominate the ritual dance that commemorates a successful killing in battle.[19]

Behind this ritual lies an assumption that life and death are interrelated. The whole experience of farming seems to have precipitated the conceptualization that without death (the burial of the seed) no life was possible and that therefore death was in some sense a positive good. (The parallel with the psychic "death" of a part of the individual via the socialization process and the necessity of this death for the good of the whole is less often noticed.) This belief is reflected in the dichotomous world view of such people and in their fertility rites. But whereas fertility rites normally emphasize sex and life as important, the ritual of war places its emphasis upon death.

For any society death has always at least some unpleasant and anger-provoking connotations, especially when it is unexpected or potentially disastrous for the survivors. The death of the very young or the senile is accepted by most preindustrial people as "natural" or unexceptionable (though in the case of one's parents it is made subconsciously painful by unresolved desires and angers). But the death of productive members of the society (mothers and fathers on whose shoulders the task of both procreation and food production for the whole tribe rests) is always viewed with realistic alarm and resented as "unnatural," regardless of whether it was caused by illness, accident, or homicide. Such fatality threatens, indeed, any assumptions that the world is an orderly place over which human beings exercise control. It is with this "unnatural death" (chaos, if you will) that ritual war is concerned.

By the logic of the ritual, what the participants do is to identify themselves with death and/or the dead ancestors, no very clear distinction being made between the two. This lack of distinction is partly the result of the tendency of human beings to conceptualize impersonal forces in personal terms; it is also partly the result of the tremendous emotional importance these peoples ascribe to the dead and particularly to their ancestors. Thus if misfortune has befallen the tribe, it is partly or even primarily the ancestor's responsibility, and in that sense they are not only dead, they are indeed death. Having made the identification, the participants then imitate the actions of death not as they have been, but as the tribe wishes them to be: that is, death is made to strike elsewhere and not within the tribe, in the belief that by such imitative and directive action, the participants can gain control of the forces of nature in their deadly manifestations.

When the ritual battle is successful, death has presumably been constrained to follow the tribal will, the proper and creative balance between life and death has been reestablished, and the continued prosperity and fertility of the tribe is assured. As the Papago warrior claims of his deeds in song:

> There did I seize and pull up and make into a bundle
> Those things which were my enemy's,
> All kinds of seeds and beautiful clouds and beautiful winds.
> Then came forth a thick stalk and a thick tassel,
> And the undying seed did ripen.
>
> This I did on behalf of my people.
> Thus should you also think and desire,
> All you my kinsmen.[20]

At this point the women, who have previously taken a minor role in the whole ritual, rush forward to greet the returning victors with cries of elation and often take a prominent and gloating role in the celebrations that follow. The men, by risking their lives, have insured that the women will have more children and that they and their children will live and live well. Indeed, part of the explanation for the widespread degradation of women among horticultural people may lie in the particular importance assigned to ritual warfare as a means for controlling death as well as life. Certainly it accentuates the voluntary and powerful role that men play in insuring the continued well-being of the group (as opposed to the involuntary if equally powerful role of women in reproduction), and the sense of gratitude and awe women may be expected to feel toward men for willingly assuming this dangerous responsibility.

The actual origin of the rite of war remains hidden in time, lost to direct knowledge. However, speculation based on indirect evidence has produced a hypothesis about the origins of human symbol- and ritual-making capacity per se that is revealing when applied to this rite. The theory stresses that both symbolization and ritual originate in the capacity for physiognomic seeing, which humans share with other complex animals.[21] The tendency to intuit from the external characteristics of an object feelings about its internal or "real" character can lead to a sense of import or awesome discovery in the observer. Such emotions are then attributed to the object that has triggered them, investing it with a sense of holiness or fearsome power. Sharing the emotions that the object induces through outwardly expressive (and imitated) physical movements enhances the attractive sense of power residing in the object and in the group itself. This hypothetical scenario is focused, of course, primarily on emotional response to a physical object, while battle rites are focused on an act, killing. Since by the time battle was institutionalized the human capacity to create symbols and rituals was well developed, the distinction is not theoretically important as long as both object and act resonate with an emotional sense of power and awe that can be shared communally. More critical is the need for a hypothesis explaining the original emotional potency of communal killing.

The My Lai incident, involving the soldiers of Charlie company during the Vietnam war, suggests at least one prototype of a situation that could have taught our ancestors about the availability of emotional power through battle. The essential element in these American soldiers' pre–My Lai experience was an increasing sense of disorientation (alienation), helplessness, and absurdity. During their first three months in Vietnam, the soldiers were ordered to perform a jumbled variety of tiring, frightening, and inconclusive tasks, in which their inability to see the enemy meant that they became "the hunted" rather than "the hunters." (The metaphor is particularly potent when transferred to a Neolithic context.) The first American death was a particularly traumatic turning point. "Suddenly we realized a guy could get killed out there."[22] Inevitably this was followed by more deaths, including a mine disaster that incapacitated 20 percent of the unit, so that their company as a whole, indeed their entire universe, seemed to be slowly disintegrating.

From the perspective of gestalt psychology, these men had been placed in a situation of extreme disequilibrium, subjected to "a continual irk of danger and frustration, interspersed with occasional acute crises and never fully resolved."[23] In such a situation the body will normally (and usefully) respond with protective attempts both to block out the unpleasant stimuli ("shock, anesthesis, fainting, playing dead, blotting out a part, amnesia,"[24] etc.) and to exhaust some of the unusable energy through hallucination, fantasy, obsessive brooding, and restless movement. When such a condition is experienced chronically at a low-tension level (as is not unusual in childhood), the result will be a body structure and character that are typically neurotic: "under-aware proprioception and finally perception, and hypertonus of deliberateness and muscularity."[25] When, as with Charlie company, the tension level is very high and the situation continuous, the pressure to act and the desire for release will be correspondingly high. In the words of one veteran of My Lai, the soldiers felt "a need to explode": "When they used to have those battles I imagine a lot of guys were really tremendously relieved. . . . [At My Lai] they could just sit there and mow them down. And that's what I guess they wanted to do."[26] In addition, hallucinations became common and took the form, not surprisingly, of "absolute revenge. Fantasies previously held by individual men now were pooled."[27]

My Lai, of course, occurred within the context of a war, but it did not conform to normal military values or game rules. Rather it and similar incidents in other wars stand out glaringly because they are essentially spontaneous actions of a community of soldiers who go "berserk" in response to their own psychic and physical needs. Nor is war the only setting in which humans experience such extreme dangers and frustrations. Natural disasters, for example—drought, earthquake, fire, plague—can also produce a sense of powerlessness and disorientation. In particular, the end of the Ice Age (and the accompanying environmental changes that undermined a whole way of life and the symbols and rituals that had conceptualized it)[28] may well have radically increased humanity's experience of helplessness and frustration and therefore the potential need for acting out unfocused rage.

In the immediate aftermath of the My Lai massacre, almost all of the participants were elated and felt a keen sense of satisfaction. In gestalt terms, their explosion had unblocked physical repressions, acted out their hallucinatory defenses, and allowed the discharge of all the previously retroflected energy. It is thus understandable in physical and psychic terms, if not morally, that they experienced a sense of significance, loosened up and relaxed, and became more effective, confident, and pleased with themselves, their actions, and their weapons. From being powerless objects of impersonal disaster, they had become powerful dispensers of death, capable of controlling their world rather than simply being controlled.

Repetition of such experiences during the Neolithic period would have confirmed the psychic potency and physical satisfaction available through such "battles" and led gradually to their institutionalization. What began as a spontaneous, expressive act would eventually be ritualized into a "dance" whose specific movements were intended to evoke (rather than express) the original emotions. The attractive sense of power was thus made available in an ongoing and easily repeatable manner. Further elaboration would create the additional symbols helpful in making the appropriate emotions available to all members of the community (rather than just the actual killers). In addition, since it seemed important that the ritual be endlessly repeated and its psychic payoff be continually available, humans devised rules to limit its actual destructiveness.

The My Lai incident is also instructive since it illuminates some of the internal psychological effects of communal killing on the killers themselves, effects to which the symbols of battle ritual consistently point. The ritual taboos in particular insist that by killing another human being the warriors have performed a good and powerful but also a dangerous and unclean act. On the one hand, like shamans, they have opened themselves to power and to mind-expanding, consciousness-altering experiences. Since contact with such power can be captured in visions, songs, or sacred objects and be made available to the tribe, the act is a good one. On the other hand:

> the first consequences of the "exemplary combat" . . . is to bring him [the successful warrior] to such a state of exaltation that he even places his own society, which he has served and must continue to serve, in danger. . . . The exploit has its good effect . . . only after a bad phase in which the power acquired by the hero appears in disordered form, either a diminution analogous to an annihilation [psychic numbing?] or an intolerable excess [berserk rage?].[29]

Thus men are perceived as returning from battle in an unclean and inappropriate condition and must be quarantined and purified for their own and their society's safety.

The psychic aftermath of My Lai falls into two similar modes. The immediate sense of power and liberation described above is certainly real, if only temporarily. Euphoria and ecstasy are true, even if amoral or nonfunctional in the long run. It is this emotional elation that warriors value. In the primitive experience, moreover, there is a "natural" identification of emotional with symbolic and practical values. Emotionally potent objects and acts are perceived as actual *sources* of life and death rather than as symbols of life and death. Such an interpretation is, of course, an illusion, but it rests on an ever-present human preoccupation with, and overvaluation of, our own ideas.

Besides this overvaluation of ideas, the potency of battle ritual is also based on the psychological desire for revenge, the attempt to claim a strength and omnipotence one does not in fact possess. The My Lai massacre, for example, did not release the American soldiers from the real sources of their danger and frustration; it did not make them truly "the hunters" rather than "the hunted," and it did not negate the losses and humiliations of the previous months (or the months to come). Similarly, natural disasters are not eliminated by ritual, nor are previous losses made good. In both situations a crushing victory that eliminates the "enemy" is impossible, though the acknowledgment of a crushing defeat is a potentially viable option.

Such a response, Perls and Goodman have argued, is the path to health and sanity.

> There is a positive peace ... in a crushing defeat, if one has gone to one's limits, exhausted every resource and not withheld the maximum of rage. For by tantrum and *the labor of mourning* the need for the impossible is annihilated. The new self is sombre but whole; that is, its animation is restricted in the new conditions but it has not internalized and identified with the conqueror. So Peguy, for instance, has beautifully described how the suppliants in Greek tragedies have more strength than the arrogant victors.[30]

In the revenge battle, however, the real truth of defeat and grief is avoided precisely by acting out a hallucinatory fantasy. (This is the point at which such an explosion differentiates itself from a tantrum.) In effect the berserker does identify with and internalize the hostile "victor/victim." The result is neither victory nor defeat but "Conquest" and the continued need to dominate both the external and the internal world.

The My Lai and Vietnam experience (and primitive ritual) make this clear. In the long run, the inner tensions of the American soldiers returned after the My Lai explosion, producing veterans who were both psychically numbed and subject to unexpected outbursts of rage, dangerous to themselves and their society. In gestalt terms, their response to the long-term, chronic disequilibrium had produced a neurotic body armor that explosion had temporarily released but not destructured. In particular, the very real losses had not been dealt with by mourning labor, while the killings themselves may well have left a residue of unexpressed horror or regret. (For example, over four years later one soldier was still haunted by nightmare visions of the mutilated bodies.) The conviction that war has a purpose and significance seems to produce a partial resolution of this internal turmoil, allowing the soldier to view his experience as a "dirty but necessary job" and his losses as a necessary grief. Certainly tribal societies offer their warriors such reassurance immediately and warmly, while Americans after Vietnam did not. Tribal ritual also provides opportunities for communal mourning that are not institutionalized in the modern world.

But tribal people go a step further. Their ritual explicitly embraces and approves the killer's psychic numbing and prescribes a way for dealing with it. The fear of intimacy, of touching and being touched that is common in battle survivors and that in the twentieth century is labeled a sickness ("shell shock," "Vietnam Vet Syndrome," etc.) is accepted and even enforced in ritual warfare as an appropriate response to the experience of inflicting death in battle. The successful warrior is usually isolated from everyone except older killers and is specifically forbidden to touch or feed himself, to experience sexual intimacy, to touch the ground, and so forth. In effect, the numbing is externalized and formalized in a series of taboos; it is prescribed as a chosen response to the ordeal. Simultaneously, the tribal warrior-killer is assured that his disorientation and hallucinatory tendencies are potentially valuable. Accepted and even sought, they can be structured into symbolic forms that will enhance the practical power of his people.

There is simply not enough evidence available to clarify the actual efficacy of the cleansing taboos in working through and resolving the warriors' psychic dislocations. The taboos, however, resemble certain modern therapeutic and religious techniques whose efficacy is well established. For example, a direct attempt to relax tensed muscles, to "force" release is usually unsuccessful; instead tension will increase as the body defends its own defenses. A more fruitful approach is to identify with the tension and deliberately contract the muscles as tightly as possible. When the deliberate contraction is released, the spontaneous stress will generally relax as well. Similarly a tendency to hallucination or brooding, when consciously embraced through meditation, can be converted to a healthy mode of discharging otherwise unusable energies.

Certainly most tribal warriors manage individually to achieve some kind of psychically viable balance vis-à-vis the battle-produced tensions. Indeed, anthropologists have reported that eminently successful warriors are not only stable members of society but often exceptionally generous and kind in their day-to-day social relations. (This may, however, simply reflect the splintering of personality demonstrated by some German death-camp commanders.) But anthropological studies also make it clear that the cleansing ritual does not always work for specific individuals. At a minimum, some warriors remain potential "berserkers," liable at any time to vent explosive rage against members of their own community.

In our own day, the combination of lack of public enthusiasm for the Vietnam war and our general insensitivity to the psychological costs borne by veterans has certainly increased the number of American men who bear such psychic scars. Forced to act during their tour of duty as ritual surrogates for the community, they were then rudely returned, without any ritual of victory, mourning, or cleansing, to the turbulent civilian community and expected to be untouched by their searing experience. A society that could not deal with the symbolic and moral meaning of either battle or defeat had neither patience nor healing to offer its sons. Nonetheless, though the American experience may be extreme, the phenomenon of "battle shock" is not, as both battle ritual and mythic history insist, new. The "Vietnam Vet Syndrome" is simply the most recent side effect of humanity's attempt to cope with the trauma and anxiety of fate and death by identifying with, and acting out, the destructive side of existence.

3
The Neolithic Revenge

> A good man feels as strongly about insults as he does about the benefits he has received. Either way it is virtuous to repay. . . . "The world tips," they say, so long as an insult or slur or defeat is not requited or eliminated. A good man must try to get the world back into balance again. It is human virtue, not an all-too-human vice.
>
> —*Ruth Benedict*[1]

If one asks tribal people "what is the meaning of ritual warfare?" they will not give the explanation outlined in chapter 2. They do not distinguish between ritual and nonritual actions as our analytic, dissecting society is likely to do. Nor do they reflect upon or build abstract theories about reality; they perform ritual acts because they are traditional, "natural," a part of the good life; their meaning is experienced, felt rather than thought. Pushed by an anthropologist for an explanation, they are likely to refer to the anger of the dead and the need for revenge—merging ideological and psychological causes. Anthropologists with a functionalist bent have a tendency to understand such wars as law-enforcing devices, comparable to the judicial and penal systems of civilized societies. From this perspective, war is simply part of the legal system, the only means of enforcing rules available to a society without a strong central authority.

What has happened, however, in the process of interpretation is that vengeance or revenge has been understood as simply the equivalent of deterrent punishment. There are three serious problems with such an explanation.

First, it ignores the fact that historically and by any strict analysis vengeance and deterrence are two very different sources of motivation for punishment, leading often to very different conclusions concerning the proper response to objectionable action. Deterrence involves a very functional or utilitarian approach: The reaction to unwanted activity must be the infliction of enough unpleasantness to deter the actual offender, and any other potential offender, from repeating the act. Revenge, on the other hand, is concerned with the personal satisfaction of the one offended, with making the injured party feel better by reestablishing the balance of pleasure and pain that has been destroyed by the offense. That deterrence may also follow is accidental and not essential. Thus criminal systems like those of early medieval Europe, which were based on the revenge motive, were unconcerned with the intent or even the rationality of the offender, so that purely accidental injury or injury inflicted by animals was handled in the same manner as deliberate human acts of hostility. Second, societies engaging in ritual warfare seldom talk about deterrence or teaching the opposing side a lesson. Indeed, the death that needs to be avenged may not have been caused by any human agency and the death that satisfied the need for revenge may be inflicted upon a clan or family with no involvement in the initial injury.

Finally, if primitive societies intend warfare as a means of eliminating unwanted violence in intertribal relations, as a means of guaranteeing peace, they are singularly unsuccessful. Rather than ending bloodshed, ritual warfare with its revenge motif seems designed to further it, since each succeeding death calls for another one. If the point of war, through retaliation, is to teach the other group to keep the peace, one would expect that either the retaliatory approach would be abandoned or the strategy of violence would escalate toward an attempt at annihilation. Instead both sides adopt all kinds of rules and restrictions that effectively limit the amount of "punishment" they can inflict upon each other, thereby assuring that war will in fact continue. Thus the Ibo of Nigeria traditionally considered it improper to use firearms in certain kinds of battle, while the Dani do not use feathers on their war arrows. Moreover, the rules of the game are often so set up as to maximize the chance that a relative balance of deaths will be achieved. Indeed, the Ibo counted up their dead at the conclusion of a war and the winner regularly compensated the losing side with money in order to balance the difference.[2]

It is hard to believe this failure to deter is accidental or the result of ineptitude. If one looks at the elaborate rules under which war is waged, it is apparent that a great deal of intelligence and cooperation between warring groups is involved. If the goal were to eliminate or minimize death or injury, surely the same intelligence and cooperation could have been exercised in a more effective fashion. Both in the blood ties created by exogamous marriage and in the shared mythical and religious systems common to such warring groups, the effective basis for punishing unwanted violence and eliminating blood feuds exists. Unless one is willing to consciously and deliberately assume that "primitive" people are so psychologically blind and so intellectually incompetent that they are unaware of their own motives and unable even minimally to achieve their desires, it would seem unwise to interpret revenge as simply the functional equivalent of deterrent punishment.

If one follows the more valid course of accepting such warring societies at their own evaluation, one is still left with a basic question, however. Is the desire for revenge a basic human motive, and if it is, why was it only 13,000 years ago that it became compelling enough and important enough to be institutionalized and indeed glorified in war?

Among most animals, anger and aggressive action intended to inflict injury upon another are normally connected with an immediate, specific, and usually physiologically based desire—to secure food, sex, or status, or to avoid danger and pain. An animal in the pursuit of any of these goals will fight vigorously and to the full extent of its capacities. Having failed or been defeated, however, nonhuman animals tend to abandon the fight and, as far as can be told from their activities, to forget the issue and the emotions connected with it. Although there may be a period of withdrawal and depression in which the loss is assimilated and seemingly grieved over, there is no attempt to pursue the offender. The defeated male buck moves on to feed in another part of the woods, the bereaved mother bear ignores the infant-killing male (and may later mate with him); the hyena driven off from its meal by lions simply seeks a new source of food. Nor can one easily see what biological function continued anger in such a situation could perform, since the initial object of aggressive energy (the female in heat, the cubs in danger, or the dead gazelle) is gone beyond recall. To remain angry is to lock emotional and physical energy into the past instead of using it to achieve physical satisfaction and growth in the present.

But revenge as a motive for action seemingly involves just such a locking of energy into the past, since it involves the desire to inflict pain upon another in retaliation for an injury suffered in the past. It serves no obvious biological function since it does not provide sex, food, or security; indeed all of these may be sacrificed to its pursuit. Instead it provides primarily an emotional satisfaction: the present pleasure in another's pain. The explanation for this neurotic, backward-looking desire seems to lie in three distinctively human characteristics: our unusually highly developed capacity for remembering and conceptualizing; our long period of dependency as children; and our dependency on learned rather than genetically coded patterns of behavior.

The first of these characteristics makes the continued desire for revenge possible; the last two make it likely because of the nature of the relation between parent and child. In particular, during that long period of dependency there are often times when the child wants or needs something from its parents (love, security, comfort, food) that it does not receive. As a result, the child is often angry and yet may be unwilling to express that anger lest it find itself further denied the very thing it wants. Unsatisfied desire and unexpressed anger are therefore interlocked in such a situation.

At the same time, in their socialization of the young, human parents often demand actions or emotions from children that are not spontaneous or self-motivated. In order to secure obedience, they may well inflict punishment—either physical pain or the psychic pain of ridicule or withdrawal of affection. In either case parents temporarily represent a felt danger to children at a time when they have no effective way of eliminating the danger. Because they are dependent, children cannot run away; because they are small, they cannot fight back; and indeed to express anger may simply increase the punishment and the demand for obedience. Small wonder if in the very act of obedience children often feel that they would like "to kill Daddy or Mommy." And yet since the persons they would sometimes like to kill are, after all, also people they love and depend upon, their own anger is threatening, almost regardless of parental attitudes. Thus they are often unable to face or acknowledge the depths of their rage, much less express it. Instead they retroflect it back against the self and feel ashamed of not being "good" spontaneously. But the anger is still there and if the situation is repeated often enough, a pattern is built up whereby they simultaneously love and desire, and hate and would destroy, their parents.

If this is experienced repetitiously, with neither desire nor anger brought to full expression or completion, a pattern or habit of holding onto both emotions is established. Indeed, one may say the child has been taught that it is a good thing to hold onto emotions, to retroflect them back upon the self. Moreover, such retroflected emotions can remain an unconscious element in parent-child relations well after the child has reached adulthood and the original desire (to suckle, for example) has ceased to actually be attainable. The adult still desires what was never given to the child and remains angry about the frustration and pain.

The intertwining of desire and anger are components of most aggressive acts that meet with frustration. What differentiates revenge is that its roots are in the past rather than the present, and that the satisfaction ostensibly desired is the effective, pain-inflicting expression of previously controlled anger. It is in the repeatedly uncompleted desires and angers of childhood (the energies held onto and retroflected because their expression seemed too dangerous) that revenge as an emotion and a character pattern is established. Moreover, to the extent that children have learned that a full expression of certain desires or angers is dangerous and shameful, a pattern of behavior has been established that will affect relations with others besides their own parents.

Unquestionably, the potential for such an individual pathology always exists within the human psyche. The most pacifistic of hunting and gathering people recognize it as an individual motive and have even institutionalized (in the song duels of the Eskimos, for example) socially safe ways for individuals to act out its angry components. But it is surely no accident that revenge as a major and socially approved emotion, and as a motive for an institution as resource-consuming as war, emerges in just those human cultures that have made the transition from hunting and gathering to farming.

The psychological roots of humans' excessive preoccupation with revenge as well as with war are to be found in the changes in the socialization process necessitated by the shift from hunting and gathering to farming as the basic means of human subsistence. The capacity to farm and to evolve a culture to support such a mode of subsistence was not in itself necessarily neurotic. It may instead have been a creative adjustment to a difficult environmental situation or to newly perceived possibilities in the environment. However, though humans were by that point genetically coded for adaptability, culture creation, and learning, they were not genetically coded (like some ants, for instance) to farm.

Like most other mammals, hunters and gatherers were adapted to a psychic/physiological system whereby aggression in the pursuit of food was closely related to, and indeed primarily activated by, hunger pangs. With the shift to farming, however, it was no longer possible to rely simply upon the self-regulating hunger needs of the body as a motivation for, or energizer of, aggression in the pursuit of food. Instead, aggressive energy (work, as it would increasingly be characterized) had to be harnessed to the time schedule of the external seasons, the life cycle of plants, and climatic conditions in general. Of course, both the hunter-gatherer and the farmer must adjust internal desires to external realities. Hunters, for example, must follow the water, the game, the honey; if, through laziness or disinclination, they miss a chance, they will go hungry for a day or a week. Farmers, however, must begin (anywhere from three months to several years before they will be hungry) to clear the land, till the soil, plant the seeds, weed and water the garden, and finally harvest and store the crops at the appropriate time, or face failure and possibly starvation. In both cases humans must respond realistically to the external environment or pay a price, but the extent of the discontinuity between hunger and the expenditure of aggressive energy is greater for the farmer than the hunter-gatherer, while the cost of this discontinuity is potentially much greater.

Ironically, the transition from hunting and gathering to farming is usually seen now (and probably was at the time) as a great advance for humans, who are depicted as moving from simply adapting to the environment to forcing it to adapt to them. What such a perspective (with its underlying euphoria of progress) ignores is the extent to which the new strategy of subsistence required a new kind of human adjustment to a new kind of external control. The fact that humans subjected themselves to greater control by nature in the process of securing more control over nature is seldom openly recognized by farmers, however, and for a very good reason. The imposition of external controls is taken over by the society, and child-rearing practices are modified so as to internalize the norms necessary for successful adaptation to farming. In the process what began as a creative mode of interacting with the environment is turned into a neurotic social structure.

In contrast to children of hunting and gathering societies, who are breast-fed until they are three or four years old and who bear no responsibility for food collecting until they have reached physical and psychic maturity, the children of farmers are weaned at one or two and are likely to be incorporated into the adult work structure at a very early age. At about five or six years they are given siblings to care for; at around seven or eight they will be given responsibility for guarding pigs or acting as scarecrows; by ten or eleven they will be sharing responsibility for weeding, harvesting, and other tasks. Moreover, these responsibilities will be specifically prescribed, and the child will be punished if he or she fails to fulfill them. In effect, children's attempts to follow their own natural inclinations will be frustrated initially by physical force and ridicule, and eventually simply by an implied or remembered danger. By the time they are adults, they will "naturally" take to being farmers. They will have internalized the norms and controls necessary if they are to energize aggressive capacity according to a time schedule other than that of their own physiological needs.

Again and again in the process children have been forced, or have felt themselves forced, to repress or inhibit their own natural inclinations. They must hold back the mouth that would suck or bite, the feet that would run in play, the eyes that would close in sleep, or the arms that would lash out in anger. To achieve this repression they must, in effect, retroflect backward against the self aggressive energy that would normally have moved outward to achieve some self-defined satisfaction. They must defeat and restrain the self lest they suffer a seemingly more dangerous defeat at the hands of parental figures. Eventually the muscular control will become automatic, though the desire and the anger will not have been eliminated. Even if not consciously recognized, they still exist as a troubling, because unsatisfied, inclination or presence within the psyche.

In effect, the transition to agriculture is accompanied by a childhood in which the desire for "revenge" against one's parents becomes an almost inevitable result of the socialization process. Because the tribal structure of such cultures submerges the biological in the social family, so that all adults are to a degree "psychic" parents to all children, the occasions for such denied anger are seldom idiosyncratic and focused. At the same time, however, refusal to conform to shared cultural norms is very dangerous, since it threatens the child with rejection by all adults. The resulting frustration and anger is no less real for being diffused among several objects. Animals with a shorter dependency period will not experience such conflicts, and human societies such as the hunters and gatherers who socialize their young with less deprivation and fewer demands will minimize their existence. It is only when child-rearing patterns consistently demand the repression of anger and deny the satisfaction of personally defined desires that holding onto past emotions and situations can become part of a consistent character pattern of the society. The accentuation of that backward-looking and biologically nonfunctional emotion we call vengeance or revenge is thus a psychic cost of the shift in socialization patterns that accompanies the shift to farming as a means of subsistence.

Although the desire for revenge against one's social parents increases with the shift to farming, parricide does not, and that is because, even in adults, love for and the desire for benefits from parents continue and hold the anger in check. But the moment of parental death is unquestionably a moment of trauma, as it is then, if ever, that individuals must face the fact that the desire will never be completely satisfied, that revenge is impossible, and that it is necessary to abandon both emotions as unsatisfiable and inappropriate. One must give up not only the aged and possibly senile parent who has actually died, but also the supportive and punitive parent of one's childhood. Even within the context of modern therapy, the process of accepting this double loss is a difficult and threatening one.

Most horticultural societies seem to have been unable to handle the problem directly; moreover, because children were treated similarly, it was a widely shared neurosis, requiring a common and socially supported solution. This was accomplished through mythic and ritual means whereby, in effect, a further and even more neurotic avoidance of the very real loss and anger was achieved. A continuing relation with the spirits of the dead ancestors, who were understood as being still present and active in the world of the living, was established, allowing the intertwined and contradictory emotions of desire and anger to be acted out in fantasized relations with the dead. The parents were thus understood as still operating as punishing, controlling but potentially nurturing figures—the feared, supportive tyrants of one's youth.

The good things desired from the parents continued to be hoped for and expected from the dead, while anger (intensified by their death, i.e., their final withdrawal and betrayal of childish needs) was denied by projecting it onto the dead. Specifically, the dead were understood as being angry because they were dead, as believing that they had in some way been injured, and of desiring to see death inflicted upon someone else in return for the injury they had suffered. The major contact point between the fantasized, angry emotions attributed to the dead and the emotional reality of the living was simple: Certainly the bereaved children had at points desired their parents' death or annihilation, but that was precisely the one desire that had never been fully acknowledged—and still could not be, since the child still desired benefits. Because that angry desire to annihilate still existed, it was projected onto external forces, and the dead were then perceived as angry in response to a deliberate injury.

Ritual warfare to "avenge the dead" allowed the living to "prove" that they did not desire their elder's death (some other person or force did) by risking life to fulfill the dead's demand. Thus the revenge never achieved directly with parents was satisfied indirectly; instead of killing the parents, the "child" killed for them, redirecting anger toward another. Finally, by killing another the child attempted to accomplish the supreme act of obedience, symbolically killing the rebellious and angry part of the self. The spirits of the parents were left happy and ceased haunting the bereaved and the village, while the living could hope for good things from their influence. Thus Neolithic war was an elaborate, potentially therapeutic ritual that allowed both the individual and the society partially to close accounts with the elders and eventually with all the dead. That the ritual was not completely successful as therapy, however, is demonstrated by the fact that a relation of desire and propitiation between the living and the dead continued to exist; any major disaster was generally understood as evidence that the dead were angry and needed to be reconciled to the living.

Obviously not all demands for revenge, even within societies that practice ritual warfare, are directly connected with parent-child relations, not even when one extends that concept to cover the relations of all the middle-aged with the departed elders of the tribe. In addition, there are also cases in which the living individual deliberately seeks revenge for other injuries. In such a case there is clearly more at stake than a childish desire to be revenged on one's parents.

If one again contrasts human and nonhuman animal behavior, the emotional meaning of such a desire for personal revenge becomes clearer. Take the case of a mother bear whose cubs have been killed or a stag who has lost its potential mate to a rival. In both cases the pain of loss and the frustration-fed anger are forgotten with relative rapidity. A human being who responds to a similar situation by desiring revenge is not only binding energy to the past (and so denying the energy to the present) but is holding on to the pain as well as the anger. One cannot remember to be angry without also remembering the hurt and anguish of the unsatisfied desire and the loss. What possible motive could be strong enough to bind an individual not just to the past, but to a painful memory from the past and to a desire that can never be satisfied?

The answer is to be found in the refusal to fully acknowledge and assimilate the loss; in the attempt to deny, in the face of all the evidence, that such a thing has really happened to one. Normal handling of loss involves accepting that it has happened, grieving for it, and then letting the loss become at most a faint memory tinged with sad emotions. But vengeful people refuse or are unable to go through this process; they submerge grief in anger and set out to inflict upon another a pain equivalent to the one they have suffered. In effect, they are unwilling or unable to accept the fact that they are the sort of person who suffers injuries or can be injured.

Such revenge is an attempt to sustain an essentially false image of oneself. It is comparable to that element in the avenging of the dead whereby one kills the part of oneself that had desired the death of one's parents. In revenge, one kills that part of oneself that is weak, vulnerable, soft, and able to be hurt, the "childish" part of oneself that one refuses to acknowledge. It is, in fact, so important to deny that one is the sort of person to whom injury and pain can happen, who cannot control or manipulate reality, that individuals devote enormous amounts of time and energy to rewriting or correcting the past. The victor in an act of revenge is that part of the personality that desires always to be correct, strong, and in control, while the real victim is the "child" who suffers.

The psychic importance of the correct self is directly related to the socialization process through which the incipient farmers are trained to ignore or distrust the promptings and inclinations of their own body. In order to train them to conquer and control nature, their own physical/animal side has been at least partially denigrated and rejected. Moreover, such societies are almost uniformly "shame" cultures. Their socialization process typically involves both the provision of a great deal of physical and psychic satisfaction through close identification with the group and heavy reliance on ridicule, shame, and rejection as the cost of failure to conform to the group's norms. When children please adults and peers, they are defined as good and rewarded with approval; when they violate social norms, they are ridiculed.

As it is impossible to reject the ridicule and demand love, children are faced either with consciously accepting their own defeat and essential badness or trying to avoid such knowledge by adopting and identifying with (introjecting) the norms and values of the culture, turning defeat into self-conquest. Since defeat in this context means unworthiness and isolation, the second alternative is clearly attractive. But it involves a splintering of the self, since the spontaneous, self-defined, and "defeated" elements in one's person still continue to exist alongside the introjected, self-controlling elements. In the slang of gestalt psychology, one has now a "top dog" (correct self) who is the enforcer of externally defined rules of conduct and behavior and a "bottom dog" (childish self) who is always in secret, and often spiteful, rebellion.

Though the retroflection of angry aggression and the introjection of external norms are intended to make one invulnerable, the personality structure built by these means is actually inherently unstable and brittle. The very retroflection of anger tends to produce a rigid muscular structure, while the introjected part remains under attack from the self-regulating elements of the personality. Indeed the more self-respecting one is, the more potentially shameful, since the very need to be right stems from one's capacity to be wrong. Moreover, the group's actual or fantasized evaluation of, and reaction to, the individual has become the explicit standard for self-evaluation. In such a situation any external injury, defeat, or suffering is likely to exacerbate the internal conflict by arousing a childish belief that one is being insulted (ridiculed) because one has been bad. Injury or pain that is "unjustified" is particularly threatening since it challenges the efficacy and correctness of one's whole rigid personality. Any loss is an insult that undermines one's self-evaluation; to refuse or be unable to reject or eradicate the insult/loss involves accepting the self as shameful and worthless.

The connection between revenge and a false self-image is nowhere more clearly demonstrated than in the conventions of "honor" and "face" that are so much a part of the value system of any warrior caste or warlike society. Both "honor" and "face" are tied up with an ideal public image or personality that, among other things, is immune to injury or offense. Since the ideal image does not correspond to reality (any human being can in fact be injured or offended by another), revenge becomes the convention by which the false self-image is sustained and the reality of the past eradicated. By killing or injuring the offender, one "protects one's honor" and "saves face." It is the need to hold onto a good self-image that gives emotional power and sustaining force to the drive for revenge. Indeed it turns the conflict from one that simply deals with the past into one that concerns the present and the future. What is achieved by revenge is not the actual satisfaction of past desires, but the preservation for the future of one's self-image as tough, worthy, and in control of things.

The act of revenge in such a situation represents a double drama. One demonstrates one's control of the external world by acting out the role of the punishing parent and at the same time transfers the internal drama of control, shame, and punishment into the external world. Whereas normally the correct self retroflects anger back against the spontaneous self, in a revenge situation the existence of such a spontaneous, uncontrolled, and therefore shameful being is projected into the external world and the originally retroflected anger is at least partially turned outward in an attempt to deny or eliminate the insult. Thus the seemingly successful revenge killing both denies the existence of the spontaneous and therefore vulnerable self of the revenger and symbolically "kills" the suffering and therefore shameful self. The actual subject of any act of revenge is therefore part of one's own person. Psychologically, however, revenge (unless carried to the extreme of actual suicide, which is an option in most shame-revenge cultures) is never completely successful. The vulnerable and self-regulating part of the personality cannot in fact ever be totally eliminated, while the environment is never completely under control. But one keeps on trying, turning revenge into a ritual of self-justification.

A psychological understanding of the desire for revenge helps to explain the origins of war in two ways. It exposes the mechanics whereby in the human psyche anger and the desire to destructure another can be divorced from immediate physical needs and become alienated and alienating emotions that can then be channeled into deliberate and socially controlled acts of aggression, as in battle. It also clarifies why the desire for revenge should be exacerbated and the institution of war created in that particular period of time when humans abandoned their original hunting and gathering way of life.

What no psychological explanation of revenge can explain completely, however, is why the desire for revenge should have been channeled by Neolithic societies into the act of war rather than being left to individual initiative, satisfied through a system of revenge-based punishments or even handled through the ritual killing (sacrifice) of scapegoats. Indeed, with the transition around 5000 B.C. to civilization (i.e., to large hierarchic, political conglomerates), when ritual warfare for revenge ceased to be socially functional, variations of all of these expedients were adopted. (Moreover, the sources of all of these outlets already existed in the customs and religious framework of the earlier societies.) The desire for revenge was not eliminated with civilization, but it was controlled and directed toward other sources of satisfaction.

No theory of individual psychology can fully explain why most Neolithic societies, rather than merely tolerating the desire for revenge and vengeance, glorified it and made the act an explicit duty incumbent upon all adult males (though usually not females) through the act of war. Indeed, in societies that practice ritual warfare, revenge becomes an obligation that may be divorced from, and even contradictory to, one's actual emotional needs. Thus it is not uncommon, as among the Maring of New Guinea, to find men required to avenge a troublemaker whose death they have consciously desired. The psychological capacity to seek vengeance may make war possible, but it does not require all men to be warriors, a fact amply illustrated by a peasant-based or technological empire. Only an ideology of power will do that; such an ideology is embodied in the ritual of battle and in the myths horticultural people have woven around the ritual itself.

4

The Destruction of Chaos

The culture-hero is Man, overcoming the superior forces that threaten him. . . . His task is the control of nature—of earth and sky, vegetation, rivers, season—and the conquest of death.
—*Susanne K. Langer*[1]

Myth, which emerges after a rite has been established, "explains" the ritual by embodying its origins in a "dream-time" act of creative potency. The war myths of tribal people carry out, though not explicitly, the revenge motif of their conscious explanation. Indeed emotion, act, and story exhibit a well-knit unity that more technologically developed and pluralistic societies might well envy.

The Yanomamo, an intensely aggressive people of South America who have institutionalized war as a focal point of their social life, tell the following story as an explanation of both their own origin and the origin of war. In the beginning there were only "original beings" who created most of the important plants, animals, and artifacts. After most of these original beings had been wiped out by flood, Periboriwa (Spirit of the Moon) was one of the few who remained.

> He had a habit of coming down to earth to eat the soul parts of children. On his first descent, he ate one child, placing his soul between two pieces of cassava bread and eating it. He returned a second time to eat another child, also with cassava bread. Finally, on his third trip, Uhudima and Suhirina, two brothers, became angry and decided to shoot him. Uhudima, the poorer shot of the two, began letting his arrows fly . . . but he missed. . . . Then Suhirina took one bamboo-tipped arrow and shot at Periboriwa when he was directly overhead, hitting him in the abdomen. The tip of the arrow barely penetrated Periboriwa's flesh, but the wound bled profusely. Blood spilled to earth in the vicinity of a village called Hooteri, near the mountains called Maiyo. The blood changed into men as it hit the earth, causing a large population to be born.[2]

In effect, the myth says that human life begins with an act of violence whereby chaos or unnatural death (the moon is out of place; it eats small children) is overcome. Moreover, the Yanomamo also believe that war itself was born in this act of violence, since they repeatedly assert that "because they have their origins in blood, they are fierce and are continuously making war on each other."[3] If one takes this story as a piece of literal history or biology, it makes no sense. But if one views it as a mythopoetic rendering of perceived reality, it points to the Yanomamo's experience of the interdependence of life and death and to a belief, which they act upon consistently, that the chaotic potential of this interdependence can be controlled by ritual acts of violence that are effective for insuring the ultimate triumph of life.

A myth from another continent tells the same story in an only slightly different way. The Hottentots, a pastoral and fighting people of southern Africa, recognize two primary forces or deities in their experience, both of whom they relate to through ritual sacrifice.[4] //Gaunab is a god or great chief, and he is also a demon or a specter; he is evil, black, the source of sickness and death—and he is identified with the ghosts or specters of the dead. He is in effect "the destroyer, the one who annihilates." By contrast, Tsui//Goab is a great hero, the All-Father, the source of rain, the thundercloud and the Thunderer. He is also the source of human life, having made the Hottentots. There is only one important story about Tsui//Goab, however, in which Tsui//Goab went to war with another chief, //Gaunab, because the latter always killed great numbers of Tsui//Goab's people. While in the fight Tsui//Goab was repeatedly over-powered by //Gaunab, in every battle Tsui//Goab grew stronger; and at last he was so strong and big that he easily destroyed //Gaunab by giving him a blow behind the ear. Again one finds the forces of life and of death opposed to one another, and a battle in which life uses death in order to subdue death. The Hottentots do not specifically identify the myth with the source of their own societal patterns, but they do believe that, though killed, //Gaunab comes alive again, and they tell the story as though the battle were "an annual event." And, of course, as they reenact it in their ritual wars, it is an annual event.

The Chiricahua Apaches of the American southwest have a similar myth.[5] In the beginning, in the dream period, humans shared the earth with animals, monsters, and certain heroic figures, including White Painted Woman (who had existed from the beginning) and her son, Child of Water. Both White Painted Woman and human beings were preyed upon by monsters, one of whom, Giant, actually consumed a number of White Painted Woman's children. When, after a divinely protected childhood, Child of Water reached maturity, he went hunting in company with his brother, Killer of Enemies, and they met Giant, whom Child of Water killed. The hero then proceeded to conquer the other monsters, such as the giant eagle and dangerous buffalo, and forced them to agree to serve rather than harass human beings in the future. Having saved mankind, White Painted Woman and Child of Water departed for their sky home, though only after having instituted the girls' puberty rites.

Clearly they had also set the pattern for ritual war: The Apache used a special language while war was in progress—a language that helped make the war efficacious. In particular, all women had to be referred to as White Painted Woman and all men as Child of Water. Thus the war repeated and reaffirmed that initial, critical act of the culture hero whereby the forces of destruction and chaos were themselves destructured and rendered subservient to mankind's survival needs, and out of which sprang the institutions and rules of human social life.

Interestingly, the Papago Indians, horticulturists of the semiarid Southwest who were one of the Apache's traditional enemies, have a very similar, though more elaborate, myth (one that was probably influenced by Aztec thought).[6] In the beginning the world was inhabited by "another people" who were led by Elder Brother. When Elder Brother seemed to become tyrannical, the "other people" got Buzzard to kill him, and Elder Brother went underground. But he returned eventually, bringing the Papagoes with him as an army. Elder Brother quickly captured Buzzard, but agreed only to scalp him (that is why Buzzards are bald), if Buzzard would teach the Papagoes the songs that make power. The Papagoes then fought the "other people," while Elder Brother sang the songs that gave the Papagoes success. After teaching the Papagoes all of the songs that give them their power and control over nature, Elder Brother finally retired to a cave in the mountains. When the Papagoes wage war, they repeat carefully all the actions that Elder Brother took when he fought Buzzard and the "other people." The story has become more elaborate, incorporating elements of the dead and resurrected god as well as historical overtones; the ruins of the homes of an alien and unknown people do dot the territory the Papagoes inhabit. But the myth still contains the conception of violence, in this case literal war making, as a necessary ingredient in the overcoming of violence and uncontrolled nature.

One could repeat such myths endlessly as they are part of the cultural heritage of almost all horticultural, tribal peoples. Despite minor variations the basic structure is amazingly consistent. In the dream time either a god or a culture hero overcame, through an act of violence, the forces of chaos and destruction. He thereby made possible the well-being and social organization of mankind, or at least of that favored group who are the "true people." In the sense that it is concerned with the interconnection between life and death, the myth bears a certain relation to that other basic myth of the dead and resurrected god. However, it is different in an important way:

The being that is killed is not resurrected. Strictly speaking, there is no transformation but rather a final destruction that, though it may then be reenacted repetitiously in a rite, is mythically complete. (That this is not a myth of the eternal return based on a lunar mysticism is made particularly clear in the Yanomamo legend where it is not the death of the moon but its severe wounding and enforced return to its normal sphere that is creative.) Moreover, the death or destructuring is the necessary prerequisite for the emergence or birth of a completely different order of creation.

Specifically, the death is not the necessary prerequisite for the endless flow of the seasons and the fruits of the earth, nor for the release of humans from this world into the world of transcendence. Instead it creates human society and the social order, which is thus seen as a once-and-for-all-times event. This is particularly clear in the Papago myth where the culture hero who introduces war is also the dead-and-resurrected god. Elder Brother's death and resurrection in themselves do not change conditions; rather it is the destruction of the buzzard and the "other people" that sets the stage of true human (i.e., Papago) existence. The myth, moreover, opposes two kinds of death-dealing figures: the one that is purely destructive and chaotic and the one that is creative and order producing. But the creative figure is creative (within the framework of the myth) not primarily out of its own capacity to be reborn or to reproduce or to transform, but simply because it is capable of destroying that which needs to be destroyed. And what needs to be destroyed is that which in its chaotic and uncontrolled aggressiveness is threatening the existence of a harmonious and orderly universe.

The acting out of this understanding of humanity's relation to the cosmos is clearly illustrated by the parallels between the myth of the destruction of chaos and the ritual of war. The signal that the ritual is needed, for example, comes primarily when an external act of chaotic destructiveness (an "unnatural" death or a dream vision) impinging upon society warns the people that the original act whereby harmony was established is losing its effectiveness. As a result the society must prepare to repeat the actions of the original drama in order that chaos may again be defeated and an orderly prosperity restored to the universe.

Since actual warfare is part of the ritual, it is impossible to predetermine exactly which role any individual warrior will actually assume. He may find himself the culture hero, the supportive brother, or, if killed, chaos itself. Rather than creating a tension between the myth and the rite, however, this ambiguity of roles reconfirms that the conditions of the myth, the dominance of undifferentiated and disorderly chaos in the universe, do in fact exist. If the ritual roles were more clearly defined (as in, say, the fertility rituals of sacrifice), then the actual terms of the myth would be violated. The uncertainty regarding the participants' roles requires, however, that they be adequately prepared to make a symbolic identification with either chaos or hero. And this is borne out by the complexity of the ritual actions. Thus the Yanomamo both identify with the carrion eaters and by simulated vomiting reject the identification, while the Zulu warrior identifies with his ancestors (earlier heroes) and swallows a foul-tasting emetic. It is, moreover, this ambiguity that sustains the mutual interdependence of the two warring tribes.[7] In effect, they need each other for the ritual to be efficacious; unless one side through the unwilling sacrifice of a member enacts the role of chaos, the other cannot produce a hero.

For the side that "wins," that produces a culture hero, the myth has clearly been acted out fully. The successful enemy-killer has made a complete identification with a very destructive primordial being and with an act of great creative potency. The victim, whether man, woman, or child, has embodied in its moment of death the tremendous destructive potency of chaos, which has now been overcome. (Thus, for the Papagoes, all Apache are "magicians," possessors of supernatural powers.) As the channel for both such enormous destructive power and for the power that creates harmony, the enemy-killer is both a possible danger to, and ultimately a savior of, his society. Hence his seclusion until he is less "hot," less potent, and the immediate celebration through which his power, in its creative aspect, is confirmed and channeled into the life of the tribe. Hence also the awe (respect and fear) with which the victim's body, belongings, or name are regarded, to the extent that parts of the body may be eaten, while his name may actually be adopted by the killer. If primordial chaos is destructive, it is also the original source of all being and hence, when properly controlled, a source of enormous fecundity and power.

THE DESTRUCTION OF CHAOS   61

For the side that "loses," which produces chaos rather than a hero, the acting out of the myth simply takes longer. The continued existence of chaotic conditions is confirmed by the loss of an additional member, but the belief in the myth is not destroyed thereby because, in even its most attenuated form, the myth makes it clear that the hero had to make several efforts before being successful. Hence the grieving side can be understood simply as being temporarily frustrated, while the myth assures that, with continued effort and faith, victory will ultimately be possible. After the proper funeral ceremonies, war will therefore be renewed and the ritual continued.

In analytic terms, it is particularly revealing that the aggression of the chaotic force expresses itself as uncontrolled oral aggression. (Thus both the moon in the Yanomamo legend and the giant in the Apache story are eating children.) This is symbolically significant because of the importance assigned by almost all primitive people to the question of who eats what and how. Indeed, one of the two earliest and most compelling ways by which human society organized itself while still at the hunting and gathering stage was through food taboos (the other being marriage rules).[8] The limitations on what one could or could not eat defined one's existence as a human being, one's relation to nature and to other human beings. The mythic monster that blatantly violates these taboos thus represents not just any form of chaos or destruction, but specifically a form of aggression that strikes at the core of any kind of harmony between human beings or between mankind and nature. It is only with the destruction of this uncontrolled aggression that appropriate and harmonious relations can be established.

Such a myth of original creation through destruction stands in contrast to the equally prevalent myth of an original Golden Age from which mankind and nature have fallen. The myth of the Golden Age is a statement about humanity's spiritual experience, a way of expressing the reality that all people at certain times, and shamans in particular, have moments of at-oneness and harmony with the universe. At the same time that these myths explain human beings' fallen state, they also call people to attempt to reestablish by ritual action or trance that transcendent experience that, though mythically placed in the dream time, is by the very logic of mythic and ritual thought capable of being eternally reexperienced. The myth of the destruction of chaos, on the other hand, is a statement about mankind's social condition. It is, to use metaphors from a later and more sophisticated mythic conceptualization, the story of the founding of the City of Man as opposed to Adam and Eve's fall from the City of God.

From the perspective of gestalt psychology, every element within a dream/myth is in fact an element in, a projection of, an unassimilated part of the dreamer/mythologizer. Thus chaos (the giant, the moon, //Gaunab, etc.) is a projection of the part of a person that operates spontaneously out of its own desires and wants; that eats what it wants to eat when it is hungry, that strikes out destructively when it is angry. Insofar as the aggression is usually oral in character, it is a particularly infantile figure since oral aggression is the first and most basic mode of human aggression. Moreover, the existence of a mother, either explicitly (White Painted Woman) or by implication (as in the Yanomamo legend), as the most directly aggrieved figure fits into this pattern, since one of the earliest forms of social aggression is likely to involve biting rather than sucking the mother's breast, while early displacement from the breast because of the greater claims of a younger sibling is likely to produce some of our earliest homicidal desires. Thus chaos is a projection of the human psyche when it is least controlled or structured by external rules or societal pressures, following simply the dictates of its own physical needs. Moreover, chaos itself possesses no father or mother; thus it acknowledges no ties to its own kind or to the rest of existence. It simply is itself. But the price of its self-assertiveness is that it is feared and unloved; it is isolated.

By contrast, the culture hero (Child of Water, Suhirina, Tsui//Goab, etc.) usually has a mother and/or a brother with whom he has close, loving, and cooperative relations. He is thus a projection of that part of the human psyche that is a good child. He is both loving and loved; he does what his mother wants him to do; and he is pained and angered by what hurts and angers his mother/brother. It is, moreover, this identification with the family (the introjection of external norms) more than any personal fear of, or threat from, chaos that leads him to do battle. He will do what the mother desires and thereby win approval. And so, after a struggle, he slays (or brings under control) the forces of chaos and spontaneity and thereby becomes a hero, a man of character, a model of appropriate behavior.

From this successful conquest flows a third element in the human psyche—the element projected into the new order of reality that emerges from the conquest. The actual embodiment of this reality differs from myth to myth, but always contains certain basic conditions. It is a projection of that part of the psyche that is both orderly and productive (creating new human beings, domesticating animals, harvesting food, etc.). It is the ideal mature self. Clearly a more complete analysis could be made of any individual myth, since each element (the mother, the destroyed children, the threatened animals, etc.) is a significant projection of the psyche. But the myths are so different in details that such an analysis would be long and eventually tedious, and somewhat pointless in terms of the concerns of this work. What is important here is the general meaning of the conflict between the culture hero and chaos and the result of that conflict.

One of the more interesting aspects of this myth/dream has to do with the process it reflects. The three parts of the human psyche that dominate the structure of the myth (the infantile, the social, and the productive) are those recognized by almost every modern psychological theory, though under differing names, as elements in the human personality or stages in development. Because of our genetic makeup, moreover, human infants must and want to learn from their elders the rules, norms, and culture of society in order to become fully functioning adults. But the ideal learning process involves the assimilation of culture by children who bite into, chew over, swallow, and eventually digest and absorb knowledge because it is natural for a human being to do so, because they are "hungry" for it. In this myth, however, the process of assimilation is interrupted and the urge to appropriate on one's own time and terms is killed; the child's own aggressive energy is retroflected back against the self by the introjected elements (i.e., elements that have been swallowed whole rather than being assimilated) of his or her own personality. The result is that the mature individual is not in fact well integrated, but remains a collection of warring elements. Thus the human society founded by this act depends ultimately for its continued existence on the repetitive reenactment of the original act, that is, on continued retroflection and on ritual warfare. The process of the myth/dream is, therefore, a pathological one.

Like any primordial myth, the myth of the destruction of chaos can be read on and contains many levels. It is, as just explained, a psychological statement. But it is also a statement about human society that explains that only when the culture hero, embodying the norms of that society, is able forcibly to overcome anarchy and private desires can an orderly and productive society exist. It is also a statement about mankind's relation with nature. The chaotic, because uncontrolled and unordered, nature of the myth is destructured and a new universe is created in which (and this is especially clear, for example, in the Apache myth) a new relation of dominance and service comes into existence between humanity and nature. This new relation is, of course, not the only existing reality, but it is the only *true* reality. Since in mythopoetic thought only the world that has been created according to an extraterrestrial archetype is given any validity, only that world has been truly created.[9]

Thus the myth of the destruction of chaos concerns itself not just with the enforced and unassimilated elements in human socialization, but connects this process symbolically with the imposition of humanity's will and design upon nature. Thus it is a myth not of the origins of human society per se but of human society based upon farming rather than on hunting and gathering. The historic event, the event in time, has simply been transformed and given meaning and permanence by placing it outside of time, making it an archetypal gesture that is always repeatable and therefore reenforceable through ritual action.

The original or "primitive" tendency of the human mind and spirit has been to deny change, to resist the understanding of time as linear, and to reaffirm as consistently as possible that the present reality merely repeats an original divine act of the "dream time." Whatever is not conformable to, or a repetition of, such creative dramas is insubstantial and unimportant. All of the critical acts of human existence (from birth through initiation and marriage to death, and including the killing of large animals, the planting and harvesting of crops, the smelting and forging of ore) are understood as repetitions of such transcendent actions and thereby take on substantiality, significance, and predictability. The truth of the world and of human experience is eternal and understandable because it repeats endlessly the actions from which it originated.

As the examples illustrate, such an attitude does not make actual change impossible. New modes of productivity and of social organization were, in fact, adopted by human beings holding such a conservative view of reality. But the importance of the change per se (and, indeed, even the memory of the change as an act in time with a contrasting before and after) was denied. Instead the change was mythically pushed back into the dream time and made thereby part of the original, significant drama. Pride in human achievement as "progress" was exchanged for a sense of pride and security in human conformity to, and reconfirming participation in, the eternal nature of existence.

The shift from tribal villages to monarchical city-states did not in itself change this tendency of the human mind and psyche. Instead the city itself, the emerging political structures, the new relation with the earth and particularly with water, were whenever possible read back into the gradually restructured myths of the beginning. Thus by the fourth millennium B.C. the city-states of Mesopotamia were understood not as emerging from a long evolutionary process involving accident and human will but as the result of a single act of divine creation, and as repeating in microcosm the forms of divine reality. (Indeed, the shift from a transcendent dream time heavily inhabited by animals and natural forces to a transcendent world of anthropomorphic gods may reflect primarily the new kinds of changes in human social structure, which needed to be sacramentalized and thereby substantiated, rather than any sudden increase in human egotism and pride.) All that was needed for this process of mythologizing conservatism to work was for the pace of change to be slow enough and contiguous enough with the past for the creative reconstruction of the myth to keep pace with it. The result was that combination of change and continuity, that impression of timelessness imposed upon creativity and flux that is so much a characteristic of civilizations like the Mesopotamian, Egyptian, Indian, and Chinese.

As a result of this tendency, ritual elements remained embedded in the war of all civilizations. Not only did both the Babylonians and the Egyptians continue to act out mock ritual battles annually as part of their major religious festivals, but among the early Mesopotamians, the king-priests (or, in periods of political pluralism, the high priests) of the city-states organized and commanded the armies, acting, in theory at least, as stewards and agents for the gods.[10] Thus their decision to wage war and the way in which it was waged was still authenticated or initiated by a dream from the gods, and the results of the war were understood as simply the working out here on earth of decisions already taken by the assembly of gods.

Similarly, the Chinese decision for war was initially a religious one, made in the temple and including calculations as to whether the heavens were propitious for such a venture,[11] while the pre-Etruscan Romans had rituals for beginning and concluding wars that were performed initially by their kings but later entrusted to a guild of priests, the Fetiales. Even under the Republic, a triumphant Roman general was presented to the public in the guise of the great god of the Roman state, while the legionnaires usually bore on their standards the sacred animals of the deities to which they were especially devoted.[12] And, of course, the ancient Israelites marched into Palestine preceded by their sacred object (the Ark) and were likely to call upon their priests to act as war leaders in battle.[13]

In addition, myths with very clear structural parallels to the Neolithic destruction of chaos stories are part of the heritage of all major civilizations. The Babylonians, for example, knew a story in which Apsu and Ti'amat, the father (sweet water) and the mother (sea) of the gods, eventually became angry at their overly active children. Disturbed in their primordial rest, Apsu and Ti'amat decided to kill their own offspring, which produced counteraction by the gods. Ea, the spirit of intelligence, subdued and then killed Apsu by a spell, using his dead body to create the earth and the waters below it. But Ti'amat was more formidable; she remarried, collected a band of followers, and rode forth to battle.

The gods tried twice to subdue her by their authority alone and failed. They then turned to Marduk, god of strength, and empowered him as their king. Under his command the gods then proceeded as an army to confront Ti'amat. Marduk pierced her heart and killed her, taking her second husband, Kingu, and her followers captive. By the counsel of the gods he turned half of her into the sky, while he and Ea together created human beings from the blood of Kingu and put them upon the earth to do the work of the gods. The creation story has become more elaborate, but it still contains a mythological battle as its central element, replacing the individual warrior with a king and phalanxes. Out of this conflict with, and overcoming of, the chaotic forces of nature, the forces of life have created mankind —or, more accurately, have created human society as the Babylonians knew it.[14]

The Indo-European tradition has a similar myth.[15] The Vedic tales tell of a period when Indra, the warrior-god par excellence and the wielder of the thunderbolt, was king of the gods and undertook for them the task of murdering the giant and semidivine serpent, Vrtra, the enormous formless Resistance who was destroying the worlds. Although Indra was successful in killing Vrtra, he was overcome by the effects of his effort and fled into the water as a lotus flower, leaving the other gods and the universe itself in a chaotic condition. Finally Saci (Indra's wife) and Agni (Fire) found and restored him to his true form. As a result of his victory, the gods all came together and there was a general sharing of rewards and authority, creating the structured nature of the universe. Agni, who had played such an enormous role in bringing the whole affair to a successful conclusion, received a major reward: the institution of the fire sacrifice by which the whole order of the universe is maintained and by which he became indistinguishable from Indra himself.

The political organization of this mythic realm is less sophisticated than that of the Babylonian tale. Though a king, Indra operates more like a culture hero than a leader of armies, a fact that seemingly reflects the less sophisticated political organization of these Vedic pastoralists. Moreover, though the basic plot remains the same (the ordering of the universe as a result of an act of creative violence), the special role assigned Agni, the patron of the priestly Brahman caste, unquestionably reflects both that caste's competition with the warrior caste (which stood in a special relation to Indra) and the incorporation into the myth of the traditional purification rites prescribed for the warrior-killer.[16]

The Hebrews, however, essentially abandoned (if reluctantly and never completely) the story of an original battle with chaos. Instead they focused on an actual historical act (the Exodus from

Egypt) by which they believed their society had been formed and proceeded to mythologize it. Thus the Hebrews remembered the Exodus as involving a cruel monster (the Pharaoh) who destroyed children, a culture hero (Moses) who set out to overcome chaos in conformity to parental (i.e., the god of the fathers) command, repetitive failures of the hero that mark but do not end his mission; and a final victory in which Moses/Yahweh uses chaos itself (the waters) to defeat chaos. Moreover, from this event flowed the rules (covenant) that founded proper relations between the chosen people and the divine. Interestingly, on a ritual level the Hebrews associated the remembrance of this successful escapade with the observance of first-fruit rituals intended to assure increased fertility and life, while one of the oldest song fragments preserved (in Exodus 15) was specifically remembered as a song by a woman in celebration of victory. If the Hebrews had essentially abandoned cosmology for history, they had not abandoned a mythic perspective. Rather they acquired in the Exodus and the covenant a new mythic pattern through which to interpret historic events.

The Roman branch of the Indo-European family handled the tension between the original myth and their historical memory in a fashion almost directly opposite. In effect, the Romans historicized mythology—and all of European civilization has been the heir to this event. By the second century B.C. the original Indo-European myths of the dream time had been turned into a history of the origins of Rome itself. The gods and heroes of Aryan myths became a line of kings, each of whom in his acts and functions embodied the characteristics of the gods, while it was understood as a sign of Rome's good fortune that the gods brought forth exactly the right man for each successive stage of state building.[17] In historicizing the myth of war the Romans attributed the qualities of the battle god (Mars, Indra, etc.) to a human king (Tullus Hostilius) who was depicted as warlike, hostile, offensive, courageous, a good disciplinarian, and the founder of the Roman military and penal establishments. Instead of being an impersonal representation of chaos and death such as Indra must contend with, his enemy was a perfidious human opponent, the Albans. The benefit accruing from his victory was not the creation of the ordered universe but the very concrete and specific political and economic expansion of Rome.

THE DESTRUCTION OF CHAOS 69

In this historicized myth, the warrior takes on the attributes of the gods, becoming the creator and controller of his own destiny so that history is seemingly freed from repeating the forms of eternity and its content is given power and importance. However, the historicization of myth does not mean its annihilation, but rather its assimilation into a new medium. The form of the original myth is in fact retained and becomes the filter through which actual historical wars are perceived and understood. The warrior-king becomes the actual cultural hero rather than his representative, while the human enemy literally becomes chaos. For example, in Virgil's *Aeneid*, Turnus is depicted as "crazy with bloodlust . . . with the criminal mania for fighting, still more, with resentment."[18] Thus in contrast to Neolithic ritual warfare where good always triumphs, because both sides are simply struggling for the same good and one always wins, war for the Romans came to be perceived as actually determining whether chaos or order would triumph in the universe.

Hebrew and Roman thought has inevitably led us from timelessness to history. Indeed, one of the major challenges to humanity's attempt to deny the historical dimension, the linear and contingent character of human experience, unquestionably came from the changing nature of war and the dramatic impact of functionally oriented battle on the life of civilized communities. Once released from its ritual limitations and given a directly materialistic goal, warfare simply could not be confined to an unchanging pattern; instead its results involved not only enormous losses of life and property, but also changes in political and economic organization, influxes of new people and cultures. War ceased, therefore, to be an obvious reaffirmation of the conservative, timeless nature of reality and became instead one of mankind's most dramatic experiences of flux, catastrophe, and change.

5
Cultures of Greed

From time immemorial, man has had an instinctive love of power. With the growth of our empire, this instinct has become a dominant and uncontrollable force.... Worldwide conquest and the destruction of all rival communities or potentates opened the way to the secure enjoyment of wealth and an overriding appetite for it.
—*Tacitus*[1]

Men are born with the love of gain; if this natural tendency is followed they are contentious and greedy.... They are filled from birth with envy and hatred of others.
—*Hsun Tzu*[2]

When one looks at civilized as opposed to Neolithic warfare, one fact stands out. The wars of peasant-based, civilized states are fought primarily for territorial rather than ritualistic goals, a fact reflected in the actual strategy of the armies involved. Moreover, in the peasant-based civilizations that dominate history from around 3000 B.C. until the nineteenth century A.D., territorial expansion involves the extension of political sovereignty over additional populations and also results in increased resources (money, raw material, and manpower) for the elite that controls the victorious political structure. The primary result of war, therefore, is increased power and material wealth for the successfully aggressive elites.

As even the most superficial student of history knows, the story of any civilization is a story of continuous and repetitive warfare involving a struggle over territorial (and therefore political and economic) sovereignty. States and contiguous civilizations compete endlessly over the positioning of their boundaries, while centralized empires collapse into their warring feudalistic components and are recreated into single units in a dreary and incredibly repetitive tale. Indeed, one of the tests of a great historian like Livy is his ability to give individuality and interest to events that are, in fact, compulsively alike. It is clear that political elites in all civilized cultures are obsessed with an insatiable desire for power and goods. What is less clear is the source and meaning of this greed.

The attitude of most twentieth-century thinkers regarding the supposed fact of human insatiability is ambiguous. While western economic and political theorists tend to assume that unlimited desire is an inherent or natural trait of human nature, they differ in their attitudes toward this supposed fact. Economic theory takes human insatiability as an acceptable good and concerns itself primarily with the problem of which economic arrangement is most efficient in producing an ever increasing array of commodities to feed this desire. Conservatives, à la Hobbes, tend to generalize from this greediness to the necessity of politics. Only a powerful sovereign can provide internal law, order, and peace; between states relations must inevitably be violent and suspicious. Liberal political theorists, however, tend to deny a connection between the desire for power and greed for material goods. While generally accepting material hunger as a good thing, they assume that humanity's insatiable drive for political power is an evil that can be contained by a government of checks and balances. The elimination of war is sought through international government, while the drive for goods is left primarily to self-regulating economic mechanisms.

Western psychological theories, on the other hand, assume that human desires are satisfiable and that insatiability (whether it be an unlimited greediness for food, power, or affection) is "compulsive" and neurotic. But even Karen Horney, the psychologist who has dealt most extensively with this problem on a theoretical level and whose thinking Perls has explicitly incorporated into gestalt therapy, believes that such compulsive drives may, under special conditions, be functional and therefore presumably nonneurotic. Thus she observes in *The Neurotic Personality of Our Time* that "If it is a monarch who develops a restless striving for power and possession, the result . . . may be reassurance and a successful life,"[3] without questioning whether the existence of a monarch and the cultural traits that approve his "restless" striving are themselves neurotic.

Horney, however, is convinced (as political and economic theorists generally are not) that ever-expanding desires for goods and power are not inherent in human nature but are traits that are encouraged or discouraged by specific cultural conditions. In this she is supported by the works of ethologists and anthropologists that make it clear that insatiability, like revenge, is not only a species-specific characteristic, but that it is a trait that becomes "natural" only at a specific point in human evolution, that is, with the development of peasant-based civilizations. Any attempt to understand the compulsion to wage war that characterizes the insatiable elites of civilization must therefore also deal with the roots of compulsive greed in general.

Any nonsocial species needs five things for survival: air, water, protection against inclement weather, food, and sexual partners. Moreover, they need them in a limited amount: Mother and children need only one den as a protected nest; a bear can occupy only one cave during the winter; physiological capacity limits the amount one can eat or drink. Even when hoarding or storing is part of the life cycle, as with squirrels or bears, only enough food to tide one over the barren cold months is useful or desired. Male sexuality in animals such as seals or horses that collect harems seems unlimited, but it is in fact checked by the limited receptivity of the female. The animal that has satisfied these physiological and genetically based needs is likely, unless it is a social animal, to be in a state of satisfied equilibrium and to spend its time sleeping, sunning, or playing—all essentially nonacquisitive activities.

In addition to these five needs, social animals desire nonsexual contact with other members of their species and will spend hours in the gentle, sensual interaction known as grooming. Among social animals, only the desire for grooming (which like sleeping, sunning, and playing is a nonacquisitive, essentially nondestructive activity) appears to be relatively unlimited or, more precisely, to be limited only by the amount of time that must be devoted to the equally essential need for food, shelter, sex, and sleep. Such social grooming, moreover, plays an important biological role, since it helps to develop and maintain those close ties among the animal band on which species survival partly depends. It is thus quite likely that the need for such sensual interaction is genetically based. Certainly experiments with chimpanzees have made it clear that to deprive a social animal of such close contact during infancy results in an adult incapable of achieving total and effective biological maturity and therefore incompetent as a perpetuator of the species.

Hunters and gatherers closely approximate the desire-acquisition-satiation pattern of other social animals. Their desire for food and shelter is closely connected with their immediate physical needs; although female sexual receptivity is constant, mature males tend to seek out one or two partners and remain loyal to them. Activities in pursuit of food and shelter occupy, on the average, only twenty hours a week. To the nonacquisitive activities of sleep and social grooming, however, Homo sapiens adds a third need: involvement in cultural interaction. Moreover, it is the dominant importance of these cultural interactions that differentiate human beings from other mammals because they arise from a genetic dependency on culture creation and culture transmission as a replacement for genetically imparted information concerning practical knowledge and forms of social organization and interaction.

Even among hunters and gatherers, the desire for such cultural interaction appears to share with the desire for social grooming the characteristic of being unlimited. Such cultural interaction may, however, take place through a variety of means: through stories, dance, ritual, and songs as well as through the meaning attached to very mundane activities such as eating, marriage, the decoration of tools and the human body, or the organization of shelter. While the conceptualizing capacity of the human species means that any physical act or interaction with the external environment can become, and perhaps necessarily becomes, a vehicle for the expression of cultural needs and values, it need not, and among hunters and gatherers does not, necessitate any significant expansion of the desire for material goods.

The reliance on physiological needs as the energizer of aggressive action in the pursuit of subsistence goods that characterizes the life-style of hunters and gatherers is, of course, broken when mankind turns to horticulture as a way of life. The necessity to plant crops or tend animals regardless of one's physiological state or desires, and the socialization necessary to insure that the mature adult will conform to nature's time schedule rather than his or her own, is unquestionably the first break in the original close connection between physiologically based and therefore satiable needs and aggressive activity. But with most horticulturalists this does not produce a general cultural pattern of insatiability. Garden plots remain fairly commensurate with the sustenance needs of the group; housing remains fairly small and starkly functional in size. The desire for personal decorations and elaborate, special clothing may increase slightly, but it seldom goes beyond the limits of what the individual may actually manage to wear on his or her own body on special occasions. Though sexual desire seems to expand, as evidenced by higher rates of childbirth, it remains limited; even the privileged males seldom acquire more than two or three wives, and monogamy generally remains the rule. Moreover, though the horticulturalist and pastoralist possibly work more hours than do hunters and gatherers, they are still far from even a forty-hour week and have enormous amounts of time available for social grooming, cultural interaction, and sleep. Thus the distribution of time among activities reflects a relatively low priority for acquisitive desires.

When conditions favor easy acquisition of surplus foods or goods, they are not hoarded. Rather they are typically collected together (often through the offices of a tribal leader or ritual figure) and then redistributed to the community in elaborate ceremonial celebrations that become the occasion for close, friendly social interaction. This is par excellence the occasion on which elaborate finery of dress, social grooming, physical contact, cultural interaction through storytelling, ritual, and general social intercourse are made available to the whole community to an intense and even ecstatic degree. The sharing of physically unneeded material goods is thus used as an occasion for the intense gratification of those relatively unlimited desires for social grooming and cultural interaction.

With the shift to peasant-based civilization, however, there is an enormous expansion of both the capacity to feed human desires and the definition of what basic needs involve. It is specifically in such communities that an insatiable desire for goods and power becomes the norm, though it is particularly obvious among the elite who are most able to attempt to satisfy their expanding desires. Typically, for example, the elite of any civilization secure for themselves numerous houses with each individual house or castle possessing an enormous number of rooms. They secure, in addition, an endless supply of clothing and jewelry, trinkets, objets d'art, amusements, gardens, and other luxuries. That such a desire is not physiologically based is made clear when even the physical capacities of the body are strained in an attempt to eat gargantuan meals or to service several hundred women in well-guarded harems. The possession of shelter, clothing, food, sexual partners, and goods in general is limited in fact, of course, by the resources of the individual or elite for acquiring them, but not, as far as one can tell from the evidence, from a sense that no more is needed or desired. What cannot be used is hoarded, preserved unused and denied to others.

Moreover, although their capacity for acquiring a plethora of goods and sexual partners is more limited, the evidence all suggests that the urban and peasant classes share something of the elites' insatiability for possessions. Unless regulatory laws or punitive taxes restrain them, the merchant, craftsman, and farmer are just as likely as their rulers to want to acquire housing, clothes, food, sexual partners, and goods to the limit of their resources and even at the sacrifice of sleep, social grooming, and cultural interaction. Indeed, whether one observes the French or Chinese peasant, the most typical pattern is a driving desire to acquire more land, bigger houses, larger families, and increasing wealth, even though the effort involved or societal norms may make any actual enjoyment of these "goods" difficult. Similarly, the desire of the lower classes to imitate "their betters" has been an age-old source of distress to the conservative moralist, anxious to preserve the externals of the hierarchical order.

The ever-expanding desire of the ruling elite to possess more material goods, and therefore the political sovereignty that makes such goods available, is not an isolated phenomenon in a peasant-based civilization. Rather it is simply one expression of a general psychological trait shared by the vast majority of the population. The very insatiability of desire, moreover, creates at any single point in time a situation of limited resources since, when everyone is insatiable, it is impossible to satisfy everyone. Within a state competition for these limited goods is normally restrained from escalating into violent conflict by the fact that the state asserts and generally acquires a monopoly on violence; between states, however, no such monopoly prevents elites from fighting over resources in what is, at any one point in time, a zero-sum game.

Since insatiability emerges as a characteristic of the human species in a particular period of time and under specific conditions, the common characteristics of peasant-based civilizations are obviously important as a source of this greed. While these civilizations vary enormously in style, all organize substantial community projects that rearrange the natural environment in an attempt to increase human control over the external world, to provide additional resources to support an expanding population, and to insure greater survival security for the human community. As a result they all develop specialized hierarchies that direct community activities and collect from the population in general a substantial surplus of goods and labor (a tax or rent) that is used both to fund community projects and to support the hierarchy itself in affluence. While ritual activity as a mode of controlling the natural environment continues to be important, it is increasingly supplemented and replaced by administrative and engineering manipulation of resources as an appropriate way of securing the good life. Simultaneously, there is a development of economic specialization and hierarchic caste ordering. Whereas in a typical primitive society there is little differentiation of roles beyond those associated with sex and age, in civilizations specialization becomes the norm. One is a priest or a warrior or a farmer or a blacksmith, but not all four. Similarly, the totemic clans of precivilized society, which interacted in an interdependent, homologous fashion, evolve into castes that stand in a hierarchic relation to each other.

Like the shift to horticulture, the shift to hierarchic, specialized social relations and increased control of nature originally need not have been neurotic. Indeed it may well have evolved out of the human capacity for play, experimentation, drama. (Certainly early civilizations radiate an aura of excitement and energy that is both attractive and suggestive.) Once institutionalized, however, the new relations between human beings and between humans and nature mean that the distance between energy activated in work and actual physical desires becomes even greater. For the vast bulk of the peasant population farming must be carried on at a level that will not only support the immediate family, but will also consistently provide a surplus to satisfy the coercive demands of a permanent elite for tithes, taxes, and other levies. In addition, peasants are often expected to participate in the strenuous physical labor involved in building canals, bridges, roads, aqueducts, temples, fortifications, castles, pyramids, and the like. While some of these activities, such as those involved in irrigation projects, will unquestionably eventually contribute to their physical well-being, in many cases the results of this labor will provide no physical satisfaction. And in no case will the connection between work and physical needs be immediate or even close.

Though they enjoy the surplus provided by the agrarian masses, the ruling elites who specialize in fighting, administration, and religious activities are similarly involved in a life-style that requires obligations to be honored regardless of physical inclination or needs. To take an extreme example, the pharaoh or the Chinese emperor may in theory be divine or all-powerful, but the functioning of his office demands that his whole life be subjected to a rigid and all-embracing series of rules and taboos and that he participate in an endless round of ritual activities of both a religious and a political nature according to traditional and oftentimes rigid time schedules. Such a time schedule is set, moreover, by the priestly and administrative elites that, though in theory the ruler's passive support groups, in practice operate as enforcers of traditional ritual norms. Since ideally the ruler should also involve himself in administrative and policy-setting responsibilities, the "good" pharaoh clearly has little free time or opportunity simply to follow his own inclinations.

Religious, military, and administrative elites are also expected to adopt a life-style that demands similar self-discipline. Beyond the tasks that their specific roles prescribe, the repetitive tedium of religious and court ritual will occupy hours of their time. Typically their life is also disciplined by the rules of *dharma, li,* face, or honor, which demand a certain form of conduct.[4] Such conduct is not optional. Rather it is an essential part of the cultural patterns that both differentiate the elites from the nonprivileged and justify their privilege.

The tendency, then, is for civilization to demand of all its participants a substantial separation of personal physical inclination and actual working obligations. In fact, the price civilization exacts from mankind for further escape from the controls and limits of the natural environment is the intensification, at all levels of society, of controls by male elites. This means that the "natural" pattern of physiologically based desire, exertion of energy in self-motivated aggressive action and satiation upon satisfaction of the desire, must be partly replaced by a pattern in which action is motivated by external commands.

While political control has long been recognized as a crucial element in all societies that create states, the small amount of violence that is normally necessary to enforce such control makes it clear that the consent of the governed is more critical to a stable civilization than the actual coercive force of the state. Comparisons with other animal species, combined with a narrow historical perspective, has led many observers to assume that the hierarchic nature of civilization is parallel to the hierarchic structure of other social animals such as baboons or horses, and that obedience is therefore "natural" to human beings.

But, in fact, dominant males in other animal groups primarily tend to demand first rights to food and sexual partners (but not a monopoly or a right to hoard), making no other attempt to control the normal activities of subordinate individuals. Their dominance, moreover, is based on physical and psychic superiority and is constantly open to challenge, while their primary group function involves directing it to good food sources and protecting it against the predatory activities of other species, even at the cost of self-sacrifice. In theory the function of civilized leadership is supposed to be of a similar nature, and it may be so in the original stages of a civilization, but the reality in an established civilization is in fact quite different, and the demands for obedience are much more embracing. Why, then, should civilized people be so willing, on the whole, to accept with relative passivity the much more exploitative and extensive control claimed by dominant human males? And how is it possible for both passive obedience and insatiable desire to coexist within an individual and a society? The answer lies in the particular patterns of family organization and socialization of the young that are common to all peasant-based civilizations and that function to adapt the young to participate effectively as adults in such a hierarchic society.

The outstanding characteristic of all peasant-based civilizations is that their family structure is, without exception, patrilineal, patrilocal, and patriarchal. While there may be minor variations of degree, the outstanding characteristic is that women lose any recognized rights to significant amounts of property or to independent action. They become instead classified as possessions, dependent upon and ideally obedient to either their father or their husband. At the same time, the role of the eldest male within a family is elevated to a position of dominance in which his control of property and his right to give orders to younger men and all women is ideally unchallengeable. Hierarchy is thus introduced into the most primary unit of human interaction as well as the secondary structures.

The pattern of child rearing is similarly affected by civilization. While the early imposition of weaning and the demand that the child engage in regulated labor at an early age is similar to the mode of socialization adopted by horticultural societies, the element of control and deprivation after the age of five or six is intensified with civilization. Physical punishment, especially by the father, for failure to work, disobedience, or simply troublesome behavior becomes commonplace, while at the same time the father withdraws from close affectionate physical relations with his children. Thus during their prepubescent and adolescent years, the major impact of civilization on children of both sexes is an increase in physical coercion and a diminution of the physical fondling that is the predecessor of adult social grooming and that is closely connected in human psychology with the ability to give and receive affection.

Any close affectionate physical contact will be predominantly with the mother. While girls will be given more physical fondling than boys in the early years, most civilizations will reverse this situation at about the time the child is five to seven years old. From then on the mother will tend to bestow more affection upon male children, while generally adopting an attitude of punitive detachment toward females. But the mother, herself subservient to the elders of the extended family and to her husband, will also be an enforcer of the general norms of society and of her own personal demands upon children of both sexes. Her bestowal of love will be contingent upon obedience and will always be merged with punitive action, usually of a physical as well as psychic nature.

Since human children are genetically coded to learn, the overall result of such a pattern of socialization is to teach children to internalize the commands of the adult world. In particular, these adult precepts include the teaching that dominant male authority figures must be respected and obeyed; thus by adulthood men and women have been programmed to demand of themselves obedience to authority as one of the proper elements of a good human character. Moreover, since the ideal image of adulthood presented is one of a father who works hard and is relatively formal, restrained, and distant in his affectional relations, the child will also have developed the image of a mature male adult as one who does not want or need constant affectionate interchange or "social grooming." Indeed, he is likely to block consciousness of his own desires for physical affection (as well as of his desire to be lazy, independent, and generally self-motivated).

But the desire for social grooming and affection, though denied release or even recognition, does not disappear. Genetically based, it remains as part of the psyche, giving rise to a continuous experience of longing. Since, as children, civilized humans experience parental affection primarily through the granting of goods, especially food, they will tend to sublimate the desire for affection into a desire for goods, goods that the culture generally associates with social prestige and approval. Moreover, since the granting of love through goods has usually had a very contingent quality (i.e., lovable equals obedient), love and control, affection and material bountifulness become interwoven and confused in an individual's perception, until the adult is literally unable to distinguish these emotions. The pattern is thus set for the socialization pattern to be repeated, for loving parents to subject their children to the same socialization process they themselves experienced, because that appears the most appropriate way to express affection and concern. In the process, of course, the desire for material consumption has inevitably been expanded beyond that experienced by a noncivilized society, since it has become confused with the relatively unlimited desire for social grooming and affection, as well as having been accentuated as a mode of cultural interaction. Moreover, the amount of goods one possesses has come to carry both psychological meaning and cultural symbolism: more goods and prestige mean more approval, more power means more love.

The description so far has been of a cultural pattern of socialization and adaptation that most twentieth-century observers would consider "normal" or "nonpathological." In order to make the desired social structure work, society has simply used the malleability inherent in the human genetic structure to increase the willingness of adults to be obedient to dominant males, while sublimating the desire for physical affection or social grooming (which might interfere with the necessary work orientation and which has a rather egalitarian thrust) into a desire for material goods (which will encourage the willingness to work and through which hierarchic meaning can be expressed). The potentially unlimited character of the sublimated desire for affection and social grooming will, however, ideally be limited by internalized societal rules governing both the appropriate methods for acquiring such goods and power and the amount appropriate to individuals in different castes. (In addition, the longing for affection and social bonding will also be directed into religious channels, which, besides providing members of the community with access to ecstatic experiences of unity, will explicitly offer consolation for the inevitable experience of dissatisfaction, frustration, and unhappiness.)

Such a system has worked with biological efficiency for large portions of the species for five or six millennia and has been, moreover, the social setting in which the monumental works of culture and art that most humans value have become possible. One hesitates (and the hesitancy is common to most psychologists, sociologists, and anthropologists) to characterize as neurotic or pathological a mode of life that is so clearly well within the range of the human capacity for adaptation. Three factors, however, suggest that peasant-based civilizations fail to produce a truly integrated social or personality structure. Obedience to established authority is repeatedly challenged by a wide range of rebellious and often physically violent acts; an insatiable desire for additional goods and power continuously surfaces among all classes of society, despite traditional prohibitions against such desires; and the elites of such civilization have tended to engage in continual and destructive warfare as an expression of both their own insatiability and of a very real, if generalized, hostility.

In effect, civilizations would work smoothly if the value norms, repressions, and sublimations upon which they depend were, in fact, truly assimilated by each new generation. (It is doubtful, however, that either control or consumption can ever be completely satisfactory substitutes for love and physically expressed affection, especially in a cultural milieu dominated by a hierarchic social structure, since the possession of goods and power is also an instrument of social distancing.) The violence and insatiability that characterize all civilizations are the indisputable evidence that for a high proportion of individuals in a civilization, socialization has been achieved through retroflection and introjection rather than assimilation. The result is a personality and social structure constantly threatened by internal, explosive conflicts.

Typically and by intent in a patriarchal household, children are expected to obey the commands of a parent immediately and regardless of their own inclinations. Since obedience to authority is one of the main lessons to be taught, allowing children to assimilate lessons at their own pace would be inappropriate. The arbitrariness of commands is accentuated, moreover, by a conscious system of discrimination that gives males priority over females and the elder over the younger. In addition, the mother typically engages in (for the child) unpredictable changes between indulgence and rejection. In conformity with societal norms she at first overly indulges and later rejects all females; with males she is likely to be secretly indulgent, protective, and an encourager of rebellion against the father, while publicly a defender of the father's rights and an angry enforcer of her own demands for affection and obedience. All of these are factors that in any civilization militate against the likelihood of children's voluntary acceptance and assimilation of adult demands as part of their own integrated character structure.

This pattern of coercion, moreover, exists for the children of elites as well as for the peasantry; indeed arbitrariness and relative deprivation of affectional relations is often even more exaggerated for the future ruler than for his subjects. While he is adulated as a future prince and urged to remember and display his specialness and dignity, he is also subjected to rigid control, especially in terms of the obedience and servility he must display toward his father. Though elite children will usually not be forced to work, they will be subjected to fairly substantial, formalized education and expected to be silent and properly restrained observers or minor participants in the ritual life of their family, caste, and/or class. In addition, the ritualized work of the monarch or feudal prince provides even less opportunity than farming or craftwork for a child's creative involvement.

Moreover, both the father's jealous possessiveness and the demands of his role often deprive the elite child even of a close relation with the mother. Typically elite children are turned over to wet nurses, governesses, and tutors, an ever-shifting group of servants who may bestow some minimal affection on the child but who are all too likely just to be "doing a job" and concerned primarily with their own advancement. Where the monarch is polygamous, relations between mother and son will be more intense, but will also, because of the competitive scheming for power that characterizes such situations, be highly contingent and demanding. In either case, affectionate physical relations between generations are likely to be even less available to the elite's children than in a peasant household, while arbitrary coercion and unjust demands are likely to be even more typical of their education.

Thus in civilized societies all children after the age of five are deliberately presented with situations in which they must act contrary to their own bodily desires or face punishment and loss of love. Any expression of anger at being coerced or thwarted is also prohibited by the adult world. The energy that would move outward in anger to achieve their desires must be retroflected against themselves and thereby blocked. Over a period of time this produces not only a rigid body armor of tightened muscles that operate to prevent many of these emotions from reaching consciousness, but also a growing reserve of unfinished situations involving unexpressed pain or anger. Such retroflection causes anxiety, both physiologically by interfering with normal breathing patterns (which are necessarily interrupted as part of the blockage of both tears and anger) and psychologically by the creation of a sense of diffused and potentially explosive anger and pain charged with a sense of potential danger (originally blocked because it was dangerous).

Once this pattern of retroflection and repression is established, the child and later the adult has, in addition to the need to survive and satisfy conscious needs, the problem of dealing with the conscious anxiety and the unconscious but present pain and anger that are the price of retroflection. Typically such an anxiety-ridden individual tries to handle these problems in four ways, one of which generally dominates: withdrawal, a search for affection, submissiveness, or a search for power (including prestige and goods). The dynamic assumption behind such a personality structure seems to be "if I am powerful (or if everyone loves me, or if I am submissive, or if I don't need anyone) then I will get what I want and I will not be hurt." Obviously different social and familial situations as well as personal idiosyncracies will affect which mode is most likely to be adopted, though of the four the search for power and goods is the most common in peasant-based civilizations, since symbolically and emotionally power/goods and affection have become intertwined, even for the "normal" members of the society.

In a society that, like the twentieth-century United States, values good feelings and popularity, the search for affection and approval can, as Karen Horney has observed, seem both natural and an indication of "good character." It will win parental approval, while undue submissiveness (especially among men) is likely to be castigated by parents because it runs counter to our high evaluation of individual assertiveness. In a peasant village, on the other hand, submissiveness to external standards (as embodied in the dominant religious-social standards and traditional male authority) is likely to be approved and rewarded as appropriate behavior. Thus among the peasant and lower classes of a hierarchic society, neurotic as well as successful socialization of the young is likely to produce an overtly submissive personality that is secretly anxious to accumulate material wealth and land.

Children of ruling elites face a situation of even greater difficulty and tension, however, because while they too are forced into actual submissiveness vis-à-vis their parents as minors, the adoption of submissiveness as a general character structure is devalued by their mentors and the demands of their future roles. They are thus in a double bind in which they are expected both to conform to the orders of their father and the ritualized norms of the elite's life, and simultaneously to exhibit and exercise the capacity to lead and exercise power over others. The anxiety and hostility created by such a dilemma are likely to be considerable. For many, withdrawal from human involvement is clearly the easiest release, a pattern exemplified in an extreme form in this century by Edward VIII, who seems to have formed only one meaningful relationship in his entire life and to have abdicated gladly to preserve it. But a similar, if less extreme withdrawal is also recognizable in the distant, formal, and relatively affectionless lives of many other monarchs: for example, Elizabeth the Great, Matthias and Charles V of the Hapsburg line, Louis IX of France, and Nicholas II of Russia.

Submissive to their parents while they lived, such monarchs are characterized predominantly by their desire to be "correct," that is, simply to conserve that which they have inherited and which tradition prescribes as their right. As rulers they seldom initiate wars, though they may respond defensively against attack. Their real defense against pain and harm lies in their affective noninvolvement with or attachment to other human beings, a pattern revealed strikingly in their secretiveness and lack of trust, their insensitivity to others' love and suffering, and their failure or refusal to form any important or loving bonds with equals. Such rulers are often judged by contemporaries and posterity as "good rulers," and rightly so because they are peaceable, just (i.e., conformable to social norms), and industrious (since busyness helps fill the void created by withdrawal). Moreover, the ritual formality characteristic of court life helps cloak, and may have been developed in part by, their tendency to withdraw from social contact. The cost in pain and loneliness that such an adjustment involves (since, like any human being, they still want affection and do feel hostility and rejection) is borne more by themselves than by their subjects. That the pain is real is attested by the number of rulers who, like Charles V of the Holy Roman Empire, have voluntarily abdicated to withdraw into the even deeper solitude and protective anonymity of monastic life.

Those rulers who seek power and its concomitant prestige and wealth follow a more turbulent career. As young men they are likely to be involved in constant conflicts with their fathers and siblings (as were the sons of Henry IV and of all the eighteenth-century Hanoverian kings). As rulers they are likely to be energetic and even ruthless in seeking to expand as much as possible their domestic and international power, even when such action defies the norms into which they and their subjects have ostensibly been socialized. While the specific personal history of most rulers, like that of their subjects, has been lost to memory, we do have information on the childhood of some of the more exceptional warrior-kings. All of it fits into the pattern psychological theory would expect to find. Alexander the Great, for example, grew up as only one of many children in a contentious polygamous household. His contacts with his royal father were minimal, but his ties with his mother, an energetic, ambitious, and rather violent woman, seem to have been exceptionally close. Given what we know of her character, it seems likely that her affection was always contingent. Granted the seductiveness and hostility characteristic of all the legends that have clung to her memory, it is understandable that only the conquest of the known world would suffice as an outlet for her son's hostility and a sop for his anxiety.

By contrast, Frederick the Great of Prussia suffered from a mousy, submissive mother who provided neither overt affection nor protection and a domineering, callous father who alternated periods of neglect with harshly critical demands that his sons conform to his barracks-style vision of masculinity. It was only when his attempt to escape from this disastrous family situation and find affection outside it was brutally thwarted that Frederick adapted and began the pursuit of power and prestige that made him one of the major military leaders of eighteenth-century Europe.

Alexander and Frederick are, of course, exceptions in terms of their capacity as military leaders and, possibly, in terms of the destructiveness of their childhood experience. But everything we know about the socialization patterns of individual royal families (such as the Romanovs, Bourbons, and Hapsburgs), and about the norms of patriarchal royal families in general, makes it clear that the difference is merely one of quantity rather than quality. For the anxious products of such families, the authority and material prosperity that civilized states normally provide for their elite is understandably inadequate as a resolution for repressed hostility and neurotic anxiety. Indeed if one is continuously driven, as such individuals are, by a sense of weakness and a fear of being "found out," then the demand for strength and the publicity that regularly beat upon leaders will heighten rather than assuage the anxious need for reassurance. As James Mills observed in the 1820s, in such a situation there is not "in the mind of a king, or in the minds of an aristocracy, any point of saturation with the objects of desire."[5] Instead rulers strive to increase the extent of their own realm, the scope of their authority over their subjects, and the material abundance achievable through these means.

For all civilizations, wealth and power come together symbolically and actually in a single object: gold. It is the goal and the prerogative of both divine and human authority. Soft, shiny, and easily workable, gold has been used to adorn the bodies of rulers in life and death, molded into statues for temples and dinnerware for courts, lacquered over walls and furniture, hoarded in vaults and the ground. It was the major lure that first drew nomadic hordes from Eurasia to sack urbanized civilizations, while as late as the eighteenth century enlightened statesmen still venerated it as both means and goal of a wise foreign policy. It is the ultimate meaning of all coinage and currency, the "surplus use-value" that still drives capital accumulation.

Part of this facination undoubtedly stems from the sheer erotic quality of gold: its smoothness, fluidity, warmth, and glow. Of all inorganic material, only silver comes close to it in sheer visual and tactile appeal; if one cannot touch a human body, it is at least a plausible substitute. But since its discovery in ancient Egypt gold has always carried a meaning beyond its pleasurable attractiveness. Glitteringly yellow like the sun and amazingly incorruptible, it has been equated symbolically with life and immortality. To possess gold, whether one hoards it in secret or displays it lavishly in public, is to possess the power of (or power over) nature and life. But the movement from the erotic reality of gold to the idolatry of the symbol is a further step in the alienation of our species from the physical reality of human bodies that must inevitably live and die. The sacralization of gold ultimately means that mankind "spends money on what is not bread, ... wages on what fails to satisfy" (Isaiah 55:2). In John Ruskin's words, the pursuit of gold substitutes "dust for deity, spectre for possession, fettered dream for life." Unfortunately, it is a dream for which many men and women have died.

6

The Satisfaction of Guilt

> For all to be accomplished, for me to feel less lonely, all that remained to hope was that on the day of my execution there should be a huge crowd of spectators and that they should greet me with howls of execration.
> —*Albert Camus*[1]

> In most of us there is a genuine longing for community with our human species, and at the same time an awkwardness and helplessness about finding the way to achieve it.
> —*J. Glenn Gray*[2]

In the sixth century B.C., Cyrus, King of the Medes, conquered much of the Middle East, including the imperial city of Babylon and the province of Palestine. His primary motive seems to have arisen from the insatiable lust for power and wealth that made him one of the first great "world conquerors" known to history. In pursuing his goal, however, he relied (as would many of his successors) on clever, manipulative use of religious and popular sentiment as well as superior military strategy. Thus the extension of his political control was typically accompanied by an ostentatious religious tolerance plus propagandistic justifications of his acts.

In Babylon, for example, his conquest was explained as the result of the action of Marduk, the patron god of that city. According to a poem Cyrus commissioned, the Babylonian king Nabu-na'id had offended Marduk by his religious policy and his unjust oppression of the merchants and the poor. When the citizens of Babylon complained, Marduk "became terribly angry.... He scanned and looked [through] all the countries, searching for a righteous ruler." Having discovered Cyrus, Marduk "declared him . . . to be ruler of all the world. . . . He made him set out on the road to Babylon, going at his side like a real friend...." As a result, the inhabitants of Babylon greeted Cyrus "as a master through whose help they had come to life from death."[3]

Cyrus, a Persian Zoroastrian, did not really accept the particular theological framework within which the story was cast, but the poem is important historically as an example of the mythic framework within which ruler and ruled could communicate about the meaning of war and the authority that power in war could bestow. It also provides a clue to the psychic and ideological means whereby elites were able to gain passive acceptance of their exploitative and warmaking proclivities from the vast peasant majority over whom they ruled.

In peasant-based civilizations monarchs were understood by their subjects (and possibly understood themselves) in a dominantly mythical and religious fashion. Whether they were hailed as Pharaoh, Son of Heaven, the embodiment of Indra, the Lord's anointed, or the Sun King, they were believed to hold the throne because they possessed certain characteristics necessary for the critical task of preserving the correct order of relations between humanity and the cosmos. By the elaborate ritual that encompassed their lives, they represented the community to the gods and thereby insured that prosperity and the good life were made available to the human community. Thus in China the emperor represented "the transcendent power that keeps the universe in balance."[4]

> The emperor at court worships a nonanthropomorphic sky god, T'ien or Heaven. Heaven requites a universal generosity for *t'ien-hsia*, All-under-Heaven, in response to the emperor's cosmic piety on behalf of mankind. The privileges of court life and nobility thus are justified in the name of Heaven's blessings on all.[5]

The monarchs also represented the gods in relation to the community; they were the final authority for "discovering" and enforcing the righteousness (laws) that the gods demanded as appropriate (rite, right) behavior among human beings. Since no distinction was made between secular law and religious ritual, it was assumed that if the monarchs carried out their dual role properly, harmony would reign between earth and heaven and on earth itself. Even as nontheistic a theorist as Confucius "was convinced that the cosmos is a moral order and that man's affairs can prosper only when they are in harmony with the moral nature of the world."[6] With a good monarch, natural catastrophes were avoided and social relations were correct; prosperity and justice reigned together and were indeed inseparable. Thus the monarch's authority to punish transgressors was also his responsibility to do so since "the wise declare punishment to be identical with the law."[7] In the words of the Code of Manu, the earliest Hindu collection of laws: "The whole world is kept in order by punishment, for a guiltless man is hard to find; through fear of punishment the whole world yields the enjoyments which it owes. . . . A king who properly inflicts punishment prospers."[8]

This mythic framework also offered an explanation for the military activities of the monarch who, as a successful commander, was obviously obeying divine command. In Mesopotamia, for example, he was typically perceived as the steward of the god's "manor," adding by his successful wars to the resources and "pleasure" of the divine. In India and China, on the other hand, it was believed that the emperor acted in a pious fashion by attempting to bring "the world" under a single earthly sovereign to match the single heavenly reality. Indeed, in China the authority delegated to the ruling Son of Heaven was such as to preclude "the need for or the legality of other political units."[9]

In all cases the monarch's personal greed was projected onto the divine and thereby rationalized and justified. Insatiability for power and wealth was not his personal need, but the righteous demand of the gods. Royal success in war was proof of his legitimacy and of his authority to decree and enforce law. The Code of Hammurabi, for example, began with a detailed list of Hammurabi's military successes, which were offered as proof of the claim that

> Anu and Bel delighted the flesh of mankind by calling me, the renowned prince, the god-fearing Hammurabi, to establish justice in the earth, to destroy the base and the wicked, and to hold back the strong from oppressing the feeble: to shine like the Sun-god upon the black-headed men, and to illuminate the land.[10]

On the other hand, any disaster was a sign of monarchical error and failure. Thus the laws of King Edgar of England begin by explaining that

> Edgar the king was deliberating what might be for "bot" in the pestilence, which much afflicted and decreased his people, widely throughout his dominion. . . . [It] seemed to him and his "witan" that a misfortune of such kind had been merited by sins, and by contempt of God's commandants. . . . He thought on and considered the divine according to worldly usage. . . .[11]

Similarly, failure in war was understood as a sign that the gods had been angered by some violation of divine ritual or law. Livy, for example, attributed the following address to the dictator Marcus Furius Camillus as an explanation of the first Gallic occupation of Rome:

> Only consider the course of our history during these latter years: you will find that when we followed God's guidance all was well; when we scorned it, all was ill. And what of this unprecedented calamity which has just befallen us? It never showed its ugly head till we disregarded the Voice from heaven warning us that the Gauls were coming—till our envoys violated the law of nations and we, who should have punished that crime, were again so careless of our duty to God as to let it pass.[12]

War was "God's beadle" that chastised the erring, regardless of the intent of the victorious army. Thus the prophet Jeremiah, speaking for Yahweh, could warn that "I am going to deliver Zedekiah king of Judah . . . into the hands of Nebuchadnezzar king of Babylon" (21:7), without assuming that Nebuchadnezzar recognized his role.

In an unsuccessful war, peasant and urban dweller alike suffered the degradations of battle on their own territory, while the king (as scapegoat for the community) was humiliated or deposed. If he was deposed, his successor was recognized as the new divine intermediary. Faithfulness to this mythic understanding of reality has, for example,

> unfortunately given rise to the basic misconceptions of Chinese dynastic history. The actual transfer of power . . . is presented as an act of abdication based on motives that are traced to Confucian ethics. The mandate of Heaven is said to have been conveyed or transferred without interruption from one legitimate holder to the next.[13]

The result of the military punishment was the assuagement of divine anger and the reestablishment of correct cosmic relations.

From a strictly functionalist perspective, such a myth seems so clearly self-serving for the elite that it is difficult to believe that it was not always a conscious rationalization. At a minimum it provided a relatively cheap and undemanding explanation for the elite's exploitation of the peasantry. It also provided the basis for creating a symbiotic relation between any conqueror and the existing temple complex and ruling castes. The traditional elites could use it as a means to justify their shift in loyalty, to preserve their historic privileges, and to constrain the conqueror and his heirs to observe the cultural and economic norms of their society. Conversely, the conquering monarch who was willing to adopt it as his own ideology was thereby assured of priestly and intellectual support in asserting his authority (rather than simply his power) to rule. Operating within this context, for example, the Chinese bureaucratic caste was able for several millennia to convert barbaric hordes to the tenets of Chinese civilization. On the other hand, the attempt of the Romans to ignore the local version of the myth in Palestine and of Napoleon to introduce new laws into Spain precipitated mass rebellions that sorely tried the military power of these imperial states.

The very effectiveness of the myth in reconciling old and new elites and establishing authority over the masses makes it clear that the myth was more than simply a clever propaganda device. It spoke at some level to a psychological reality that gave it tremendous emotional potency. Moreover, its near universality among preindustrial civilizations suggests that it reflects social and psychic processes present in all peasant-based cultures.

On the psychological level, the mechanics of guilt are fairly simple: Guilt is essentially resentment turned inward. Like other specifically human psychic phenomena, it has its roots in the processes of socialization. It arises in the difficulties and tensions human children face in moving from the dependent confluence of the infant (where ideally there is no perceived boundary between the baby and the supportive environment) toward the independence and ability to sustain separateness and conflict that are the attributes of maturity.

In a child-rearing process where coercion is minimal and childish anger and rebellion are accepted as normal, it is possible for this transition to be accomplished in a fashion that produces adults who are both integral parts of the social fabric (whose norms they have assimilated) and independent beings capable of enduring isolation and conflict. When, however, as in peasant-based civilizations, parents are both coercive and punitive, consistently prohibiting independent action or the expression of direct anger, children receive little support for the development of independence. Instead they are likely to retroflect anger and resentment against themselves as guilt, while introjecting the parental prohibitions as part of their own character structure. This introjected parental command becomes an isolated and potentially controlling part of the psyche, ready to direct retroflected resentment toward (that is, to judge as guilty) any element in the psyche that threatens to interrupt the desired confluence with the parents. Because the suffering and pain necessary to develop independence has been abandoned, a rigid character structure evolves, which will tend in later years to introject other social norms as well and to respond to interruptions of familial or social confluence in a judgmental fashion. Any significant conflict will be considered bad; resentment for the interruption will either be retroflected on the self as guilt or directed against others as a demand that they feel guilty. Thus the pattern is likely to repeat itself in an intensified fashion in the child-rearing norms of the next generation and to reinforce itself socially.

Beyond this, a felt connection is established between punishment and community. At the time when punishment is first inflicted, it is usually intended by parents as a method of teaching the child that a particular mode of action is unacceptable to adults. But the child also learns a different lesson, especially since anger and punishment are followed by reconciliation. The lesson, often unconsciously assimilated, is that confluence and harmony can be achieved by accepting guilt and punishment, which thus becomes a passive technique for controlling others. Punishment becomes a method of eradicating conflict and reestablishing cohesiveness. As Perls describes the situation:

> If a confluence between Persons A and B is interrupted, A will think that either he or B interrupted it—and is, therefore, guilty. If he feels that he himself has done it, then he must make restitution to B in order to restore the confluence; but if he regards B as guilty, then he feels resentment, feels that B has to pay him something, which may range from an apology to a willingness to accept punishment. In German, *Schuld* means either guilt or debt. . . . The aim . . . is to restore the upset balance and mend the intolerable situation of broken confluence.[14]

Instead of perceiving conflict as an opportunity for creating a new relationship or mode of interaction, the guilt-addicted personality uses punishment as a means of recreating the preconflict status quo. Thus punishment is never, and is not intended to be, creative. Rather it is essentially a conservative, controlling response to a situation: rigid, infantile, and backward-looking.

We do not know enough about the history of families and childhood socialization in archaic civilizations to be certain as to when or how this pattern of dependent, guilt- and resentment-laden character structure was institutionalized by the socialization process. Certainly in the early centuries, if the new engineering and religious projects and their concomitant social hierarchies were freely and enthusiastically chosen responses to environmental needs and opportunities, it may well have been lacking. If hierarchy and group cooperation were freely chosen by adults as an appropriate way of life, then there was no need and no benefit to be achieved by guilt-laden child-rearing patterns.

However, if one looks at the records of the Mesopotamian basin as a fairly well-documented example of the earliest civilizations, it is clear that social harmony no longer existed by the third millennium B.C. Instead the quasi-democratic state socialism of the early Sumerian cities had given way to a more exploitative and stratified society, while an increase in epidemics and floods (the "natural" consequences of civilization) made life less joyful and secure. Nor was assent to the social structure any longer a matter of willing assent; rather civilian rebelliousness and violence had become a common phenomenon of the great urban centers.

Moreover, guilt as an important part of character structure is discernible as early as the second millennium in Egypt and the first in Mesopotamia. In the latter, for example, both Sumerian and Akkadian "Penitential psalms" and "letters to Gods" stress confession and self-laceration.

> Your servant who has sinned, have mercy on him!
> He has bowed down and loudly implored you.
> For the wrong he committed he shouts a psalm of penance.
> . . . .
> He has sinned, all his conduct he lays open.
> The weariness with which he wearied himself he recounts![15]

The story of the Davidic succession preserved in II Samuel marks the entrance of guilt into Hebraic consciousness in the ninth century B.C., while the fifth century Platonic dialogue, the *Crito*, carefully draws the distinction between a shame ethic and the guilt ethic of the Socratic daemon or conscience. Similarly the Hindu conception of "the stain" of sin involved in violating dharma, a stain to be "wiped away" by suffering and amendment in future lives, involves a comparable conception of guilt and punishment. Civilization thus came to rest on an introjected personality structure compounded of submission and guilt.

With the development of civilization, public trial and public punishment replaced the taboo system as the major ritual for defining social boundaries, enforcing critical political and economic rules, and resolving personal conflicts. The king and his delegates theoretically functioned as divine intermediaries in upholding the rites and rules of the cosmos, while private revenge (as an act of personal passion) was outlawed. The trial was perceived as a divine ritual, incorporating sacralized ordeal, torture, and battle as divine aids to discovering the truth in obscure situations, while public punishment satisfied the divine demand for vengeance and purity.

The public punishment that concluded the ritual, moreover, not only reestablished harmony between the human community and the divine but reestablished community boundaries in a manner that reincorporated the punished deviants as well as "the good" in a renewed bonding. This was particularly clear in the case of a ritual execution. Typically the doomed individual was for the day a hero, the "bridegroom," whose words were treasured and whose touch (like that of the king himself) was believed to possess a healing quality. Thus the act of execution was turned by the general public into an act of reconciliation and intense involvement between the condemned and the condemning. Punishment as a public ritual overcame alienation and distance and reestablished both the human and the cosmic community.

However, the very civilization that created the public trial as a mode of defining boundaries also produced substantial economic conflicts and real differences of interest between individual subjects and classes. Thus the crime of theft, for example, was created by the establishment of great economic disparities that were not fully accepted by the society as a whole. The boundaries of such a society contained groups that potentially threatened to separate themselves into geographically discrete entities or to reorganize the society entirely. The defining of boundaries in such a situation was necessarily repressive and controlling, a technique for repressing anger and conflict.

The repressive character of trial and punishment was most clear in the aftermath of an unsuccessful rebellion when a symbolic group of rebels was ritually tried and publicly killed. In such a situation, it is clearly the ruling elite that has been offended. For example, at the conclusion of the Palestinian rebellion of A.D. 66–71, the Romans held a "triumphal procession" to celebrate the reconquest of Jerusalem. Captive Jewish prisoners adorned with "elaborate and beautiful garments" formed part of the parade, which ended at the Temple of Jupiter Capitolinus.

> It was an ancient custom to wait there till news came that the commander-in-chief of the enemy was dead. This was Simon son of Gioras, who had been marching in the procession among the prisoners, and now with a noose thrown round him was being dragged to the usual spot in the Forum while his escort knocked him about. That is the spot laid down by the law of Rome for the execution of those condemned to death for their misdeeds. When the news of his end arrived it was received with universal acclamation, and the sacrifices were begun.[16]

The lesson ritually taught to the masses by such punishment was that the price of resistance to established authority was death and mutilation.

Rather than allow social and psychological conflicts (with all their destructive and recreative potentials) to develop, the authority elements in both the social and psychic structures interrupted the conflict, limited or controlled the potential for change, and attempted to preserve the status quo through projected scapegoating and retribution. Potential deviants, threatened or "deterred" by the ritual punishment, introjected anew the lesson as to the kind of behavior expected by the divine and its regents, while public trials provided an opportunity for enjoyably reaffirming membership in the good community.

> Crime brings together upright consciences and concentrates them. We have only to notice what happens, particularly in a small town, when some moral scandal has just been committed. They stop each other on the street, they visit each other, they seek to come together to talk of the event and to wax indignant in common.[17]

Indeed public justice provided for the members of society exactly the satisfactions of neurotic self-conquest: identification with the "virtues of the authorities [the introjected "good" self], strength, rights, wisdom [and] guiltlessness."[18] Ritual punishment was thus ultimately an infantile attempt at the social level to avoid the pains of continued social growth. Once established as a conceptual pattern for the good life, it interacted with socialization techniques and individual psychic structures in an ever-tightening circle.

The aftermath of a successful peasant jacquerie, moreover, makes it clear that ruler and ruled shared certain assumptions about reality and the appropriate way to handle conflict. Typically such rebellions were justified by the supposed existence of a bad or misinformed (i.e., guilty) ruler. The goal of the rebellion was not the demolition of the hierarchic structure per se but its purification. When the rebellion succeeded, the system (complete with tax collectors and armies) was simply recreated with new personnel. Peasants thus betrayed both their continued willingness to obey the good ruler and their conviction that conflict must always have its locus in guilt and its resolution in punishment and a return to the hierarchical bonding of the status quo ante.

The situation is ironic since, with the development of civilization, mankind had abandoned the relatively timeless and changeless world of nature. In its original context the liking for, and commitment to, the timeless and the repetitive that was a part of our "primitive" psyche was nonneurotic and innocent. But in a civilized society, where mankind opposes human will to natural rhythms and substitutes engineering for adaptation, timelessness becomes a fantasy, and the attempt to avoid change and conflict always has a neurotic character. Conservative civilizations are, in fact, engaged in sterile social control, just as civilized people who cling to conformity and confluence are engaged in regressive self-control.

In this context the understanding of war as punishment takes on several layers of meaning. On the most obvious level, the punitive theory of war is a method of avoiding resentment directed toward the institution of war itself and the gods who supposedly sanctioned and originated it. At a minimum defeat that brings suffering inside the territorial bounds of the community itself cannot help but provoke anger and doubt regarding the gods who are supposed to protect a society and bring it victory. Such doubts, for example, dominate the Babylonian "Lament of Ur" from the third millennium B.C. and such anger permeates the brutal humiliation of the enemy's deities characteristic of victorious armies in Mesopotamia during the second. Because the social and economic structures of any advanced civilization are intimately intertwined with the worship of its gods, real rejection of the divine myth threatens the continued existence of the religious complex and other elite groups. Moreover, as the individual subject's whole understanding of reality and the conceptual framework for self-identification are provided by the religious myths of his or her society, the breakdown of religious belief in the absence of an alternative myth inevitably threatens people with anxiety and existential despair.

Thus, giving full rein to resentment toward the gods would have been costly and painful, forcing upon society a real reorganization of its social, religious, and psychic structures. This potentially dangerous course was avoided by the simple device of projection. Human resentment was projected onto the gods and then retroflected back onto the self as a charge of sinfulness and guilt. If defeat and disaster were understood as a justified retribution, then the desired confluence with the gods could be reestablished. The disorder of sin and error (now understood as human and not divine) was paid for by punishment so that the harmony of cosmic order (in theory, if not in fact) could be reaffirmed.

The imagined scenario of crime and punishment did not always encompass the totality of a society. Thus in most of the Mesopotamian epics and in the priestly histories of Kings and Chronicles, the sin had been the monarchs', even when the punishment had involved the whole society. In part, of course, this simply reflected an identification between king and people (he "represents" them) so intense that his sin was perceived as their own. But dynastic defeat in war also made safe the expression of longstanding social conflicts and resentments. It certainly was no accident, for example, that the crimes of which the monarchs were specifically accused were usually those that infringed on the prerogatives of the priestly caste. War as divine chastisement thus satisfied the resentment of the temple complex, while providing a fine moral tale with which to instruct and frighten future rulers.

The priests may also have spoken for the masses, whose generalized resentment found indirect satisfaction in warfare (especially when the use of professional armies minimized the impact of such war on the peasants themselves). The understanding of war as a just punishment of evil elites allowed the peasantry to satisfy their class resentment, as others performed the acts of humiliation and destruction that the peasants had been unable or unwilling to engage in on their own behalf. Understandably, a high percentage of peasant rebellions occurred in the aftermath of unsuccessful wars.

The main discussion so far has been of understanding war as punishment that arises after the event. But the history of the Hebrew prophets makes it clear that such understandings are not necessarily simply rationalization. Instead the early prophets are a clear example of guilt attributed and punishment foretold before actual defeat in war had occurred. Their sense of communal guilt and the desire for punishment clearly arose from a consciousness of a collapse of valued communal cohesiveness. If the Hebrews would not heal the breach within the covenantal community voluntarily, Amos and Jeremiah, for example, looked to war and defeat as a way of restoring national unity and the divine order on which it was ideally based.

This was not a case of sadistic longing for others to be punished, nor were the prophets talking about or desiring personal revenge. Rather they clearly identified themselves with the Hebrew people; what happened to the Palestinian community would also happen to them as members of that community. They hoped, moreover, that the community would turn from its errors in time to avoid the need for punishment. Indeed, it is fair to say that the prophets desired the punishment of war because they perceived punishment as a form of reconciliation, a mode of restoring confluence and harmony. In this they were not unique. In fact, they may well have spoken to a more general neurosis in their community and in mankind in general; that is, to neurotic guilt feelings and the masochistic longings for punishment and pain that stem from them.

Since the development of a guilt-laden character structure arises from an abandonment of the effort to develop mature independence, it represents a retreat into an infantile dependency. But no societal structure and no perfectionist striving can ever produce complete harmony and universal good will; hence the dependent adult is constantly being disappointed in his or her infantile desire. This will produce vague moods of resentment as well as a general sense of guilt. Because a sense of guiltiness is also uncomfortable, it is often accompanied by a desire (usually unconscious, but nonetheless acted out) for the punishment that will cancel out the guilt and reestablish confluence and unity. Guilt produces, in effect, a form of masochism.

It may be objected that no nation or community ever consciously wants to be punished or deliberately initiates war in order to be defeated. But then guilt-ridden neurotics do not consciously punish themselves either; instead they perceive their suffering as inflicted by external forces and caused by their unworthiness. Indeed, consciously they strive to avoid guilt and pain, laying ever more rigorous perfectionist demands on themselves, even as they increase their suffering by hypersensitivity to disapproval or difficulties. But beneath this overt action, a different process is at work. As Karen Horney observes:

> a neurotic person may feel definitely more at ease, even lose certain of his neurotic symptoms, if an adverse event occurs, such as losing a fortune or incurring an accident. Observation of this reaction, and also the fact that sometimes he seems to arrange or provoke adverse happenings, if only inadvertently, may lead to an assumption that the neurotic person has guilt feelings so strong that he develops a need for punishment in order to get rid of them. . . . [However], neurotic suffering, inasmuch as it serves certain functions, is not what the person wants but what he pays, and the satisfaction he aims at is not suffering itself but relinquishment of the self.[19]

Because this masochistic wish for punishment arises from a desire to avoid the experience of individuality and separateness, war is a particularly effective social solution to dependence on punishment as a path to confluence or unity. On the one hand service in the army (and particularly the danger and risk of battle) provide one of the most intense experiences of community known to humans. Thus Shakespeare has Henry V rhapsodize before battle on the pleasure and the payoff that the imminent carnage holds for

> We few, we happy few, we band of brothers;
> For he to-day that sheds his blood with me
> Shall be my brother. Be he ne'er so vile
> This day shall gentle his condition.[20]

In a similar vein, speaking for the veterans of World War II, Glenn Gray observed of the "experience of communal effort in battle" that

> ... We are liberated from our individual impotence and are drunk with the power that union with our fellows brings. In moments like these many have a vague awareness of how isolated and separate their lives have hitherto been.... With the boundaries of the self expanded, they sense a kinship never known before. Their "I" passes insensibly into a "we." ... At its height, this sense of comradeship is an ecstasy....[21]

While psychologists and theologians may disagree as to whether the ecstatic unity of mystic experiences has its roots in infantile regression, it seems clear that the appeal involved in the loss of self in battle is connected with just such an avoidance of maturity. It is, in theological terms, a form of "cheap grace."

War also has its rewards for the civilian community since, by drawing attention to the differences that separate the enemy from one's own group, it publicizes and strengthens the boundaries of the community, making people aware of the interests and values they share. In addition, war and defeat produce misery, a misery often so intense that all the minor pains and disappointments of everyday life fade into insignificance; it is narcotic. Moreover, the misery of war and defeat, because it is shared by a whole community, tends to create confluence within the community. Under the impact of external pressures, cliques and disagreements and even hierarchic separateness often disappear, to be replaced by the general sense of belongingness and the reality of a common effort.

One of the popular slogans of the Flower Children of the late 1960s asked: "What if they gave a war and nobody came?" Certainly one of the great puzzles of history is the fact that the masses of mankind have been so willing to tolerate and even support wars whose material rewards have been reaped by an elite minority, leaving to the ordinary subject only the chaff of death, destruction, loss, and hardship. One answer would seem to point to an institutionalized, neurotic masochism. Part of the attraction of war seems to arise from civilized human beings' infantile guilty consciences and their unconscious, regressive desires for the pleasurable confluence achievable through punishment.

In 1215 the Catholic church took a momentous step. It forbade any further clerical participation in trials by battle or ordeal. While admitting that such priestly sanctification of the judicial ritual had become a tradition, it dismissed it as a concession to the prejudices and ignorance of northern converts. God, the council insisted, does not interest himself in such trivial matters, nor does he provide victory for the righteous; sacralized violence as a path to truth rests on heresy. While law and justice are virtues, their implementation is a human responsibility. Humans must rely on their own intelligence.

The implications of this decree are broader than they appear initially. In effect, through this one act the church was undermining the ancient assumption of a close and practical connection between human action and divine reaction, between ritual and prosperity. If the divine was unwilling, however, to determine the outcome of judicial ritual and insure the punishment of the guilty, then he was also presumably equally unconcerned with using natural disasters or wars as instruments of chastisement. Conversely, neither the physical world nor divine authority could be manipulated any longer by postures of guilt and masochistic suffering. Instead humans had to accept responsibility for themselves and deal as well as they could with the problems and conflicts of earthly life.

Unfortunately, theology alone cannot produce maturity or psychic health. It took several centuries of firm intervention to eliminate clerical participation and public belief in trials by battle and ordeal. The conviction that war was God's judgment died even more slowly. Thus as late as the seventeenth century the Puritans saw the King Philip's war with the Indians as "the greatest of all outward Judgments."

> We have ignored earlier warnings and lesser judgments, declared the General Court of Massachusetts in November 1675, and hence "God hath heightened our calamity, and given commission to the barbarous heathen to rise up against us, and to become a smart rod and severe scourge to us." Increase Mather . . . agreed

that God had brought the war as a just punishment for His back-sliding people. John Eliot suggested that the sin of over-security compelled the Lord to chastise New England to remind the people of His ultimate power.[22]

Unconsciously they had also expected war as a remedy for their growing disunity and loss of cohesiveness.

By the twentieth century, the conscious ideology of war as divine punishment for social guilt had died along with God himself. The Germans in 1914, for example, did not prophesy war as divine judgment, nor did they in 1918 accept defeat as a divine punishment. But psychological forces are not dependent upon an adequate ideology. Thus the Germans, condemned in the 1920s to live through the revolutionary changes and the class conflicts of the Weimar republic, came all too easily to look back with nostalgia to the war years when the nation had seemed to be "truly one." It is hardly surprising that those years, despite their enormous actual cost in destruction, pain, and loss, were remembered primarily as times of excitement, national unity, and good feeling, or that the Nazis' skillful use of military symbols was so attractive.

Like most neurotic processes, punishment is ultimately unsatisfactory and nonproductive. Though it may create symbolically and temporarily an emotional sense of community and of internal harmony, it does not and cannot eliminate the actual divisions present in any civilized personality or society. The real estrangements and conflicts are temporarily avoided, but they are not eradicated.

7
Honor and Glory

> Military honor is both a means and an end. The code of honor specifies how an officer ought to behave, but to be "honorable" is an objective to be achieved for its own right.... The effectiveness of military honor operates precisely because it does not depend on elaborate moralistic justification.
> —*Morris Janowitz*[1]

If the strategy and tactics of primitive peoples have seemed opaque to historians and anthropologists familiar with the norms of civilized war, so have the battle rules of feudal or aristocratic societies. Though the armies of such castes have at times clearly pursued economic and political objectives, they have also sporadically been inclined to ignore or undervalue such important and "civilized" strategic principles as the need for hierarchy of command, cooperation between arms, concentration of resources, and surprise. Instead these soldiers would, with fair regularity, seek each other out in a leisurely and open fashion, arrange their total forces in broad, parallel formations, and then plunge bravely and ferociously forward. Typically the result was a mixture of confused melée and individual duel, characterized (in the words of the great medievalist Sir Charles Oman) by a blend of arrogance and stupidity.

The warriors who fought such battles and who had been trained from childhood for the exercise displayed no such doubts about the intelligence or intelligibility of their acts. Moreover, when their primary concern was to extend political control over new territories, they routinely resorted to siege operations against fortified castles and towns and displayed a high degree of strategic and technical competency. But the recognized effectiveness of long-term blockades and of battering rams and catapults was never allowed to overshadow or eliminate the importance of open-field, formalized battles. If we are to make psychological sense of this situation, we must turn again to the warriors themselves for a clue to their motives. In particular, we must listen to the records preserved by contemporary poets and historians who observed their deeds and heard their words.

For example, one very detailed account of late medieval warfare comes down to us in the writings of Sir John Froissart, an aristocratic raconteur and amateur historian who accompanied Edward II of England on his expedition into France and was present in 1346 at the great English victory of Crécy. At the end of the day, when the English had successfully broken French resistance and taken many prisoners for ransom, the Prince of Wales gave a formal banquet to which the King of France, his son Philip, and numerous captured French aristocrats were invited. The English prince personally waited upon his royal prisoners and assured Philip in particular that

> "In my opinion . . . you have this day acquired such high renown for prowess, that you have surpassed all the best knights on your side. I do not, dear sir, say this to flatter you, for all those of our side who have seen and observed the actions of each party, have unanimously allowed this to be your due, and decree you the prize and garland for it."

At the end of this speech there were murmurs of praise heard from every one; and the French said, the prince had spoken nobly and truly, and that he would be one of the most gallant princes in Christendom, if God should grant him life to pursue his career of glory.[2]

By the time of Crécy, of course, both artistocratic feudalism and medieval modes of warfare were on the wane, particularly in the increasingly centralized and bureaucratized English monarchy. But the more archaic and individualistic French style of fighting obviously still had meaning for the English as well, and it embodied for both sides the language of renown and glory, garland and prize—words and values that were, even in the fourteenth century, thousands of years old. Moreover, if one accepts that the point of battle is to demonstrate individual prowess and bravery under conditions of extreme physical stress, then the strategy of these aristocratic warriors becomes perfectly logical. The prearranged but uncontrolled and unconcentrated broad-front battle plan was designed to give each warrior a relatively equal chance to display his capabilities and win the prize of honor.

We have argued previously, however, that prestige per se cannot be a goal of battle, since prestige is instead a social discipline for inducing humans to engage in valued activities. What then is the psychological or cosmological value that warrior castes had discovered in individual battlefield prowess? What made such an experience seem glorious and deserving of praise? Fortunately, two of the earliest major pieces of literature, the *Iliad* and the *Mahabharata*, are products of the late Iron Age, a period when nomadic hordes from central Eurasia conquered the older Bronze Age civilizations and then established themselves as a superior warrior caste. Both embody the value systems and the visions of life of those warrior people in terms that are still compelling.

Both epics reflect, moreover, the transitional character of the age that produced them. For example, the underlying stories are ostensibly tales of politico-economic wars, yet battle is depicted as embedded in a transcendent and ritualistic framework that is essentially an anthropomorphized version of Neolithic myth and ritual. More important, the epics focus precisely on the aspects of warfare that contradict the older Neolithic and civilized values and myths. Thus in the Indian legend the very consanguinity of the combatants makes it impossible to view the war as a simple conflict between a hero and chaos, while the Greek-Trojan contest is also ritually dubious as victory does not bring life and fertility to the victors, but further years of exile, danger, and death. Both epics, in fact, clearly raise serious questions about the effectiveness of war as a ritual instrument for overcoming chaos and establishing material prosperity.

Neither the Trojan war nor the Indian war of the Kuru cousins can have been their civilizations' sole experience of the ritual and moral ambiguity of warfare. However, instead of restructuring memory so as to bring actual events into closer parallel with the basic myth, the affronting elements are accentuated. Thus in the *Mahabharata*, the royal court is packed with advisers and relatives whose loyalties will be torn, while the misadventures of the Greeks multiply into soap-opera proportions. It is as if at a certain point in time the contradictions between inherited myth and present reality became too great to be simply ignored and began instead to be remembered and insisted upon, even by members of a caste whose way of life and whose power and prestige rested upon their role as warriors.

"Of the wrath, sing, goddess, of Achilles Peleus. . . ." Thus Homer opens his epic *Iliad*, announcing with swiftness and brevity the thematic issue on which he chooses to focus: wrath and revenge. Wrath and revenge are also the major emotional themes of the entire Trojan war: the revenge of Hera and Athene for the slighting of their beauty and prizes; the revenge of Menelaos for the abduction of his wife; the revenge of the Danaans for the Trojans' violation of the armistice and for the ills they have suffered in besieging Troy. Even the events precipitating Achilles' wrath involve a fusillade of revenge motifs: the revenge of Apollo for the slighting of his priest and the revenge of Agamemnon for being constrained to return Chryseis, his prize of honor, to her father. For Homer, however, these issues become merely background, relatively unanalyzed and peripheral; instead he focuses on the single figure of Achilles and his conflicts with his own people and then with Hector.

In his treatment of Achilles, Homer produces as perceptive a picture of the revenge-driven personality as one can find in literature. Achilles is not motivated primarily by a desire to regain Briseis, the prize concubine Agamemnon has taken from him. No words of real affection or desire for this particular woman escape his lips, and he rejects Agamemnon's offer to return her "untouched" as easily as he rejects the additional goods and women with which the hard-pressed

Danaans attempt to assuage his wrath. It is not goods or sexual objects that Achilles has really been deprived of or wants: instead it is honor. He has been dishonored, his public and private self-image has been wounded, he has been shamed.

> Not me, I ween, shall Agamemnon son of Atreus persuade, nor the other Danaans, seeing we were to have no thanks for battling with the foemen ever without respite. He that abideth at home hath equal share with him that fighteth his best, and in like honor are held both the coward and the brave; death cometh alike to the untoiling and to him that hath toiled long.[3]

In effect, Achilles has been a conforming member of the warrior caste; he has controlled his own actions but he has not been able to control his world or to get that respect and affection that he desires. Agamemnon has treated him as if he were a coward and a stay-at-home, a "worthless sojourner."

As a result, Achilles says that he will be satisfied only when Agamemnon has paid him back "all the bitter despite" he has suffered; that is, when Agamemnon has suffered equivalent bitterness and pain. But in the end, even Agamemnon's suffering is not enough, since Achilles' understanding of what he has suffered has expanded. As he exclaims to his comrade Patroklus,

> For would, O father Zeus, and Athene, and Apollo, would that not one of all the Trojans might escape death, nor one of the Argives [Danaans], but that we twain might avoid destruction, that alone we might undo the sacred coronal of Troy.[4]

That is what the desire for revenge, unchecked, must lead to: solipsism. Since the world has witnessed Achilles' shame, his sense of self-righteousness and invulnerability can only be restored by destroying his world, including, inevitably, that part of himself that is attached, and therefore vulnerable, to the harsh reality of pain and loss.

Retribution follows fast upon this moment of hubris. Patroklus, his one bond of close attachment to the world and the alter-ego who is still willing to risk love and pain, enters the battle to aid the Danaans and is killed by Hector. Immediately the focus of Achilles' wrath shifts, for now he has been injured in his spontaneous affections. (One cannot imagine him turning aside a chance to regain Patroklus as lightly as he refused that simple prize of honor, Briseis.) Now he is willing, indeed eager, to die if only he may also destroy the one who has injured him. Thus the myth surrounding Achilles insists, with real psychological insight, that for him (as for all humans), the real meaning of revenge is self-destruction.

Achilles does not die, but the death and humiliation of Hector brings him no relief. Though he thinks he has destroyed the external world that injured him, Hector (his body kept ever fresh by Aphrodite) haunts Achilles, an incubus he cannot abandon and that will not disintegrate and disappear. Achilles is, in fact, caught in a trap of his own making; as long as he clings to his need for revenge he must cling to his own pain, and find relief for neither one.

It is only when Priam arrives to plead for his son's body and reminds Achilles of his own father that the hero can give way to real grief. With his painful acceptance of his own vulnerable humanity, his desire for revenge is ended. Priam and Achilles, brought face to face, recognize in their shared beauty and nobility and in their parallel pain the bonds of their common humanity. Moreover, at this moment of catharsis Achilles is again both a child longing for his father and a man who understands, and can share and grieve for, his own father's helplessness. And so he breaks through at last to an understanding of reality that transcends his previous limited conceptions:

> For two urns stand upon the floor of Zeus, one filled with his evil gifts, and one with blessings. To whomsoever Zeus whose joy is in the lightning dealeth a mingled lot, that man chanceth now upon ill and now again on good, but to whom he giveth but of the bad kind him he bringeth to scorn, and evil famine chaseth him over the goodly earth, and he is a wanderer honoured of neither gods nor men.[5]

Achilles' wrath is buried in his acceptance of the fact that not all of his valor or toil or energy can control the workings of an impersonal fate; that he is indeed a person to whom these destructive things can happen.

Until this point the battle between Achilles and Hector has

generally followed the prescribed ritual of warfare. It has been precipitated by an "unnatural" death; Achilles enters the fight after establishing close communion with his divine mother and bearing weapons that are divine or sacred objects; and Hector's death has been followed by a Danaan victory celebration. Only the momentary confrontation on the battlefield between Achilles and Apollo has suggested that the ritual is ineffective; when Achilles would slay Apollo (the actual slayer of Patroklus, the real figure of death) he is warned off. "Me thou wilt never slay, for I am not subject to death."[6] The destruction of Hector thus does not mean the destruction of chaos. Hector is in fact only a man; he is not chaos, but hearth and home, a symbol constantly insisted upon by Homer. His death will in no way constrain the chaotic, erratic, violent actions of the gods or of fate itself. The celebration of Hector's death, therefore, is hollow and meaningless. The real end of the battle, as of the *Iliad* itself, is the grief of the Trojans and the funeral of Hector, tamer of horses.

Whereas Homer dealt with the Trojan war by examining a single, potent element of it in detail, the compilers of the *Mahabharata* pursued a radically different aesthetic ideal. The Indian epic, slowly evolving over hundreds of years, is a sprawling, variegated, seemingly chaotic work, containing within its loose structure everything from minute rules of religious and caste conduct and collections of folktales to a major religious treatise. And yet, for all its looseness and eclecticism, the *Mahabharata* is not unstructured or unfocused. Though the larger framework of the story involves a fight between two neighboring kingdoms, the Panchalas and the Kurus, the epic gives primary attention to the internecine struggle between the related Kuru cousins as the real cause of the war and the emotional focus of the work. Moreover, over the centuries the multiple authors have clearly perceived one figure as the major hero, attesting his importance both by the attention focused on him and by using him as the ostensible fountain of the priestly and caste laws with which the epic has been encrusted. If Achilles is the announced hero of the *Iliad*, Bhishma is the acclaimed hero of the *Mahabharata*, whose biography encompasses and embodies the tragedy of the war between his half nephews.

Personally Bhishma is the embodiment of the Hindu ideal of filial and family loyalty. Though as a young man he was the natural heir to his widowed father's throne, he renounced all his rights of succession in order to facilitate his father's second marriage, accepting instead the role of celibate adviser and war leader for his two younger half brothers and their numerous offspring. As the prime minister of the royal court, he has become the embodiment of political and ethical wisdom, a man of virtue who deals evenhandedly and lovingly with both the five virtuous sons (Yudhishthir, Arjuna, Bhima, and the twins) of his eldest half brother (Pandu) and the jealous, greedy, and rapacious Duryodhan, the eldest son of King Dhriata-rashtra (his younger half brother).

Because of Bhishma's loyalty to the family as a whole and his concern for righteousness within the kingdom, he is continually confronted with dilemmas and tragic problems as the jealous Duryodhan seeks by chicanery and violence to supplant and destroy Yudhishthir and his brothers. The ambiguity of Bhishma's situation reaches its peak when Duryodhan breaks his pledged word and refuses to return half of the kingdom to Pandu's sons upon the completion of their twelve-year exile. As a result Yudhishthir and his father-in-law, the king of the Panchalas, declare war, and Bhishma faces his final personal and moral dilemma.

As an uncle he should deal evenhandedly and lovingly with all of his kin; as the prime minister and war leader of the Kurus, he owes loyalty and service to the regent of the kingdom, Duryodhan; as an ethical man he knows that the ultimate right in the battle is with Yudhishthir and his brothers. Torn between conflicting goods, he responds as an upright Hindu should and follows the rules of caste: a warrior by birth, he fights for his ruler. But he does so without denying the pull either of his emotional ties or of more universal justice. Thus when Duryodhan sneeringly charges that he is not fighting to his fullest ability because of his affection for the Pandu brothers, Bhishma denies the accusation and warns Duryodhan:

> Vain our toil, unwise Duryodhan! Nor can Bhishma warrior old,
> Nor can Drona skilled in weapons, Karna archer proud and bold,

> Wash the stain of deeds unholy and of wrongs and outraged laws,
> Conquer with a load of cunning 'gainst a right and righteous cause. . . .
>
> Meanwhile since he leads thy forces, Bhishma still shall meet his foe,
> Or to conquer or to perish to the battle's front I go.[7]

Bhishma, then, is the stylized image of the warrior caught between conflicting rights and duties; he knows he fights for the forces of chaos and yet believes that to deny his responsibility to those forces would breed greater chaos. He fights with his full strength, therefore, in a cause that he not only believes should, but hopes will, be defeated. The moral ambiguity and tragedy of the sacrificial ritual of warfare, in which the very act of righteousness involves the evil of shedding blood, has never been more clearly personified in a single human figure. Moreover, the tension is heightened by the fact that Bhishma is indeed a peerless warrior, so that during the twelve days that he leads Duryodhan's forces, he is slowly destroying the forces of righteousness.

Only one release is possible from this situation: death. Though Bhishma is practically invincible and possesses control over the time of his own death, he too possesses his Achilles' heel. As he reminds the Pandu brothers who come to him asking for mercy and love,

> Bhishma doth not fight a rival who submits, fatigued and worn,
> Bhishma doth not fight the wounded, doth not fight a woman born.[8]

Though he is armored by the rules of caste and religious precept, the very rigid structure of his personality contains its own chink. Since he will not fight against a woman, young Sikhandin, born a girl and transformed by the gods into a warrior, is able to overpower the unresisting hero. But his destruction (though it insures the ultimate defeat of Duryodhan) is not a cause for happiness, nor is it treated as the defeat of evil. Rather Bhishma is raised onto a bed of Arjuna's arrows (symbolically the platform of a self-transcended guru) and mourned by all his relatives. He dies slowly as the war continues, in the process becoming a fount of wisdom concerning the requirements necessary for a good society and the good life.

The dilemma of Bhishma is, of course, the dilemma of all the major actors in the war. Bhishma's successor is Drona, who has been the teacher of all the Pandu brothers, a relation so close that Arjuna simply announces that he will not fight his beloved preceptor unless Yudhishthir's life is literally in danger. Even Karna, who has long been an angry rival of Arjuna and whose fight with him is reminiscent of the Hector-Achilles confrontation, is revealed at the end to have been a half brother, born of a mating between Arjuna's beloved mother, Drupadi, and the Sun-god.

Duryodhan is also accorded honor. Though he comes closest of any of the figures in the epic to being a simplistically evil personality, his final battle and death are attended by those miraculous and supernatural events that attest to contact with the divine. The war between the Kurus and the Panchalas may have destroyed an embodiment of chaos, but the cost of Duryodhan's destruction has involved the creation of an even more chaotic conflict of loyalties, as well as further loss, grief, and heartache. Granted the close ties between the contestants, it is small wonder that the battle ends not with a victory celebration but with an enormous funeral in which friend and foe unite in their shared grief.

For all their perceptiveness about the psychological emptiness and ritual ineffectiveness of battle, neither the *Iliad* nor the *Mahabharata* are antiwar epics. Instead they are simultaneously glorifications of war and the warrior. The beauty of the fighters, their armor, weapons, horses, and chariots, the drama and pageantry of the battles and the courage and skill of the heroes are repeatedly and even repetitiously insisted upon. If the modern reader finds it difficult to maintain enthusiastic involvement with the endless and essentially very similar descriptions of individual fights and deaths, it is clear that neither the authors nor the original listeners and readers were so easily satiated. The warriors are indeed heroes, surrounded by due glory and fame; their names and exploits are meant to live on in memory as a fitting tribute to their strength, daring, and, above all, their bravery: their willingness to risk death.

But if battle is so morally and practically dubious as an exercise of human ingenuity, and if the cost to noncombatants, to wives and children and parents, is (as both epics insist) so high, what can justify such pain and suffering? If the warriors cannot be understood as bestowing upon their people material prosperity, what is the value that makes the warrior's actions truly courageous rather than simply foolhardy? Certainly it is not the economic or political rewards to be gained by the victorious. The Danaans seek no political control over Troy, and Achilles is explicit in distinguishing this war, which is potentially glorious, from a mere cattle raid that may bring loot but no honor. Indeed, in the *Iliad* goods are valued primarily as symbols of bravery and honor.

Similarly in the *Mahabharata*, both Yudhishthir and Arjuna (unlike the evil Duryodhan) are depicted as ultimately unconcerned with wealth or power. They can live as beggars in the jungles, or as servants in disguise, and stake a whole kingdom unconcernedly upon the roll of a dice. Moreover, their duty to wage this war is one that both Yudhishthir and Arjuna openly question. The answers of the two epics as to why men do and should fight are both similar and unalike, reflecting both the universal values of the warrior caste and the particular cosmologies of their different cultures. Both epics see the desire for revenge and justice and battle itself as simply part of reality, created and sanctified by the nature of things.

Thus in the *Iliad* the desire for revenge is not simply human, it is a divine trait. The gods themselves are so motivated, and, indeed, when humans fall into an excess of wrath (as of cowardice), it is often perceived as the result of the direct intervention of a god, carried away by a parallel excess. Of course, the gods are not convincing figures to modern readers, and perhaps not wholly so for Homer. In their anthropomorphic state, they have lost the mystery and power of earlier naturalistic conceptions of divinity and not yet evolved into the abstract personifications of qualities that they become in some later Greek literature. Nonetheless they remain essential to the epic as the explanation of events and motives that the characters of the story feel to have been outside human control.

They are, in effect, symbols for the fatality of events and of personality that drive and buffet the human race.

Thus the essential vision of human experience in the *Iliad* is pessimistic. As Achilles comments to Priam at that high moment of personal reconciliation: "This is the lot the gods have spun for miserable men, that they should live in pain; yet [the gods] themselves are sorrowless."[9] And this same theme had been enunciated earlier when Glaukos proclaimed, in a simile that was to echo through all later Greek poetry:

> Even as are the generations of leaves such are those likewise of men; the leaves that be the wind scattereth on the earth, and the forest buddeth and putteth forth more again, when the season of spring is at hand; so of the generations of men one putteth forth and another ceaseth.[10]

Lasting order and prosperity and happiness are beyond the reach of mankind; the very ritual for constraining chaos and destruction is simply another occasion for loss and pain, a fated element of existence.

But "an enduring soul have the Fates given unto men,"[11] as Apollo observes. "Wailings and lamentations" are appropriate only up to a point; beyond that to be truly human involves accepting fate and enduring its blows with dignity simply because one can endure them. And if suffering and hardship and risk are the normal lot of mankind, they find their expression in the most intensified, dramatic, and poignant form in battle. War thus becomes a focal symbol of the human condition, and the warrior the purest embodiment of the capacity of humans to handle death and loss by voluntarily confronting them. Battle is also a means whereby the ontic anxiety of nonbeing is converted into the fear of a specific danger, a fear that can then be met with courage.

The warrior may bring his community no material prosperity through his actions, but he can provide spiritual consolation as a model of what humanity may be. Chaos, even that chaos lurking within the human soul, is not destroyed but denied potency by the affirmation of humanity's capacity to risk and endure. Rather than a ritual of control, war becomes a rite for attesting to human nobility, bravery, and endurance, while for the warrior the goal of battle becomes the immortality of glory. As Achilles prophesys: "If I abide here and besiege Troy, then my returning home is taken from me, but my fame shall be imperishable."[12]

If ultimately the *Iliad* contains a humanized and humanly tragic view of life and war, the *Mahabharata* restores to war an element of religious significance, but only by denying any importance to its material purpose or results. From a ritual for insuring prosperity and order, war is transmuted into a yoga through which the individual warrior may purify himself and merge with the divine eternal. This view of war was certainly not explicit in the earliest compilations of the epic. But the addition in around 500 B.C. of the religious poem known as the *Bhagavad Gita* to the *Mahabharata* provided a resolution to the tensions always implicit in the epic, enunciating a view of war and the warrior that provided for them a place of honor and utility in the Hindu cosmology.

The *Gita* section begins with a clear statement by Arjuna of the moral and emotional dilemma that this war, and by extension all wars, presents. Looking over the army arrayed against him, Arjuna is horrified by the fact that in this battle he must strive to kill his relatives, friends, and teachers. As he explains to his charioteer (who will reveal himself in the dialogue that follows as an avatar, or divine incarnation), "I have no wish for victory, Krishna, nor for a kingdom nor for its pleasures. . . . These I do not wish to slay, even if I myself am slain."[13] Krishna's answers lead Arjuna and the reader through three levels of discourse into increasingly sophisticated understanding of the significance of battle.

The first level of response is, in the Hindu context, a fairly naive, traditional one. As a member of the warrior caste, it is Arjuna's duty to fight for a righteous cause; if he does not he will be guilty of cowardice, dereliction of duty, and dishonorable conduct. Moreover, he need have no compunction about killing his kin and friends because "If any man thinks he slays, and if another thinks he is slain, neither knows the way of truth. The Eternal in man cannot kill: the Eternal in man cannot die."[14] This response Arjuna dismisses. In battle he will be destroying a family, and from this will spring the destruction of ritual, of female purity, and therefore of social and caste purity. Only chaos and hell can result from this (and possibly any other) battle.

So Krishna leads him to a second level of discourse, which argues that for the warrior, battle can be an appropriate karma yoga; if he is free from the bonds of desire, battle is a path to wisdom and serenity through action. Ideally the result of fighting should be indifferent to the wise man:

> It is greedy desire and wrath, born of passion, the great evil, the sum of destruction: this is the enemy of the soul. . . . Be a warrior and kill desire, the powerful enemy of the soul.[15]

Arjuna's concern, however unselfish, reveals that he is still caught in the web of consequences. The true yogi would be able to renounce any concern with the rewards of his actions (even the reward of righteousness) because he would understand that action, while inescapable, is part of the unreal, delusionary world of immanence. The person who can achieve such a perspective, who is

> free from the chains of selfish attachments, free from his lower "I am," who has determination and perseverance, and whose inner peace is beyond victory or defeat—such a man has pure Sattva [existence, being]. . . . He is one with Brahman, with God.[16]

Freed from the wheel of endless rebirth, he attains nirvana, deliverance from existence.

One question still remains: How can battle be an appropriate karma yoga? As Arjuna asks, what has battle to do with "supreme Brahman, Light supreme, and supreme purification, Spirit divine eternal, unborn God from the beginning, omnipresent Lord of all"?[17] For Hindu thought, this is a critical question. The caste system was the superstructure of society and it contained a specific warrior caste, the Kshatriya. If action (karma yoga) was as effective as ritual or contemplation for salvation, it should bring the actor into contact with the divine. Krishna's answer at this third level of discourse is twofold. First he provides a string of similes that are "manifestations of [his] divine glory."[18] Of these seventy-eight manifestations, twelve are specifically concerned with war and destruction. Then, in answer to Arjuna's plea for further enlightenment, Krishna manifests himself in his supreme divine form, the "radiance of the whole universe in its variety, standing in a vast unity in the body of the God of gods."[19] And while his manifested being contains creativity and beauty and knowledge and infiniteness, it also contains destruction and death. Arjuna reports:

> When I see thy vast form, reaching the sky, burning with many colours, with wide open mouths, with vast flaming eyes, my heart shakes in terror: my power is gone and gone is my peace, O Vishnu! . . . [All] enter rushing into thy mouths, terror-inspiring with their fearful fangs. Some are caught between them, and their heads crushed into powder. . . . The flames of thy mouths devour all the worlds. Thy glory fills the whole universe. But how terrible thy splendours burn![20]

And Krishna, who in Hindu cosmology is particularly an avatar of the loving elements of the divine and who teaches the special yoga of devotion, or Shakti, responds approvingly:

> I am all-powerful Time which destroys all things, and I have come here to slay these men. Even if thou dost not fight, all the warriors facing thee shall die. . . . Be thou merely the means of my work.[21]

Hindu thought, then, had come to comprehend ultimate being as encompassing both creation and destruction, both order and chaos. To be one with Brahman involves knowing and accepting both the attractive and the horrifying aspect of supreme being. In this context war becomes merely one manifestation of the multiple nature of the real rather than a means for controlling chaos. The yoga of the warrior involves selfless immersion in this aspect of the divine. Carried through with the proper love *(bhakti)* and detachment, battle becomes a discipline as austere as that of any contemplative and as effective a path to Brahman:

> These are the works of a Kshatriya: a heroic mind, inner fire, constancy, resourcefulness, courage in battle, generosity and noble leadership. . . . A man attains perfection when his work is worship of God, from whom all things come and who is in all.[22]

The only way to overcome chaos and destruction is to accept it as an ultimately unreal (because one-sided) manifestation of the unseen reality that is beyond any duality.

The *Iliad* and the *Mahabharata,* then, offer views of reality and of human existence that reflect the deeply diverging cultures of the two societies. While the *Iliad* stresses the human, material reality and the tragic as the stage on which mankind's nobility and capacity to endure and understand can find fullest expression, the *Mahabharata* moves beyond a concern with the merely natural and values the materialized world simply as a path by which salvation, union with the unchanging and undivided eternal, can be achieved. For the Greek humanity remains caught in the dividedness of human nature; for the Hindu the division can, even if only through many lifetimes of endeavor, be transcended.

For all the contrast between the two cultures, the *Iliad* and the *Mahabharata* ultimately provide a very similar understanding of battle and the values of the warrior. Both epics, for example, agree that the perfect warrior possesses constancy, resourcefulness, courage, generosity, and leadership. Neither are too concerned if he resorts to clever tricks or duplicity, but both insist upon an attitude of respect and even compassion for the men he would fight and kill. The desired foe shares with the ideal warrior his enlarged humanity, his involvement with the destructive elements of the godhead. The limitations or rules of warfare are those that will make possible and enhance the proper attitudes and actions of the warriors themselves. Thus warrior codes are "chivalric"; the death of women, children, and inferiors is an embarrassment rather than a source of satisfaction.

Similarly, both epics accept war as not only inevitable, a manifestation of one aspect of the cosmic whole, but also as an event that allows individual warriors to transcend the normal limitations of existence and the human personality. The psychological roots of this high evaluation of the battlefield were spelled out with self-conscious clarity by a twentieth-century soldier. In 1917 Pierre Teilhard de Chardin, already a priest and scholar, had been serving on the front as a stretcher-bearer for three years. While perfectly aware of the destructive side of battle, he also possessed enough self-awareness and honesty to write:

> The front cannot but attract us, because it is, in one way, the *extreme boundary* between what you are already aware of, and what is still in the process of formation. Not only do you see there things that you experience nowhere else, but you also see emerge from within yourself an underlying stream of clarity, energy, and freedom that is to be found hardly anywhere else in ordinary life. ... This exaltation is accompanied by a certain pain. Nevertheless it is indeed an exaltation. And that's why one likes the front in spite of everything, and misses it.[23]

This "underlying stream of clarity, energy and freedom," this "exaltation," is Homer's "joy of battle." Men caught in such an experience move with grace and strength like a lion or a wild boar; they are like a "fierce fire on some parched mountainside ... and the wind driving it whirleth every way the flame"[24] for they glow with energy.

Ironically, what is being described and honored is very close to the healthy sanity idealized by gestalt theorists.[25] Particularly among children at play or adults absorbed in a self-chosen task, there are moments of complete (or unblocked) contact between the self and the environment in which emotions, actions, and awareness are totally integrated. At such points in time the most pressing, unfinished gestalt has spontaneously assumed dominance, while other possibilities or introjections are ignored or silenced. Hunger, conscience, self-images, or the expectations of others are swept aside by the compellingness of the present situation, and the total organism (including all of its energy) is committed without reservation to the activity. Thus children intrigued with a demanding new toy or game are oblivious of other attractions, the passage of time, or even the presence of other people. Attempts to interrupt their involvement will be shrugged off as irrelevant distractions, while the demand that they come to the table or go to bed will be passionately resisted. At the same time distinctions between mind and body, self and environment, disappear, so that "there is no sense of oneself or of other things ... [only] one's experience of the situation."[26] Thus for the pianist or the dancer, the setting (be it concert hall or bare practice room) disappears and there remains only a moving, feeling body that is at one with the music.

We have all seen examples of such "good contact," especially in the lives of children, creative artists, and dedicated athletes, and we have personally experienced such moments of total spontaneous attention to the task at hand. Many of us also remember the particular power of such a response in a situation of "extreme emergency" in which all of our energy and capabilities have been called forth, and we have learned "who we really are" because we were then so completely present. The battlefield produces just such an emergency situation, in which the very life-and-death struggle easily dominates all other unfinished or distracting gestalts while neurotic anxieties and "blocks" are overridden by a clear and present danger or demand. Thus the warrior "passionately feels and takes pleasure in the fight," "there are no mere means and ends; with regard to every part of the process, there is a well-rounded but on-going satisfaction."[27]

Such an experience is different from the explosive tantrum produced by a combination of high-level frustration and danger discussed in chapter 2. The "joy of battle" is the product of a danger that produces a clear gestalt and an endangered individual who possesses the physical strength, skill, and psychic energy necessary to deal effectively with the problem. If the danger becomes overwhelming, the gestalt will change; in Homer's terms, men "forget their delight in battle," they are apt to flee (panic), become confused, withdraw into themselves, fantasize about alternatives. (Hector, trapped by Achilles, is a good example of a man caught in such a situation.) Heroes, on the other hand, are heroes precisely because they are exceptionally capable of dealing with the battle situation; they seldom find that its demands overwhelm their capacity to respond, while their very effectiveness tends to rally other men.

It is unquestionably this centered, focused action, this loss of self-consciousness, that recommended battle as a yoga to Hindu thought. The connection is even more explicit in the tradition of Zen Buddhism, which developed martial exercises and disciplines specifically to insure the centeredness, spontaneity, and effectiveness of samurai warriors in battle. In all cultures it is this "exaltation," the grace, excitement, and glowing energy of the warrior-hero, that communicates a sense of power and glory, convincing the observer as well as the actor that he is "godlike," immortal, at one with the Brahman.

The high evaluation of the warrior-hero transcends cultures.

Some version of it is to be found (even when most honored in the breach) in all civilizations. Its ultimate impact varies, however, according to the degree of power and prestige accorded the warrior caste. Thus in China and India, where the Confucian bureaucracy and the Brahman caste managed to depress the warriors' pretensions and to elevate their own ethics as the justification for hierarchy and exploitation, military caste values were always subordinated to an insistence on concern for familial piety or religious transcendance. By contrast, Europe, Japan, and the Islamic world preserved and revered the warrior code well into the twentieth century.

Nor has the transition to a more egalitarian, democratic society and army resulted in the annihilation of the warrior's ethics. Destroyed as a caste, warriors have become soldiers and officers who still value the archaic code and way of life. As Morris Janowitz, the dean of military sociologists, points out in his study, *The Professional Soldier in America*, "Heroism is an essential part of the calculations of even the most rational and self-critical military thinkers. . . ."[28] Moreover, such military traditions involve "a rigid commitment to the political status quo, a belief in the inevitability of violence in the relations between states, and a lack of concern with the social and political consequences of war."[29]

Such a value system is, of course, ultimately the value system of a caste and not of the community as a whole. The psychic beneficiary of battle is the heroic individual, not the society; indeed, the military code absolves the warrior from any concern with the impact of his actions on those who are not his equals. When the results of action are perceived as necessarily so ambiguous and obscure, any military objective is acceptable as long as one's actions in battle conform to the prescribed norms and produce the desired psychological results. Thus one young officer of the Prussian Junker class wrote, in what he knew was to be his last letter from the battle of Stalingrad:

> In thinking over my life once more, I can look back on it with thankfulness. It has been beautiful, very beautiful. It was like climbing a ladder, and even this last rung is beautiful, a crowning of it, I might almost say a harmonious completion.
> . . . No halo, please; I have never been an angel! Nor do I want

to confront my God as one; I'll manage it as a soldier, with the free, proud soul of a cavalryman, as a Herr! I am not afraid of death; my faith gives me this beautiful independence of spirit. For this I am especially thankful.[30]

But some young German warriors, even as they clung to the values and honor of the military code, came to understand the moral ambiguity of their battle and their death, as well as the moral bankruptcy of the Nazi regime.

> . . . You are the wife of a German officer; so you will take what I have to tell you, upright and unflinching. . . . I cannot deny my share of personal guilt in all this. But it is in a ratio of 1 to 70 millions. The ratio is small; still it is there. I wouldn't think of evading my responsibility; I tell myself that, by giving my life, I have paid my debt. One cannot argue about questions of honor.
> . . . I am not cowardly, only sad that I cannot give greater proof of my courage than to die for this useless, not to say criminal, cause.[31]

The words are words that Bhishma and the priestly authors of the *Mahabharata* would have understood and respected.

How can one condemn as neurotic an experience so close to health, so widely valued by human societies, so honored by men as sane and creative as Homer and Teilhard de Chardin? If one parallels battle with other emergency situations (a child trapped in a burning building, for example), it is clear that the capacity for a total, spontaneous, and effective response to danger is intrinsically valuable as well as "delightful." The ability to defend self or others in a life-and-death struggle with either human or nonhuman forces is, at a minimum, useful for survival.

The neurotic element emerges, however, with the addiction to, and overvaluation of, the joy of battle. In a healthy organism each completed gestalt leaves the individual open to newly emerging gestalts and to spontaneous, unplanned growth in interaction with the environment. It leaves one precisely at "the *extreme boundary* between what you are already aware of, and what is still in the process of formation." A compulsive commitment to battle, embodied in the self-fulfilling myth of "the inevitability of war," effectively limits the future and attempts to control the unknown that is "in the process of formation." Thus at the end of the *Iliad* Achilles is momentarily a man who has brought a complicated gestalt to a creative conclusion and is potentially open to a variety of new experiences. But instead he returns to the battlefield, retracing old paths until they literally become a dead-end for him.

This habitual attachment to battle is ultimately connected with the social climate that leads to an overvaluation of the warrior-hero at the expense of other examples of creative courage. The more socialization techniques and the ordinary demands of social life inhibit spontaneity, substituting neurotic self-conquest for healthy self-regulation, the rarer and therefore more valuable these moments of "good contact" and total involvement become. When humans are normally caught in a situation of low-grade frustration and danger, the high-level danger of the battlefield becomes excessively attractive and the individuals capable of courageously dominating it become uniquely impressive. Thus the nonwarrior pays the heroic fighter the homage of honor and glory; to be so totally alive seems a sign of godliness, a guarantee of immortality. In effect, battle is still being loved for its (individual) psychic rewards and valued as a ritual means of overcoming death.

What is being transcended is not, however, biological death, which (like Apollo) cannot be killed. Instead, the joy of battle temporarily overrides the life-negating retroflections and introjections that have conquered and numbed our ordinary day-to-day capacity for living. Ironically, once the life-and-death struggle is institutionalized, battle and the military life become part of the very social controls that deaden the spontaneous life of the ordinary human mortal. Thus our inability to be totally alive in the present seduces us into embracing a lively death as the lesser evil.

8
Harrowing Hell

> Fanaticism is the correlate to spiritual self-surrender: it shows the anxiety which it was supposed to conquer. . . . The weakness of the fanatic is that those whom he fights have a secret hold upon him; and to this weakness he and his group finally succumb.
> —*Paul Tillich*[1]

There is a theme much beloved by orthodox Christian art in which the newly resurrected Christ is depicted emerging from hell, holding his cross as if it were a sword and leading the liberated patriarchs by the hand as if they were children. In that one scene are caught the ambiguities toward war that have plagued Christianity from its beginning and made the civilization founded upon it both more pacifistic in intent and more profoundly violent in action than any other culture that has existed. The ambiguity lies in the question of whether one sees the cross (the acceptance of suffering) as replacing the sword as a means of dealing with chaos and sin, or whether one sees it as simply a new and more effective sword with which to destroy the forces of evil.

In its earliest formulation (and in its ongoing mystic tradition) Christianity was a profoundly unwarlike and indeed antiwar religion, a posture grounded in the Christian myth itself and in its identification with certain prophetic teachings about the nature of war and punishment. Chapter 6 pointed to the neurotic projection involved in the Hebraic understanding of war. But there was also a creative element in the prophetic response that makes it distinctive. In one sense the prophets were just as reactive, conservative, and punitive as the priests and monarchs of their own and other civilizations. But they also held on to a vision of Yahweh as reconciling and loving. Thus they added to the conception of punishment a creative element: repentance, a turning around, change.

The Hebrew prophets rejected the idea that war in any way represented ultimate necessity. Truth was not something imposed upon human beings but something freely chosen. War was a punishment but also a reminder to which the proper response was change and growth toward a correct covenantal relation with Yahweh, who demanded neither ritual correctness nor outward conformity to rule but rather a change of heart expressed through reformed social relations. "What is good has been explained to you, man; this is what Yahweh asks of you: only this, to act justly, to love tenderly and to walk humbly with your God" (Micah 6:8). If Israel could respond to this demand, then a new covenant would be possible: "Deep within them I will plant my law, writing it on their hearts. Then I will be their God and they will be my people" (Jer. 31:33). Thus the prophets called for an assimilation rather than an introjection of the divine norms. The law (social, moral, or divine) that we have written within our hearts is the law we have (to use a different metaphor) chewed over, digested, and made part of the very nature of our own being. (Biblical language, in fact, often uses the terms "heart" and "bowel" interchangeably.) Such assimilated material, becoming part of the centered core of an individual, is a source of strength and independence as well as of social cohesiveness. This social and religious perspective rooted in a profound sense of human potential reached its peak in the prophecies of Deutero-Isaiah, the anonymous prophet whose writings were appended (as chapters 40 to 56) to the earlier work of Isaiah.

We know very little about the life of Deutero-Isaiah except that he lived through the latter years of the exile in Babylon and that he was thoroughly steeped in the writings of his people. The triumphs of Cyrus and the sudden possibility of experiencing the long-promised return to Jerusalem led him, in a wave of joy and excitement, to a new understanding of sin and punishment. Thus he boldly rejected the conception that the sufferings of Israel could be understood simply as divine punishment for past sins. Instead he insisted that though

> ... we thought of him [Israel] as someone punished, struck by God and brought low, yet he was pierced through for our faults, crushed for our sins. . . . Though he had done no wrong and there had been no perjury in his mouth. (Isaiah 53:4–5, 9)

Thus Deutero-Isaiah abolished the simple equation between suffering, guilt, and punishment. Israel's suffering was neither a sign of guiltiness nor an occasion for resentment of Yahweh; rather it was a new experience of the divine nature. If Israel could accept this new insight into the nature of transcendent reality, accepting both suffering and release as gifts, then the Hebrew people could become a witness to all nations of the true character of the divine.

> I have appointed you as a covenant of the people and light of the nations, to open the eyes of the blind, to free captives from prison, and those who live in darkness from the dungeon. (Isaiah 42:6–7)

What Deutero-Isaiah asked for as a response from the Hebrews (and mankind in general) was an abandonment of their previous infantile dependency on Yahweh, their longing for repetitive dead-ends, their long-harbored resentments, and their attraction to punishment as the means to confluence and unity. Instead Deutero-Isaiah insisted that, if people could only see it, this was a new exodus, a new beginning; if the Hebrews could let go of both resentment and guilt, they could respond to the exile as he did, as an opportunity for creativity. Moreover, it was an opportunity that could affect both domestic and international policy, making available to all mankind the psychic and social liberty Yahweh had just offered the Hebrews.

Understandably, early Christians, reflecting on the meaning of a criminal death, insisted upon a close relation between their own experience of the divine and the prophetic words of Deutero-Isaiah. For them the Lord's anointed was not a king or a warrior; he was certainly not an imperial dispenser of justice or triumphant in material terms. Rather he was a provincial carpenter, condemned by imperial justice, who ended up on a cross like a slave. The parallels to Israel's exile were obvious; by their insistence that Jesus was in fact an embodiment of God himself the new Christians clarified and expanded the prophetic insight.

In the process the traditional mythic relation between guilt and punishment (and therefore the meaning of war) was completely overturned. God, in the humanity of Jesus, suffers and dies; suffering is not divine punishment but simply a part of human finitude that the divine willingly assumes. Specifically, such punishment as Jesus bears is not a sign of unrighteousness but a result of human choices; indeed the priestly elite and the Roman governors who condemned him are thereby revealed as themselves the sources of unnecessary suffering.[2]

To the extent that one identifies one's personal suffering with that of Jesus, *imitatio Christi,* one is reassured that it is indeed all right to be the kind of person to whom undesired and destructive things happen, since they say nothing about the true nature of one's own being. Any illusory identification with the conqueror or the victor is rejected precisely because it is false: Satan is a liar; evil is a lie. Instead Christianity demands "that one accept suffering with courage, as an element of finitude and affirm finitude in spite of the suffering that accompanies it."[3] Suffering accepted in this spirit becomes charged with the meanings symbolized in the resurrection; a path to growth, change, and joy.

> Truly, truly, I say to you, you will weep and lament, but the world will rejoice; you will be sorrowful, but your sorrow will turn into joy. When a woman is in travail she has sorrow, because her hour has come: but when she is delivered of the child, she no longer remembers the anguish, for joy that a child is born into the world. (John 16:20–21)

Such an acceptance of suffering, as well as the rejection of any God who is less than pure love, has always been preserved most strongly in the thought of the mystics: Philhelene, Johannes Tauler, Meister Eckhart, Thomas Münzer. Moreover, such a stance pushes one, as Münzer's example suggests, toward social change and even revolution, since it inevitably raises the question of whether one suffers for God or for the Devil.

> That "God is always with the one who is suffering" entails not only consolation but also strengthening: a rejection of every ideology of punishment, which was so useful for the cementing of privileges and for oppression. There is a mystical defiance that rebels against everything ordained and regulated from on high and holds fast to the truth it has discovered. . . . That is the extension of Paul's thought: Nothing "can separate us from the love of God." (Romans 8:39)[4]

Unfortunately such mysticism has always been suspected by both the Christian church and state as potentially heretical and politically dangerous.

From this perspective, however, war is simply one of the side effects of human error, a sign that humans' separation from their true nature has not been overcome. Certainly once God is understood as love, war ceases to have any mythological meaning or transcendent imperative, since it imitates no divine gesture. Thus St. Augustine, when he observes that the City of God is founded on an act of loving grace and the City of Man on an act of war, makes brilliantly clear the extent to which Christian mythology desacralized and therefore devalued war. "Whatever part of the city of the world raises the standard of war, it seeks to be lord of the world: in fact, it is enthralled in its own wickedness. . . ."[5]

Certainly there is little in Augustine that glorifies war. He recognizes three possible kinds: the conflict between two good but imperfect men, the conflict between two evil men, and the conflict between an evil and a good man. Were it not for the existence of this last possibility, the good man would "be under compulsion to wage no wars at all." Even in waging a just war, the Christian must see it merely as a lesser evil in the chaotic conditions of earthly life; any sense of triumph and glory in victory must be muted by a sense of anguish at the fallen state of mankind. In psychological terms, Augustine recognizes the right and need of defensive anger, but he warns sternly against avoiding grief and pain by false identification with the conqueror. Affliction falls upon both the good and the evil; "the difference is not in what people suffer, but in the way they suffer."[6]

But Augustine also brings human history back within the embrace of the divine as a drama in which Divine Providence is working itself out. Human history (and particularly human wars and empires, which he understands as comprising most of history) thus acquires at least an element of sacredness. It becomes a hierophany through which God's meaning and intent is revealed to mankind. Chronological history reveals, moreover, not a loving and suffering but a just and righteous God (a perspective Augustine and other Christian intellectuals adopted from Stoic thought).

In the process of explaining war, Augustine relies primarily on the older prophetic and Roman notion of war as a divine mode of correction and instruction, which "will test, purify and improve the good, but beat, crush, and wash away the wicked." He offers very little reason though, to assume that even Christians can consider themselves among the righteous for whom war is simply a testing of one's mettle. "The fact is that everyone, however exemplary, yields to some prompting of concupiscence: if not to monstrous crimes, abysmal villainy, and abominable impiety, at least to some sins, however rarely or—if frequently—however venially."[7] Thus suffering in war becomes a sign and a reminder of one's existential sinfulness, to which the proper response is a spiritualized form of masochism. (In the context of the fourth century, it would have been difficult to ask whether one "suffers for God or for the Devil" as war had taken on the inevitability of a natural disaster.)

Nevertheless, Augustine is unwilling and unable to despise completely the City of Man and human emotions and to deny any purpose and meaningful action to its citizens. Though the City of Man has no ultimate reality, he believes that "while history lasts, it has a finality of its own. . . ." "For, however lowly the goods of earth, the aim, such as it is, is peace. The purpose even of war is peace. . . . When victory goes to the side that had a juster cause it is surely a matter for human rejoicing, and the peace is one to be welcomed."⁸ Thus the City of Man, though resting on violence and self-deception, can move toward justice, which is an element of love. Even war can be an instrument of good when pursued, with grief and sorrow, as a defense against the injustice of an evil aggressor. Unfortunately, in his discussion of a just war, Augustine implies that a good man is under the necessity of waging a just war. Augustine does not develop this idea, but it has haunted Christianity ever since. To say that one *must* fight a just war is to begin to imbue such a war with holiness, to imply that the action is right because it is a rite action—that is, that it imitates a divine gesture. On an individual level this may be true of angry aggression; one thinks, for example, of Jesus cleansing the temple. But it opens up a dangerous potential when applied to human institutions, which Augustine recognized as inherently unjust but which will always claim to embody justice.

For many new converts in the first centuries, the impact of the gospel was of such therapeutic strength as to produce significant personality changes. Unfortunately, for even more individuals conversion left much of the old character structure intact. Among other things, it did not eliminate the conflict between the controlling and the spontaneous self, and therefore it did not eliminate a sense of guilt or a fascination with punishment and revenge. Thus as early as A.D. 80 some of the saints were calling on God to avenge them and punish the guilty nonbelievers.

The failure of the new faith in this respect is hardly to be wondered at. After all, with those who were converts late in life, there was the whole pattern of retroflection and introjection developed by their previous socialization to be overcome, while to raise children in imitation of God the Father's loving gesture and in light of the new understanding of human "all rightness" would have required a complete reevaluation of existing family structures and child-rearing patterns. While gestures were made in this direction, the traditional biases of the leadership and their belief in the imminence of the second coming muted any effective desire to challenge such existing social structures as slavery, imperialism, and the patriarchal family.

Moreover, the basic Christian myth itself unwittingly helped to sharpen the thrust toward self-control, and with it the sense of guilt and the need for justificatory punishment. For example, the myth records no defensive violence or resentment on the part of Jesus in reaction to his seizure, trial, and crucifixion. If one ignores the anguish and anger of the Garden of Gethsemane, in which the human meaning of pain and defeat is dramatized, the isolated story of Jesus' trial and death leaves the ordinary human animal who attempts to imitate it faced with severe restrictions on defensive anger and sorrow in the face of danger and pain. (Jesus, in fact, becomes totally divine.) Within the total context of the myth, the most healthy response is to feel and express defensive (or desirous) anger in the understanding that God loves and accepts one in one's bodily form, while accepting loss or pain when that is inevitable. Such a response is consonant with the stories that record Jesus' earlier expressions of anger, fear, grief, and despair. To the extent that the Christian church eventually institutionalized confession, penance, and ritual forgiveness, it opened a channel for dealing with the psychological chasm between the strictly divine gesture and human limitations. But by continuing to insist upon an essential chasm between human sinfulness and divine purity, the church nonetheless left the adult with a need for punishment and revenge as a mode of insuring human and cosmic at-oneness.

The desire for the punishment of divine vengeance can, of course, be handled in various ways. In the early years of the new sect, when it was powerless and persecuted, it seems to have been handled primarily through fantasy. The second coming was envisioned as an occasion of retribution and punishment in which the sinners and persecuters would suffer. Thus St. John of Patmos fantasized:

> And when he had opened the fifth seal, I saw under the altar the souls of them that were slain for the word of God, and for the testimony which they held: And they cried with a loud voice, saying, How long, O Lord, holy and true, dost thou not judge and avenge our blood on them that dwell on the earth? (Rev. 6:9–10)

Psychologically the picture is neither very healthy nor very pretty; rather than being expressed immediately and let go, resentment and anger are held on to for eternity: "And the smoke of their torment ascendeth up for ever and ever: and they have no rest day or night, who worship the beast and his image" (Rev. 14:11).

Unfortunately, within the context of this psychological tension certain minor images or myths emerged that, becoming part of the corpus of sacred Christian texts, helped eventually to reestablish the conception of aggressive war as a divine gesture. Specifically, St. John drew upon certain traditional images to create a mythic warring hero, St. Michael.

> And there was war in heaven: Michael and his angels fought against the dragon; and the dragon fought and his angels, and prevailed not: neither was their place found any more in heaven. And the great dragon was cast out, that old serpent, called the Devil and Satan, which deceiveth the whole world: he was cast out into the earth, and his angels were cast out with him. (Rev. 12:7-9)

The meaning of this vision for St. John is unclear, as is that of a horseman "called Faithful and True," who in righteousness "doth judge and make war."

> And he was clothed with a vesture dipped in blood: and his name is called The Word of God. And the armies which were in heaven followed him upon white horses, clothed in fine linen, white and clean. And out of his mouth goeth a sharp sword, that with it he should smite the nations; and he shall rule them with a rod of iron; and he treadeth the wine press of the fierceness and wrath of Almighty God. (Rev. 19:13-15)

Since this warlike figure is intimately connected with Christ himself (The Word of God), the judgment and destruction he brings may be no more or less than the impact of truth on the illusions and deceptions of consensus reality. Nonetheless, warlike imagery had been reincorporated into the Christian cosmology as part of the divine action of the final days, while the God of Love had been resymbolized as an Almighty Divine Warrior—and a sadist.

For centuries the fantasies of St. John remained just that: a vision of the final days and a source for private hopes of vengeance.

Heirs to a dying empire, western Christians fought primarily defensive (i.e., just) wars and generally lost. As Christianity spread northward and as Europe suffered successive waves of barbarian invasions, Augustine gave meaning to unavoidable suffering and a rationale for increasing (where possible) the power of monarchs who might restrain or eliminate the liking for internecine wars of vengeance and loot that were part of the Germanic and Slavic traditions.

In the process, however, the church found itself increasingly involved in warfare. Not only did its bishops become feudal landholders with military obligations, but the church allowed itself to become involved in the ritual trappings of war. Knights meditated before the altars as a part of their initiatory ritual; priests blessed armies before battle and invoked God's aid in securing victory; the image of St. Michael merged easily with pagan myths of other dragon-destroying culture heroes. The result is the enormous ambivalence of a church like Mont St. Michel, built like a fortress around a crucifix, and of an institution whose monks retreated to pray for peace and whose bishops buckled on the sword and fought. It is the ambiguity of a church militant dedicated to the prince of peace.

As the barbarian threat receded, the church found itself implicated in a culture of greed and war directed by Christians against Christians. Its initial response was to impose ritual limits, establishing sanctuaries, demanding nonviolence on Sundays and certain holy days, insisting that only just wars were appropriate. But simultaneously it became a leader in crusades against pagans and heretics and the patron of new militant monastic orders. Moreover, a specifically Christian existential anxiety surfaced that fueled the annihilating hatred for the opposition characteristic of the crusades of the high medieval period. Epics such as *The Song of Roland* embody its mythic and psychic roots, while the ferocious attacks on Albigensians and Jews exemplify this hatred in practice.

The Song of Roland is one of the great medieval epics, which became in its time an immensely popular story whose heroes and events were known, sculpted, and admired throughout Europe. It is, moreover, one of those interesting examples of the way in which an actual event (an eighth-century ambush carried out by Christian Basques on the rear guard of Charlemagne's army as it was withdrawing from a successful campaign in alliance with Spanish Muslims) can be mythologized by popular thought. In all such cases the manner in which the event is reworked clearly reflects the more basic mythic patterns within which popular thought moves. In this case the Christian Basques were converted into Muslims and a deceitful Muslim plot was invented to explain Charlemagne's decision to withdraw. Count Roland emerged from obscurity to become a major figure in the drama, while his treacherous stepfather, Count Ganelon, was a pure creation of the popular mind. The epic ends with a wholly imaginary trial and the execution of Ganelon and the thirty relatives who have stood as sureties at his trial.

On the surface *The Song of Roland* seems only superficially Christian. Charlemagne is clearly a traditional shaman-warrior or priest-king; the actions of battle are prevalidated by symbolic dreams; the weapons of battle are ritual objects into which bits of the cross and other "fighting stones" have been incorporated; and the ethics of the fighters emphasize universal warrior values such as loyalty, courage, glory, and fighting according to the rules of war. But on its structural level the epic is specifically Christian, if not Christlike, in a number of important ways.

On the most obvious level, the chanson is a retelling, in more contemporary and human terms, of the fight between St. Michael and the dragon whose name is Liar. The listener/reader is apprised of this early in the epic when the Muslim king's messenger reminds Charlemagne that he will soon be solemnizing by a high feast "great St. Michael of Peril-by-the-Tide." In keeping with this underlying mythic structure, the Muslims, though their individual bravery and skill as warriors are perceived, are consistently depicted as enslaved to false gods whom they themselves do not trust or, ultimately, defend. In fact, when defeated in battle they turn on their false idols and destroy them. And, of course, nothing happens. Thus the Muslim side is depicted as resting on a lie as well as embodying the disloyalty, anarchy, and ultimate defeat that go with deceit.

Peace with the Muslims can, therefore, rest only on a deception. Indeed, in initially accepting it Charlemagne has committed (regardless of Muslim honesty or intent) a major sin. He has been disloyal to God since "Never to Paynims may I show love or peace." Embodying as they do a mini-vision of hell on earth, it is only fitting that the Muslims should upon death be carried off by Satan to their proper home in hell, while the Christian warriors, returning their pledge to God, are escorted royally into heaven. (In contrast, both the *Aeneid* and the *Mahabharata* depict slain warriors from both sides of the war as mingling in the same abode for the dead.)

But *The Song of Roland* is also and more subtly (because here it clearly comes close to heresy), a retelling of the story of the crucifixion and Last Judgment, with Charlemagne as God the Father and Roland as his Son. The most direct clue to this mythic overtone resides in one event, the fact that as Roland's death approaches

> Throughout all France terrific tempests rise . . .
> And true it is the earth quakes far and wide . . .
> Right at high noon a darkness falls like night,
> Save for the lightning there's not a gleam of light;
> None that beholds it but is dismayed for fright,
> And many say: "This is the latter time,
> The world is ending, and the Great Doom is nigh."
> They speak not true, they cannot read the signs:
> 'Tis Roland's death calls forth this mighty cry.[9]

To the medieval audience such events could have only one parallel, the earth's response to Jesus' crucifixion when "from the sixth hour there was darkness over all the land unto the ninth hour" and "the earth did quake, and the rocks rent" as Jesus descended into hell to rescue the saved among the Patriarchs.

Roland, then, is the Christ, delivered to the forces of chaos by a Judaslike figure from among his own kin and comrades. And the response of Charlemagne, who like God the Father has knowingly sent his envoy to his doom, is to turn back and avenge his death. First Charlemagne defeats the unbelievers (consigning them either to the perdition of an unbaptised death or bringing them by his grace into the fold of the saved) and then he judges and punishes the traitors within the Christian community. The execution of Ganelon's kin is confusing if taken as literal history since killing sureties or kin was never a part of medieval judicial practice. It makes perfect sense symbolically, however, as a part of the final judgment on those whose loyalty is divided. Moreover, if read in this light, the judgment scene carries the analogy between Roland and Christ one step further. Ganelon's defense is that he was never disloyal to Charlemagne but only sought revenge on Roland; the prosecution's reply is

> Your officers are sacred in their persons,
> And to betray him was treachery and murder;
> It was to you, sir, Guenes was false and perjured.[10]

In effect, Charlemagne and Roland are one, and to deny the Son is to deny the Father.

An actual historical event has thus been mythologized and turned into a drama in which the primal myths of the society are reenacted. It is also turned into a model by which future wars may be experienced and understood. In the process, war with nonbelievers or heretics has become "Holy War" in which the opposition is invested with horrifically demonic aspects and war acquires an apocalyptic character, while Augustine's insistence that even the most just war must be fought in a mood of anguish and regret is completely abandoned. Moreover, since the image of the Last Judgment points to the future, the event in time becomes important as a means of moving mankind toward its inevitable future. Any war against evil may be the harbinger or the catalyst by which the final and complete overthrow of chaos and sin is accomplished.

To believe that such final destruction of sin is possible, however, requires that sin be viewed as nonessential to existence. And, indeed, within the terms of the Judeo-Christian myth, sin is almost accidental; it is not a precondition of creation that was in itself purely good. Rather than being the undifferentiated material out of which existence emerges, evil or chaos is the absence of good, a deception that accounts as worthwhile what does not, in fact, truly exist. To equate the human opposition with the dragon of Satan is thus to perceive them as embodying the absence of good, the deceiving void that stands in the way of final beatitude. Ultimately, of course, two kinds of response to a false illusion are possible. One is to ignore it in the understanding that, because it is untrue, it cannot really harm one. This is, in effect, the response of Jesus on the cross, mythically justified in the resurrection. By contrast, the response of rage and annihilating anger reveals an underlying fear: One is not secure from deception but threatened by it. The enemy is a psychological foe, an internal temptation that cannot be ignored.

Historically, this was certainly true of the relations between Christians and Muslims by the eleventh century. Facing the Christian countries across the Mediterranean and the Pyrenees, the Islamic states unquestionably presented an appetizing attraction to the more backward Christians. Their trading vessels redistributed the wealth and luxury of a far-flung empire and their cities were crowned with architectural jewels and secular wealth. Christian scholars were already beginning to benefit from the Islamic reclamation of classical thought, and Christian elites would, in the next few centuries, borrow much from Muslim culture. Christian knights, trapped between the pacifistic ethics of the church and the aggressive values of their caste, must have been envious of a religion that glorified conquest (*jihad,* or "holy war") in God's name and promised paradise to those who fell on the field of battle. Indeed the temptation must have been strong to go a step further and adopt a creed and way of life that was so materially prosperous and culturally creative.

Mythically this attraction is acknowledged by the role of Ganelon, who not only acts and speaks deceitfully but also enters into an actual pact with the enemy. The psychological but unconscious truth of the revenge and punishment motifs (that the enemy one seeks to destroy is in effect part of one's own psyche) is thus removed from the shadows of the unconscious and made symbolically explicit. Ganelon and the Muslims are brothers under the skin; at least part of the Christian community and part of the soul of the Christian pilgrim serve false gods.

The result of this knowledge is existential anxiety, for the continued existence of evil and falsehood within the Christian is understood as a barrier to eventual salvation. Unquestionably it is this anxiety that makes it impossible to conceive of a peace or truce between the Christian and the heretical forces of evil. The slaughter of nonbelievers and heretics can awaken no pity or spark of human sympathy, because what is being destroyed is perceived as so dangerous spiritually. Thus Christian aggression had little of the warm and appetitive quality of much "pagan" destructiveness, and none of the tolerance of heretics that characterized Muslim conquest. The opposition must not be assimilated; instead it must be vomited forth. Only the kind of annihilating rage that literally destroyed the community and culture of the Albigensians and drove the Jews eastward seems an appropriate response to an "evil" that is also an alluring deception.

If Christians could never be sure of their essential goodness, nonetheless there was one way in which Christian men could, uncontrovertably, imitate the divine gesture. They could die in witness to the Faith. Thus Archbishop Turpin reminds Roland's threatened rear guard that

> Soon, very soon we all are marked to die,
> None of us here will see to-morrow's light;
> One thing there is I promise you outright:
> To you stand open the gates of Paradise,
> There with the holy sweet Innocents to bide.[11]

The analogy with the Holy Innocents sits ill with most twentieth-century readers, since there seems little in common between the powerless innocence of babies and the violence and joy in battle of these crusading knights. But from a medieval perspective, the Holy Innocents and the slain knights share both the fate of being slain for Christ and the beatitude of his martyrdom. Shriven by the priests, the knights enter battle in a state of purity. Their aggressive actions from then on theoretically partake of a selflessness that assures them of salvation.

The seriousness of this understanding of the role of battle (holy war) as a path to salvation is nowhere better expressed in the Christian tradition than within the "Paradiso" of Dante's *Divine Comedy*. There as Dante rises from heaven to heaven, he beholds in the realm of Mars, the fifth of nine levels, a ruby-red, bright cross composed of the souls of martyred warriors (including that of Roland). And through this cross Dante catches his first vision of Christ. Symbolically these warriors who have taken up their cross share with Christ the triumph over death, a triumph metaphorically embodied in the song that swells from the warriors' cross:

> For some high song of praise I knew it, since
> "Arise" and "conquer" caught my ear, although
> I heard it not with full intelligence.[12]

The death of these warriors has been a means of "conquering" chaos, of harrowing hell.

To accept frustration and pain and even death as simply a part of reality is healthy both biologically and psychologically. To glorify death in an aggressive war as a martyrdom insuring salvation is to glorify (however unconsciously) suicide. In psychological terms, the annihilating rage of the Christian community turns, in the end, back against itself. The hell that must be harrowed and ultimately destroyed exists within its own soul.

The sadomasochistic elements present in this high medieval vision of God were not overcome by the Reformation. If anything, they were strengthened, as in John Calvin's assumption that all suffering was a sign of sinfulness and his faith that God was fattening the ungodly "like pigs for the slaughter." Moreover, Calvin's punitive attitude toward sinners was paralleled by a deep self-hatred, revealed in his belief that humans were "miserable sinners, conceived and born in guilt and sin, prone in iniquity and incapable of any good work."[13] At the same time, child-rearing patterns were modified toward greater harshness, discipline, and control, thereby increasing the internal sense of retroflected guilt and the need for punitive anger.

The profound ambivalencies and temptations of the Reformation period were particularly stark in Martin Luther, who was deeply aware of the nascent capitalism and greed of his society and rejected it as a lie and the work of the Devil. But Luther was also despairingly aware of the extent to which he himself was tempted by the Devil, who "rules the world." When, as with the papacy or rebellious peasants, he could project this temptation onto a human foe, his ferocity and desire to destroy were unlimited. The alternative, after all, was to "voluntarily take upon oneself and bear the hate of the Devil, of the world, of the flesh, of sin, of death," "to be resigned in every deed to hell."[14]

Similarly, the Puritans believed the native Indians were "the snare of the Devil," "men transformed into beasts," and "the very bond-slaves of Satan."[15]

> John Underhill, a captain of the New England troops in that [King Philip's] war, referred to the Pequots as "these devil's instruments," and was certain that "the old serpent, according to his first malice, stirred them up against the church of Christ." . . .[16]

(Such a perception certainly made it possible for the new Americans to ignore their own responsibility in precipitating conflict, that is, their greedy invasion of another people's territory.) Some Puritans, of course, stressed their obligation to convert the heathen, while others found the Indian way of life attractive. But the majority would "admit no distinction between one Indian and another" and "distrusted all such English as were judged to be charitable to them."[17] Thus the groundwork of greed and existential anxiety that produced the genocidal Indian policy of the nineteenth century was laid very early. The parallels with Hitler's genocidal attack on the Jews, whom he both hated and admired for their enduring strength as a people, seems too obvious to need explication.

The power of the mythic framework and its endurance can be seen also in the American response to the aftermath of World War II. Unable to recognize or accept that the expansion of Russian influence in Eastern Europe and Maoist influence in China was an almost inevitable result of the power exigencies of the war, Americans instinctively sought an explanation in Judaslike treachery and found it in the left-wing Democrats and socialists within their midst. Thus the judicial and political witch-hunting of the McCarthy era (with its paranoic fear of, and its attempt to exorcise, the interior evil) was seen as a necessary parallel to the "Cold (i.e., nonappetitive) War" with godless Communism. The ultimately suicidal self-hatred that motivates such a policy surfaces explicitly in a favorite slogan of contemporary Christian fundamentalists and right-wing patriots: One is "better dead than Red."

9
The Cadence of Time

You're inches away from death every time you go on a mission.
How much older can you be at your age?
—*Joseph Heller*[1]

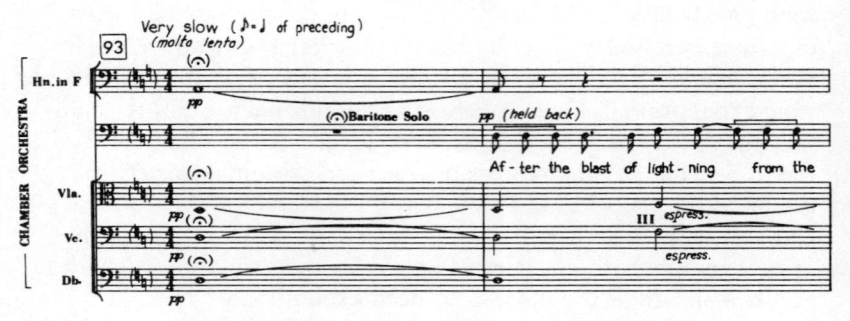

[musical score excerpt for Chamber Orchestra, measure 93, Very slow (♪=♩ of preceding) (molto lento), with Baritone Solo: "Af-ter the blast of light-ning from the"]

After the blast of lightning from the East,
The flourish of loud clouds, the Chariot Throne;
After the drums of Time have rolled and ceased,
And by the bronze west long retreat is blown,
Shall life renew these bodies?
—*Benjamin Britten and Wilfred Owen*[2]

In 1789 the French National Assembly euphorically abjured wars of aggression, denouncing them as relics of Europe's aristocratic, feudal past. Three years later, in 1792, the French Legislative Assembly declared war on Austria, Russia, and Prussia. Aside from the fallacious (and contradictory) domestic goals that secretly motivated the monarch and his Brissotin ministers, two ideas seem to have swayed the majority of French representatives in deciding to fight. One was a heritage from the warrior past, the cult of honor and revenge: "A Louis XIV could declare war on Spain because his ambassador has been insulted . . . and we who are free, should we for a moment hesitate?"[3] The other was a new perception of war as an instrument for change: "It is that expiatory war which is to renew the face of the world and plant the standard of liberty upon the palaces of kings, upon the seraglios of sultans, upon the chateaux of petty feudal tyrants and upon the temples of popes and muftis."[4] Understandably, the language of the newspaper, the *Patriote Français*, was that of traditional war myths (renewal, expiation), but the context was revolutionary. Specifically, the concept of renewal had lost its ritualistic, cyclical connotation; it pointed instead to the creation of a radically different stage of human development.

French politicians were not alone in this belief that war could be a rite of transition. When, several months later, the untried army of the revolution successfully survived a Prussian cannonade at Valmy while firing 20,000 rounds in a great artillery battle, the German poet Goethe had essentially the same reaction. Asked for his understanding of the day's unexpected events, he explained to the officers of the Saxon army that "From this place and from this day forth commences a new era in the world's history, and you can all say that you were present at its birth."[5] Over a decade later the German philosopher Hegel expressed the same idea when, watching the conquering Napoleon ride by after the battle of Jena, he believed he had seen "the world-spirit," which would dominate the next stage of history, "on horse back."

In effect, a new myth was in the process of being created, a myth that still undergirds twentieth-century reflections on military might and warfare. Thus on August 5, 1914, José Ortega y Gasset would write that "History is trembling to its very roots, its flanks are torn apart convulsively, because a new reality is about to be born,"[6] expressing an apocalyptic vision soldiers of all countries shared. But as we have seen earlier, myth is closely connected with ritual. If a new myth of war emerged in recent centuries, it must have had its roots in changes in the actual pattern of warfare. Moreover, since the myth concerns time and history, one would expect (and find) that the new military tactics and strategy were also connected with controlling or using time.

The new faith in progress rested originally on a very practical belief (enunciated by Francis Bacon in the late sixteenth century) that knowledge was power and that a correct understanding of the workings of nature would allow humans to dominate their physical environment. From the beginning, moreover, this faith was partly grounded in the concrete examples provided by the fruitful interaction of scientific knowledge and military practice. Side by side with the imitation of classical military models, there developed in the sixteenth century a very pragmatic and innovative willingness among rulers to use scientific knowledge to solve military problems and an interest among scientists in solving them. Starting with Leonardo da Vinci, a long line of engineers (Errard, Lazare Carnot), mathematicians (Nicolo Tartaglia, Girard Desargues), chemists (Vannoccio Biringuccio), and physicists (Jean Richer) combined practical military involvement with their more abstract theoretical concerns. Increasingly sophisticated fortifications and siege operations, as well as more effective and stable gunpowder, stronger cannon metal, and the invention of the bayonet flowed from this early wedding of the scientific and technological spirit with the monarchical drive for power. Nor did the benefits flow all in a single direction. Galilei Galileo, for example, worked out his groundbreaking laws of dynamics in the process of solving some basic problems in military ballistics.

The metaphor that informed and to some extent made possible this striking advance in technology was that of the machine, a metaphor used both to delimit (as in the theorizing of Galileo and Descartes) the area capable of systematic investigation and to describe (as in Fontenelle, Pascal, or Leibnitz) the actual nature of the universe. The machine also operated as an analogy for the drive toward standardization and centralization that shaped monarchical reforms during these same centuries. Since human beings, as a part of nature, were also machines, it followed that productive results could be achieved by training them to perform with precision and predictability. Understandably, the first real applications of this idea were made by benevolent despots concerned to improve their military organizations.

The process was a slow, continuous one. For example, as early as the sixteenth century both the battle squares of the Swiss and the Spanish, with their subordination of the individual to the mass, depended for their effectiveness on a regimented response from soldiers. But squares were large masses with little in the way of articulated function, difficult to maneuver, and slow to act. By contrast, the self-conscious experiments of Maurice of Nassau and Gustavus Adolphus in the mid-seventeenth century demonstrated that the division of the army into small units with specialized functions was more effective (a lesson also applied to the organization of the arms factories Gustavus Adolphus established in Sweden).

In the long run the actual tactics used in these prebayonet armies were less important than the new attitude that informed them. The square, like the classical phalanx, had simply attempted to utilize typical human reflexes under stress. Their cohesiveness rested on the "sheep-like instinct which causes every man to crowd upon his neighbor, because he thinks to put himself out of reach of danger by it."[7] The reforms of the seventeenth century, on the other hand, depended for their effectiveness on the assumption that the natural tendency to crowd or flee could be overcome and that rote training could be used to mold and control human responses. Gustavus Adolphus's actual tactics were not widely imitated, but his emphasis on drill and training were standard procedure by the end of the century.

In the eighteenth century this process was carried a critical stage further, while its implications were partly masked by an aristocratic ideology insisting on the radical chasm between the "dumb, animal masses" and the fully human elite that officered and directed them. Minutely regulated drills were devised, correlated to mechanically timed cadences, and forced by brutal discipline upon the peasant armies. In the process soldiers were deliberately turned into automata whose individual bravery and intelligence were irrelevant as long as they responded efficiently to the order of command. Indeed the real technological breakthrough of this period was precisely in the realm of human material: the ever-increasing subtlety with which human bodies were taught to move according to very rigid and often quite complicated patterns. In its most extreme form, in Prussia, this involved a distinctive way of holding the body (the "goose step"), different march steps for every possible contingency, and minutely detailed patterns for firing and reloading guns. In theory, and often in practice, this meant that at any one moment a thousand men might be making precisely the same movement and drawing the same breath. Until this period, only religious orders had so carefully disciplined actions and so rigorously adapted humans to the demands of a timetable. In both cases, moreover, such conformity to the clock was clearly a symbolic, if unconscious, means of gaining access to the power of the divine.

Such military reforms were essentially conservative in intent. Tied to their cumbrous wagon trains and fortified supply depots, royal armies moved slowly and predictably across the countryside in an attempt to intercept each other's supply lines. Battles were few, though sieges were numerous; battle lines and siege operations were drawn up according to convention and followed routinized patterns. To the soldiers slogging out these interminable marches and countermarches or digging endless, geometrically precise trenches, little seemed to happen, and indeed in the treaties that concluded these wars, little territory changed hands. But to the choreographer directing events from the capital or the commander's tent, movements took on the quality of an elaborate minuet in which dancers moved forward and back, circled and curtsied according to the established "rules of the game." In this sense war imitated (or was imitated by) the Baroque fugue, in which variations on a single musical theme chased each other according to the formal pattern that characterized the Being of the ordered, hierarchic world of Enlightened Despotism.

The aesthetic (and therefore symbolic) character of these military developments is further clarified if one observes the visual quality achieved by armies fighting "set battles" in which both brilliantly uniformed sides were drawn up in ordered lines before any major fighting began. In this regard it is important to note that, though details differed from regiment to regiment, the typical eighteenth-century uniform involved a striking color contrast between coat and breeches, a coat with a tail so tapered as to create an inverted V in front, with contrastingly colored sashes, cross-belts, and facings on the coat further contributing to the vertical, geometric quality of a soldier's appearance. If large numbers of men, all dressed in approximately this fashion, are lined up in long rows, they turn into the visual equivalent of columns. An almost architectural façade is created whose basic characteristic can be described as severe regularity allowing great variety and elaboration. There is thus a similarity in feeling and inner vision between the façade of, say, Versailles and the French army at Ramilles or Blenheim.

This concern with visual effects explains the eighteenth century's relative neglect of skirmishers and of close coordination of arms as part of the tactics of battle. Skirmishers were not unknown before 1780, while the much-studied example of Gustavus Adolphus had clearly demonstrated the military advantages of mingling horse, foot, and artillery. It was not out of ignorance that these techniques were neglected but rather as the result of an almost deliberate oversight, as the intermingling of different arms and a "haze of skirmishers" would have destroyed the desired appearance of regularity and order.

That the stiff drill of the eighteenth century satisfied nonmilitary needs seems further suggested by the comment of an English soldier, Sergeant Roger Lamb, that "it is indeed surprising to see how soon an awkward young man becomes well-disciplined, performs his evolutions with a neat agility, and handles his arms with graceful dexterity."[8] The connection between warfare, class structure, and aesthetic sensibility is further clarified when one remembers that one of the major peacetime duties of an army in this period involved ceremonial functions at the royal court, while it was just such qualities as "agility" and "gracefulness" that were held to differentiate the aristocrat from the bourgeois. The effect of such aesthetic and social considerations on the method of fighting is nicely demonstrated by the memoirs of Edward M'Gauran, an Irish soldier of fortune who volunteered for service with the British army during the American Revolutionary War. When a progressive young captain attempted to introduce the company to the tactics of skirmishing, M'Gauran dismissed them as

> Whimsical modes practiced by cowards and savages. . . . This exercise of . . . sprawling on the ground, was ridiculous in my opinion. However, in these harlequin exhibitions . . . we passed some weeks to our mortification and the abhorrence of the whole army.[9]

In fact, the late seventeenth and the eighteenth centuries, perhaps in reaction to the excesses of the previous century, seem to have come to desire a close relation between power and order and to have imposed this vision of reality upon both their battlefields and architecture. If this order and harmony, essentially foreign to the nature of battle, meant that armies were militarily less efficient than they need have been, it may still have been psychologically necessary: Power may not have seemed worth fighting and dying for if it was devoid of the element of order and control.

During the eighteenth century, however, a more time-conscious attitude emerged that eventually overwhelmed the static world of mathematics and monarchs. On the theoretical level the Christian concept of human history as embodied in a linear time span divided by a critical event was secularized, and the turning point was moved from the life of Christ to a relatively contemporaneous period. In the thought of men as diverse as Hume, Voltaire, and Gibbon, the previous centuries were essentially "dark ages" characterized by passions, prejudices, priests, and superstitions, while the present and future represented the working out of the scientific spirit and reasonableness. The effect of the new knowledge and rationality would ultimately be comparable to the Day of Judgment (Enlightenment), ushering in a utopian city of truth.

On the surface the new myth seems to break with Christian thought by assigning a critical, determining role to mankind. Whereas in orthodox Christianity all of history and human effort is subordinated to Divine Providence, which controls the pattern and the results, Enlightenment theorists seemed to be saying that humanity makes its own destiny. As with Stoic thought, however, the concept of divinity remained, hidden in the guise of nature. Human beings determined their own future only because they had or could discover and conform to the hidden (scientific) laws that govern the universe and the hidden (historic) patterns that control time.

On a conscious level, then, the effective power behind the expected change sprang from the realm of ideas. Humanity was learning to recognize the rules of nature; such knowledge was power and would produce, through human control over nature, material abundance. Rational consciousness would also overcome passions and insure human happiness. Though the philosophers disagreed as to whether change was to be inaugurated by enlightened despots or an educated citizenry, most believed that the essential struggle was internal, occurring in the realm of ideas and domestic politics; culture, education, and knowledge provided the critical fulcrum for change. By contrast, war was usually seen as a characteristic of the unfortunate past; at best battle (as in Kant's thought) was viewed as a tool of nature for pushing human beings toward conscious reason, morality, and freedom.

The practical side of this new attitude toward time was expressed in a self-conscious concern with saving time, increasing the pace of events, and escaping from inconclusive, repetitive rituals into decisive, history-determining actions. Unfortunately one aspect of this "conquest of space and time" involved the introduction of the flintlock, reducing the ninety-eight motions required for loading a matchlock to less than thirty and speeding up the firing process by 300 percent. This increased rate of firepower (combined with the bayonet) made it possible to reduce military formations from eight to three lines and therefore allowed armies to occupy a much larger front. Since a longer front meant more protection for vulnerable flanks and greater possibilities for encirclement, rulers in response expanded the size of armies, which grew from about 70,000 at the beginning of Louis XIV's reign to 200,000 at its close. In effect, greater speed increased the space that could be dominated by fire, and this domination was countered by increasing the mass of men and gunpower on the battlefield.

Because highly trained soldiers were expensive to produce, the search for a faster rate of fire continued. In 1718, for example, the parsimonious king of Prussia, Frederick William I, equipped all of his infantry with double-ended iron ramrods, making it possible for them to fire twice as rapidly as those armed with wooden ramrods (as were the Austrians). The pay-off on this capital investment was secured in 1740 when Frederick the Great was able to sweep the Austrians out of Silesia by the speed and volume of his infantry fire. This technological advance in the conquest of time and space led, of course, to the expanded manpower created by the alliance of Austria, Russia, and France. With Prussian manpower resources stretched to their limits in the 1750s, Frederick turned to horsepower and created the first lightweight horse artillery, the increased rapidity of which restored missile superiority to the Prussian forces in the Seven Years War. When in 1776 Jean Baptiste de Gribeauval was appointed Inspector General of the Artillery of France, one of the losers in the Seven Years War, his first significant action was the creation of a horse artillery. Moreover, he went on to improve upon the Prussian model by designing more efficient gun carriages and an elevation screw that further accelerated the rate of fire.

The increased capacity to use ammunition and guns that resulted from this emphasis on conquering time and space produced a demand for more and cheaper armaments. Special arms factories were established by all major powers during the seventeenth century. By the eighteenth century the French and English arms factories had introduced division of labor and the use of waterpower as normal means for speeding up production, while muskets, cannons, and shot were standardized by caliber and reduced in variety to simplify problems of repair and supply. In the 1770s Gribeauval went one step further and insisted that all French artillery and gun carriages be produced with interchangeable parts, while in 1785 Nicolas LeBlanc produced mechanical designs for applying the same technique to French military muskets. In effect, the new attitude toward time and space that had been introduced into warfare began to infect the workshop.

Until the 1780s these technical changes did not radically affect the actual strategy of war, which continued to be limited in its goals and to produce minimal profits. By the 1750s, however, a new theoretical school of impatient military writers emerged (especially in France) that began critically to reappraise existing practices and devise new strategies as a means to more decisive victories. Professional soldiers as diverse as Marshal Maurice de Saxe and Pierre de Bourcet wrote speculative treaties, philosophers such as François Mesnil-Durand and Jacques Guibert popularized new theories, and the royal war games at Vaussieux in 1778 were used to test the validity of competing tactical hypotheses. (Thus war and the military again became one of the areas in which Bacon's dream of government-supported scientific experiments was in fact realized.) Moreover, the character of military practice slowly began to change as a result of this intellectual ferment. The proposals of Guibert and Bourcet were partly adopted by the French royal army in the Provisional Ordinance of 1788, ratified by the National Assembly in the Ordinance of 1791, and brought to perfection on the battlefield by Napoleon.

Following the line of thought established by Saxe and Bourcet,

Guibert's *Essai général de tactique* (published in 1772) abandoned the static, siege-oriented approach of contemporary royal armies and emphasized instead rapidity, mobility, and the drive to battle. Imagining an ideal general addicted to bold movements, rapid forced marches, and fluid battle lines, he predicted that such a man would cut himself free from supply lines and magazines in his drive for victory. "Coming within reach of the enemy . . . the troops . . . form for battle in an instant, beginning their attack before the enemy has had time to determine the point where the blow is being aimed or . . . to change his dispositions to ward off the blow."[10] Constantly harassing the enemy, outmarching and outthinking him, such a general could force battle on his own terms and conquer Europe "as the north wind blows down the frail reed."

Obviously Guibert's proposed changes in military strategy called for an end to the minuet or fugue quality of earlier campaigns, just at the time that the European bourgeoisie became enamoured of the new sonata form. Originally used in operatic overtures, the sonata (with its developmental ABA form, its explicit conflict of contrasting themes, and their final resolution) had in the 1750s and 1760s become the organizing structure for the newly popular symphonies, concertoes, and quartets. Guibert's most famous pupil, Napoleon, insisted that a campaign, like a good play, must have a beginning, a middle, and an end; the same could be said of any sonata-based musical composition. In effect, then, on all levels of culture, there was a shift in the second half of the eighteenth century from Being to Becoming as the primary mode of conceptualizing reality—and military thought and action were part of this critical transition.

Guibert was convinced, moreover, that his proposed strategic changes could best be effected by an army composed, like that of the Roman Republic, of citizen-warriors. His *Essai* thus began with the vision of an ideal state in which the administratively simplified machinery of government had been turned over to the populace at large, while a brave citizen army guarded its borders. Though he later lost faith in the possibility, as a young man Guibert hoped that such a radical change might be carried out by a prince of great genius. He also hoped that this scientific Solon would then voluntarily withdraw his control, keeping for himself only "the honors of the crown, the right to propose wise laws, the power of executing them when you [the people] will have ratified them; the absolute authority, the dictatorship in all crises which threaten the state."[11] Guibert's faith in the creative political genius, his belief that freedom could emerge from despotism, has generally been dismissed as a failure of insight, the result of psychological ignorance. What is less generally recognized, however, is that his vision of domestic politics is perfectly consonant with his understanding of war as necessarily dominated by a great general and with his proposed reforms in military tactics.

Guibert insisted that his strategy required tactics replacing complicated drills and elaborate maneuvers with movements designed for simplicity and speed. (His shift from 60 to 80 paces per minute for normal or parade-ground marches parallels, interestingly, the contemporaneous acceleration of ordinary tempo in instrumental music.) In particular, he advocated a single, simplified column that could be used for a variety of functions and deployed into lines or squares at four to six times the rate of any columns then in use.

These tactics, in addition, could be employed by the most uncommitted, monarchical army, as long as the soldiers had received rigorous, thorough instruction. Thus Guibert did not eliminate training procedures; instead, by simplifying tactics, he made training easier and less costly. Codified in a manual, Guibert's tactics could be (and were) taught by the greenest of young officers. Requiring only five months rather than five years (as in the armies of Frederick) to become effective, they made democratic conscript armies possible in 1792 and substantial loss of life in combat economically feasible for the state. In effect, soldiers, muskets, and the cloth for their uniforms came to be mass produced during the same decades.

Guibert's skillfully written *Essai* was an immediate popular success in France and was translated into all of the major European languages during the 1770s. It provided a general perspective by which a later generation could view wars and prepared the ground for Talleyrand's portrait of Napoleon as the liberator of Europe. In this context it is understandable that when in 1802 Beethoven began his third (Eroica) symphony (an ambitious and revolutionary new expansion of the older sonata form), he intended to dedicate it to Napoleon as an embodiment of the heroic spirit. That Beethoven, learning Napoleon had taken an imperial title, later withdrew the dedication in disgust is historically less important than his initial identification of mankind's golden destiny with the bloody victories of a military genius.

While the universal, democratic, and humanistic aspirations of the great composer are undeniable, nonetheless Beethoven was constrained, as were most of his contemporaries, by the fact that in Europe the warrior still remained one of the two valid models of the heroic maker of history. The regimentation of the French armies, moreover, can hardly have seemed unnatural to a man who composed for professional orchestras, expected string sections to have been drilled in a single technique of playing and a uniform use of the bow, and whose works had no place for improvisation but demanded strict adherence to a detailed score. Indeed Beethoven, one of the earliest devotees of the mechanical metronome, had much in common with the Napoleon who conducted the battle of Austerlitz with watch in hand.

In a similar fashion Napoleon can be called a Romantic artist par excellence. For example, Napoleonic cavalry included no less than nine different types of regiments, ranging from the heavily armed cuirrassiers and carabineers through the dragoons to the light troops of hussars, chasseurs, lancers, and so forth. As it is difficult to rationalize the need for more than two or perhaps three different types of cavalry in terms of military uses or armament differentiation, the question arises as to why these multiple categories were created. The question is made more pressing by the fact that the real brunt of battle was borne, and the real results were achieved, by the infantry and artillery. Each cavalry category, however, had its own special uniform; such uniforms were invariably dramatic in their use of sashes, feathers, and capes; and these units included such exotic specimens as the Polish lancers and the orientally garbed Mamelukes. The connection between the burgeoning Romanticism of the era and Napoleon's use of his resources seems difficult to ignore. In terms of power the Napoleonic battlefield was undoubtedly dominated by the cannon and the foot soldiers, but in aesthetic terms its mood was set by the sweeping charges and flamboyant color of the cavalry. Unquestionably this was an illusion, but then Napoleon's political power also rested on skillfully exploited illusions. Indeed, Romanticism itself may be considered an attempt to combine the illusion of naturalness and freedom with the actuality of control and design.

This illusion (the masking of the naked power of technology behind the flamboyance of color and ornamentation) is one that the nineteenth century seems to have struggled to maintain both militarily and artistically. Though the mask slipped at times, as in the American Civil War, the deception of highly carved mass-produced furniture, elaborately ornamented steel and concrete buildings, and brilliantly uniformed soldiers carrying repeaters and Lewis guns was generally supported until World War I. The surrender at Appomattox, moreover, is nicely symbolic of the ambivalent character of the Civil War. As Grant later reported,

> General Lee was dressed in a full uniform which was entirely new, and was wearing a sword of great value. . . . In my rough traveling suit, the uniform of a private with the shoulder straps of a lieutenant general, I must have contrasted very strangely with a man so handsomely dressed.[12]

The parallels between Lee's elaborate uniform and the highly mannered strategy favored by Lee (and by Grant's predecessors), and between Grant's deliberately drab uniform and his direct, massive strategy of attrition, seem too marked to be simply accidental. As long as one confuses the aesthetic sensibility with delicacy, or the aesthetic temperament with the aesthete, it will, of course, seem difficult to imagine Grant, the bluff, hard-drinking, unintellectual solider, being affected by aesthetic considerations. But if he literally did not care how he looked, he could very easily have continued to wear the traditional officer's uniform. Moreover, Grant's aesthetics, like his military practice, lead us into the twentieth century.

Since 1800 the strategic core of western military thought has been "mass multiplied by velocity" means victory. This is most explicit in the nineteenth-century writings of Clausewitz, Jomini, and Foch:

> Modern war proceeds from Napoleon's views, as he was the first to throw light on the importance of preparation and on the omni-

potence of *mass* multiplied by *impulsion*, with the object of breaking, in a battle sought from the outset of the war, the moral and material forces of the adversary.[13]

With later writers the formula tends to be simply assumed, so that attention can be focused instead on its specific application in the present state of technology. Thus Liddell Hart, whose thought dominated the second quarter of the present century, stressed the need

> to attack the enemy's command (Concentration) prior to attacking his fighting body, so that his fighting body, when attacked, would be paralyzed through lack of command. The means was to pass *powerful columns* of *fast-moving* tanks, *strongly* protected by *aircraft* through the forward areas. . . .[14]

Tactically, once national conscription was accepted as the norm, mass continued to be expanded by technological advances. Increased destructive power was sought in TNT, napalm and fire bombs, claymore mines and HEAT rounds, atomic and thermonuclear warheads, while heavy howitzers, planes, and rockets were developed to increase effective missile range. And, of course, the potential speed of an individual soldier was accelerated by breech-loading rifles and cannons, machine guns, and self-loading tank guns. As in the past, increased mass produced increased defensive capacity and therefore pushed forward the search for more offensive mass. By 1916 at least, armament had come to dominate the battlefield, while manpower increasingly functioned primarily as supporting servant to the explosion-propelling machine. If the seventeenth-century rulers disciplined the battlefield, modern armies have mechanized and industrialized the act of killing.

At the same time general staffs have devoted sustained attention to the task of getting this mass rapidly to the correct battlefield and keeping it moving. Communications have been speeded up by the shift from semaphore to telegraph, radio, and finally electronic computerized equipment, while transportation has followed a similar accelerating path. From 1833 to 1914 effective impulsion for the mass was sought in the steam-engine railway and battleships; from 1918 to 1945 the solution seemed to reside in gasoline-driven tanks, armored cars, submarines, and airplanes. Since 1945 military hope has fastened on jet-propelled planes and rockets; helicopters, tanks, and armored personnel carriers; intercontinental missiles and Polaris submarines as the means to achieving a victorious first strike kill.

Such a mechanized army can be used, moreover, as it was in Grant's Wilderness campaign, the Somme, Stalingrad, Kursk, and Normandy, "as if it were a battering ram, without consciousness and without feeling...."[15] And it continues to work, even though each square mile of advance or retreat costs 8,222 men (as it did the British at Third Ypres) or 11,000 (as at Iwo Jima). This is a result of the fact that the physical coercion of officers, which characterized the battles of earlier centuries, has been replaced by that of the battle itself; "the fire which nails him [the soldier] to the ground or drives him beneath it, the great distance which yawns between him and safety, the onward progression of a vehicular advance or retreat which carries him with it willynilly."[16] Its discipline, moreover, can come to seem rooted in "the nature of things" rather than being the result of human choice. Thus a British noncommissioned officer wrote of the Battle of the Somme:

> It was not a noise, it was a *symphony*.... It seemed as if the air were full of vast and agonized passion, bursting now with groan and sighs, now into shrill screaming and pitiful whimpering ... vibrating with the solemn pulses of enormous wings.... It did not begin, intensify, decline and end. It was poised in the air, a stationary *panorama of sound*, a condition of the atmosphere, not the creation of man.[17]

The symphonic metaphor brings us, of course, back into the realm of aesthetics, despite the fact that it has become a convention to say that contemporary warfare is ugly. Such a charge (which tends to emphasize the drab tones of twentieth-century uniforms and the lack of ornamentation on modern weaponry) rests, however, primarily on a nostalgia for the aesthetic standards of an earlier era. In fact, twentieth-century uniforms and weapons do possess a type of beauty, the beauty of functionalism. Like Bauhaus designs, their appeal rests upon simplicity and appropriateness of form. More important, the dullness and starkness of modern uniforms and weapons are undoubtedly offset by the tendency of our battlefields to be visually as well as aurally dominated by the effects of firepower: the graceful curve of shell or bomb, the blinding flash of the explosion, the upward thrust of billows of smoke or fountains of earth. One can describe the effects of firepower in terms that make connection with our conventional ideas of beauty, but to do so would be misleading. The aesthetic appeal of firepower is ultimately that of the sublime as opposed to the beautiful: that is, the appeal of transcendent power and awesomeness as opposed to that of design or regularity or grace.

The impact of such an experience of the sublime creeps into the records of our recent wars again and again, even into the reminiscences of men who have, on the whole, hated war. Thus Frederick Manning, in his novel of World War I, *Her Privates We*, recreates a night in the trenches in these terms:

> The boy on the firestep watched his front intently. The expectation that he would see something move, or a sudden flash there, became almost desire. But nothing moved. The world grew more and more still; the dark became thinner; soon they would stand to. He could see the remains of the building now, almost clearly. There was nothing there, nothing, the world was empty, hushed, awaiting dawn. And then, as he watched it less keenly, something from the skies smote that heap of rubble, the shadowy landscape in front of him blurred and danced and a solid pillar of darkness rose into the air even before he heard the explosion, spreading out thicker at the top like an evil fungus; spread, and dissolved again, and the heap of rubble was no longer there.
> "Christ!" said the boy. "That were a good 'un."[18]

Although at first glance they might seem quite disparate, there is in fact a twofold relation between the sublime and the functional. On the simplest level, functionalism reflects an idealization of the mechanical, a glorification of means; that is, it reflects the motivation that has made our highly sophisticated technological developments possible and thus has brought about the domination of our battlefields by firepower. The fascination with pushing up ever higher buildings and the tendency, observable in both world wars, to cram the battlefields with mechanical contrivances both seem to reflect an aesthetic desire to experience the results of industry and technology to the fullest. The tendency in World War I to call repetitiously and wastefully for more and more shells is too well known to need comment. It is perhaps less generally recognized that World War II was similarly dominated by firepower. In fact, however, a typical battle was determined by the American and Russian fascination with and excessive reliance upon tanks used as artillery, as well as their preference for direct, broad-front strategy as compared to the indirect approach or the concentrated thrust.

On the deepest level, of course, both functionalism and the fascination with the sublime reflect a particular vision of the nature of mankind and of reality. It seems hardly coincidental, for example, that the adoption of drab uniforms has coincided with a tendency to both emphasize firepower and subordinate the individual to the group, while the group is then viewed as an instrument in the service of some high ideal (the union, democracy, the nation or race, the proletariat) whose victory is inevitable and necessary. Whether as cause or effect, the experience of the sublime on the twentieth-century battlefield seems to demand and to authenticate such an understanding of reality. In this respect Guy Chapman, in writing of World War I, records a particularly instructive experience:

> Questioning the countryside, I caught in my glass a grey ant crawling over the edge of the railway cutting, followed by another, and then more. The sun polished their steel helmets into a row of little shining discs. More and more were now coming out of the cutting. . . . They came crawling in three lines, about six hundred strong. They were just starting down the forward slope when something flashed in front of them. A column of bright terracotta smoke was flung upwards so high, that there shot into my memory the pictures of the djinns in an old copy of the Arabian Nights. Another and another rose until an arcade of smoking pillars seemed to move across the hill-side. Already the grey ants had thinned. The first line was hardly there. It merged with the second and mechanically the whole inclined southwards to avoid the shells. But the guns followed the movement and another line of smoking columns fountained into the air. At last, reduced to one line, the minute figures turned and stumbled back over the crest of the hill. A little puff of white smoke danced gallantly in the air. In ten minutes the counter-attack was broken, smashed, and

tossed in the air like a handful of dust: and up here everyone was whooping, laughing, and hollowing.[19]

Though fascination with unlimited power is undoubtedly a perennial human response, like functionalism it is particularly appropriate to a culture that tends to submerge the individual in the mass. They are related and integral parts of our twentieth-century style of life, closely connected with our view of the world and with the massive, overpowering quality of most twentieth-century public buildings. Moreover, this fascination with functional sublimity, which Henry Adams sensed at the turn of the century and expressed in his vision of the dynamo, is unquestionably closely related to our century's insistence upon viewing nonhuman reality as an "it," while we attempt to humanize the transcendent. Thus the Union, Democracy, the Nation, the Race, or the Proletariat—that is, humanly defined abstracts—become our substitute names for the sublime and the holy.

But even as we idolize our own species, we pay a price: We turn ourselves into columns of "grey ants." Yet on the battlefield, if not the assembly line, we can find the experience, because sublime, aesthetically and emotionally satisfying and compelling. As Glenn Gray has observed about the battlefields of World War II:

> The awe that steals over us at such times is not a feeling of triumph, but, on the contrary, a recognition of power and grandeur to which we are subject. . . . This ecstasy satisfies because we are conscious of a power outside us with which we can merge in the relation of parts to whole. . . . In losing ourselves we gain a relationship to something greater than the self and the foreign character of the surrounding world is drastically reduced.[20]

Thus the aesthetic experience of the sublime on twentieth-century battlefields makes sense emotionally, if temporarily, of our mechanistic and anomic way of life.

The conviction that properly concentrated mass multiplied by velocity means victory has led each generation to an almost unquestioned faith that its wars could and would be short and decisive.

Thus while truly prodigious effort has gone into planning the first stage in great detail, little attention has been given in peacetime to long-term needs or second-stage strategies. Joffre's initial lack of interest in infantry helmets in 1914 (because he believed the war would not last long enough for them to be mass produced) and Hitler's failure to provide winter clothing for his Russian army are not personal idiosyncracies; parallels can be found in the thought and action of all major military organizations. Since knowledge is power, the country that most efficiently applies the scientific rules of warfare should win the prize and win it quickly.

Unfortunately, the theory has not worked out in practice. With the exception of the Prussian wars of 1865 and 1870, when Bismarck deliberately limited both political goals and military actions, modern wars have tended to be long and desperate struggles. Moreover, they have not produced decisive results, even for the victor; no general has for long been able to sweep aside the enemy "as the north wind blows down the frail reed." Though territorial boundaries have been more radically altered than in the eighteenth-century, the primary results have been destruction so enormous as to rupture the very fabric of society, undermining existing monarchies, constitutional democracies, and laissez-faire economies, while shifting power centers outward from Europe itself. In addition, it has become clear since 1945 that the strategy of mass multiplied by velocity depends on an enemy who fights by the same rules, who is also eager for battle. When, as in Vietnam, the enemy refuses to "stand and fight," then mass times velocity has proven singularly ineffective as a means to secure victory.

The failure of the formula, even when both sides are playing the same game, stems in the end from two factors. In the first place, as in the eighteenth-century, increasing both mass and speed inevitably increases the size of the space to be conquered. Thus the 2.5 mile front of Waterloo had expanded by 1914 to cover 475 miles of trenches. Simultaneous with its lateral spread, the space of war deepens. Since both mass and velocity depend on machines, the industrial base becomes part of the true battlefield. Thus blockades, bombing raids, and missiles become necessary if one is to conquer the internal space, the heart of the enemy. At the same time the very conquest of space also brings into contact forces previously separated by time and distance. European wars became true world wars, while campaigns evolved into theaters that stretched across continents and oceans. In effect, the more one conquers time and space, the more time and space there is to be conquered. Even a thermonuclear holocaust that wiped out existence on this planet might not solve this technological problem, as some military minds are already toying with the idea of moving fighting machines to space satellites and other planets.

In the second place, the increased velocity of the past century is illusory, even in the "blitzkrieg" initial phases of modern war. Compare, for example, the pace of some famous campaigns in which little or no effective resistance was encountered:

Campaign	Miles Per Day
Marlborough's drive to Bavaria in 1704: 250 miles ÷ 41 days	6
Napoleon's descent on Ulm in 1805: 210 miles ÷ 11 days	19
Kluck's First Army, from French border to Chantilly in 1914: 240 miles ÷ 11 days	22
German conquest of Poland in 1939: 300 miles ÷ 30 days	10
Von Kuechler's 18th Army, from French border to Paris in 1940: 360 miles ÷ 32 days	11
German clean-up operation in southern France: 200 miles ÷ 12 days	15
Hackett's imaginary Russian plan to conquer West Germany in 1985: 200 miles ÷ 9 days	22

Napoleon's pace (determined by the marching capacity of physically healthy men carrying sixty pounds of material) has not been improved upon significantly, and many of his successors have moved more slowly. This is partly due to the fact that increasing mechanization has meant increasing logistical problems. Men may go hungry or forage for themselves; machines bereft of fuel or ammunition simply cease to function. Armies therefore become tied to the pace of the railroad-building engineer or of motorized transports confined to existing roads and bridges. The result has been compared "to an arm pinned from the shoulder to the wrist with only the fingers free...."[21] Moreover, the fingers are inevitably so swollen with men and material that it is difficult to secure effective concentration, while any sudden change of plans is generally doomed to hopeless entanglement.

Besides the difficulties of supply, mechanized mass armies also present incredibly complicated command problems. Composed of numerous specialized components with narrow functions and different speeds, such armies pose elegant chess problems in coordination during peacetime. Once the "fog of war" descends, however, the task becomes nightmarish. General Sir John Hackett's description of the battlefield of the future is convincing and terse precisely because it reflects the repeated difficulties of the past:

> When should the [Russian] infantry dismount? How were the varying *speeds* of tank, BMP, SP gun and foot soldier to be related? How was the fire of tank, BMP, SP gun, divisional artillery and helicopter gunship, with tactical air support thrown in, to be coordinated? .... [The] heaviest load of all lay on the battalion commander. In a reinforced motor-rifle battalion with a minute staff of four officers, one NCO and eight men, he would be attempting to control a force of some 700 strong, with a company of thirteen tanks, a battery of six guns (or even a battalion of eighteen), a mortar battery, anti-air weapons, an ATGW platoon, reconnaissance and engineer elements, thirty BMP, sixty light machine guns and 356 assault riflement. It was a tall order.[22]

Like his optimistic predecessors, Hackett hopes that NATO's technical superiority in electronic communications will solve the problem of "varying speeds." But his description of electronic effectiveness remains impressionistic, wistful, and unconvincing; the imagined NATO advantage seems instead to stem primarily from the simplifications of decision making that go with being on the defensive.

The problem of coordinating a variety of different speeds and rhythms was first consciously faced by musicians during the nineteenth century. Then the drive toward complexity, drama, and universality begun in the eighteenth century by Haydn and Mozart led eventually to the music-dramas of Wagner and Richard Strauss and the massive, dramatic symphonies of Bruckner and Mahler. In the process, however, music burst through the ABA structure of the sonata and began to find its form in variations on contrasting themes and rhythms (as in Hector Berlioz's *Symphony Fantastique*). By the time of Wagner, this tendency crystallized into a reliance on rhythmic gestalten or *leitmotif* whose multiplicty and complex interactions carried forward both the music and the poetic drama. But at the same time that the variety and pace of rhythmic invention speeded up, the actual tempo of music (as reflected in harmonic modulations and sheer length of composition) slowed. Thus Bruckner needed two hours to develop a symphonic idea, while Wagner's major opera took sixteen hours to reach completion.

This outcome was foreshadowed in the symphonic works of Schubert—a contemporary of Beethoven and Napoleon and, like them, a major influence on nineteenth-century culture. Behind their seemingly classical form and romantic lyricism, Schubert's symphonies introduced a new approach to time from which such diverse composers as Wagner, Bruckner, and Brahms drew inspiration. One critical element in this new style was Schubert's use of rhythm rather than melody as his main musical building block. In particular, he was especially fond of a heavily accented four bar rhythm that carried "the frightful sound of sheer physical repetition," and is probably one source of the nineteenth-century's exceptional liking for marches. In addition, Schubert tended to introduce three different speeds in a single section, while at the same time lengthening the scale of his harmonic and tonal operations. The result was a "duality of pace—two speeds running concurrently."[23]

In Schubert's hands, the allegro slowed but it still moved. By the end of the century, however, musical thought was so rapid that the pace of a composition became the slowest of andantes, while its drama expanded to embody Bruckner's still, radiant world of Creation and the timeless ecstasy of Wagner's *Liebestoden*.[24] The human brain, like the cosmos itself, has its own time, which is not that of the clock, the metronome, or the computer. In effect, musicians learned before Einstein that time and space are relative to the perspective of the observer. Our military strategists and war-making politicians are still unconvinced.

Between the eighteenth and the twentieth century, western societies experimented militarily with the potential effectiveness of new ritual acts. Unfortunately, the revolutionary wars of France did not "renew the face of the world"; the Great War of 1914–1918 did not lead to a "new reality" or act as a rite of regeneration. It did not even make the world safe for democracy. Progress, it seems, is not inevitable, nor is history so easily subject to human control. However, despite all the evidence suggesting that the rite is ineffective and the myth an illusion, neither has been abandoned. Nations that pride themselves on their secular rationality and objective efficiency, that are typically contemptuous of "mere ritual," have nonetheless been incapable of thinking or acting in a reasoned fashion when it comes to warfare. As in our study of earlier cultures, the question thus arises as to the nature of the psychological need that both undergirds and motivates humanity's continuing desire for battle.

10
The Danger of Fear

> I've done my best to live the right way
> I get up every morning and go to work each day
> But your eyes go blind and your blood runs cold
> Sometimes I feel so weak I just want to explode
> Explode and tear this town apart
> Take a knife and cut this pain from my heart
> Find somebody itching for something to start
> —*Bruce Springsteen* [1]

In 1795 Immanuel Kant wrote in *Perpetual Peace* that a republican (i.e., representative, constitutional) government was the one most likely to secure an end to war.

> The reason is this: if the consent of the citizens is required in order to decide that war should be declared . . . nothing is more natural than that they would be very cautious in commencing such a poor game, decreeing for themselves all the calamities of war. Among the latter would be: having to fight, having to pay the cost of the war from their own resources, having painfully to repair the devastation war leaves behind, and to fill up the measure of evils, load

themselves with a heavy national debt that would embitter peace itself. . . .[2]

He thereby expressed pithily the expectation of the eighteenth-century Enlightenment and the hope of nineteenth-century Liberals. Since wars of the past had been occasioned by the greed of an exploitative elite, they would become outmoded and irrelevant when foreign policy was subordinated to the interests of the ordinary citizen, who could not hope to benefit materially from violence or territorial expansion.

The experience of the nineteenth century seemed to offer support to these hopes. As one European nation after another adopted some form of constitutional government, wars between the European powers became fewer and less costly. Violence, indeed, seemed to be moving to the peripheries of civilization, to colonial areas, and presumably it was explainable there as the result of undue pressure from the greedy new commercial and industrial elites. More democracy and greater public control of foreign policy, or the overthrow of capitalism, could thus be seen as the practical solution to violence.

Unfortunately for these hopes, in the summer of 1914 a war erupted between the five major powers of Europe that was approved by close to 95 percent of the elected parliamentary representatives of the states involved and hailed with enthusiasm by the vast bulk of the population. It was a war, moreover, of a scope, destructiveness, and deadliness such as the world had never seen before. It took the lives of over 5 million men; involved direct costs of $186,333,-637,000 and indirect costs of $151,646,942,560; wrecked the economic and social structures of the European powers; and destroyed the political structures of Russia, Germany, the Hapsburg monarchy, and (indirectly) Italy. Its outbreak left statesmen, intellectuals, and historians concerned to understand "why."

From the beginning most analyses of the events of that summer have been colored by one of three assumptions. Some have assumed that the real motivation for initiating war is inevitably material greed and have been frustrated by their inability to produce clear documentary proof if its influence on the events of July and early August 1914. Others, such as the framers of the Treaty of Versailles and more impartial historians, have assumed that the quasi-Christian, quasi-legalistic distinction between just and unjust, moral and immoral acts, is a useful tool in understanding violence, and have attempted to distribute praise and blame according to this criterion. This approach has forced the publication of an enormous amount of normally secret archival material and destroyed the simplistic villain-hero dualism of 1918. By the 1950s most historians agreed that every major state bore (though to differing degrees) some responsibility for the evaporation of peace.

The third assumption is that a *realpolitik* analysis, focusing on pragmatic national interests, will both clarify the course of events and allow more realistic evaluation of the actors. But the consistent fascination of such diplomatic historians with the details of proposals, demarches, interviews, and foreign office telegrams has only tended to obscure the motivation for action. One can, for example, read all three volumes of Albertini's monumental treatise on the origins of World War I, only to learn that "European diplomacy, which in the course of the July crisis had so often demonstrated its ineptitude, was hence forth silent. It was now the turn of the big guns to speak."[3] Now, ineptitude may explain why diplomacy failed; it does not explain the more important question of why nations fought! One seems to have moved very little forward from the exclamation of Bethmann-Hollweg in the heat of events: "[It] is sad to have to say that a war that was desired by no national was possibly being unchained to a certain extent by elemental forces and by the long and lasting stirring up of strife between the Cabinets."[4]

The seeming inability of war makers or contemporary observers to name the common psychological need driving countries to war has remained a distinctive characteristic of both World War I and the numerous democratized and mechanized wars that have followed it. In the cultures we have previously discussed this has not been true. Instead, whether the motivation was revenge, greed, or the desire for a glorious adventure, both the soldiers and their peers have been aware of its operation within their own psyches and those of their opponents. By contrast, twentieth-century societies have usually been both convinced that important motivational differences separated them from "the enemy" and deeply divided as to the exact nature of their own psychological state. (Hence, undoubtedly, the current popularity of genetic explanations, which are a quasi-scientific version of Bethmann-Hollweg's "elemental forces.") This blind spot in modern vision is striking—and, in terms of gestalt psychology, important as it points to a very basic and neurotic avoidance, an inability to maintain contact with one's emotions and feelings.[5]

Yet only individuals themselves can tell us, through their own words and actions, about their internal motivational state. In the absence of self-awareness one is therefore forced to observe carefully. For this purpose the events of 1914 are critical, as the eruption of World War I is not only a decisive turning point in modern history but also an event whose every detail has been laid open to observation. Instead of retracing the work of diplomatic historians, however, I intend to adopt an analytic procedure devised by sociologists of violence.[6] This methodology requires that one begin by looking for those points at which humans decide that they (their countries) have to resort to physical action, as it is these decisions that determine that a violent incident (war) will occur (rather than simply that diplomacy will fail). Having spotlighted these crucial decisions, it is then necessary to look at the explicitly expressed motivations (the individual perceptions, perspectives, emotions, and goals) that lead people to decide they must abandon verbal for physical interaction. In the process one typically discovers that every conflict is perceived differently by the supposed aggressor and victim; it is really two conflicts. At the same time one also discovers that most war-making individuals in 1914 were driven by rather similar emotional states and psychological needs.

The first step along the road to war was the decision on July 19, by a full Ministerial Council of the Hapsburg Monarchy, in reaction to the assassination of the Archduke Franz Ferdinand by Serbian terrorists, to deliver a forty-eight-hour ultimatum to Serbia in the early evening of July 25 and, if the Serbs rejected any part of the ultimatum, to break off relations with that state and begin mobilization directed against it on the evening of July 28–29. The terms of the ultimatum were deliberately framed so as to destroy Serbian sovereignty and were expected to be rejected. The goals of the war were to transfer substantial portions of Serbian territory to Bulgaria, Greece, Albania, and possibly Rumania, with some slight boundary modifications in Austria's favor.

THE DANGER OF FEAR

In the Hapsburg Ministerial Council meeting of July 19, the voices of three men were decisive: the chief of staff, Conrad von Hötzendorf; the Austrian foreign minister, Leopold Berchtold; and the Hungarian premier, Tisza. Conrad, who had held his post almost continuously since 1906, had long been convinced that

> The unification of the South Slav race is one of those nation-moving phenomena which cannot be denied nor artificially prevented. The only point is whether this unification shall take place *within* the control of the [Dual] Monarchy . . . or . . . *at the cost of the Monarchy*. . . . This loss in territory and prestige would depress the Monarchy into a Small State.[7]

He had continually urged war on Serbia as the only method of remedying the situation:

> It was not a question of a knightly duel . . . nor of punishment for the assassination. It was much more *the highly practical importance of the prestige of a Great Power* . . . which, by its continual yielding and patience . . . had given an impression of impotence and made its internal and external enemies continually more aggressive. . . .[8]

Until the assassination of Franz Ferdinand, Conrad had been frustrated by the resistance of the archduke himself, who believed that a peaceful solution of the problem was possible. With the death of the heir to the throne, the highly susceptible Berchtold was almost immediately converted to Conrad's assessment of the situation. Thus in privately asking the Germans for support, Berchtold warned them that "the Monarchy must in future look to the persistent, implacable and aggressive enmity of Serbia. It is all the more necessary for the Monarchy to tear asunder with a determined hand the threads which its enemies are weaving into a net over its head."[9]

Before Conrad and Berchtold could pursue this policy, however, they had to persuade the Hungarian premier, Count Tisza, that the planned war-provoking ultimatum was so necessary as to be worth the acknowledged risks. As late as July 14, Tisza was vigorously opposed to their plans, primarily because he believed Hungarian/

Magyar interests demanded that no more Serbs be brought within the boundaries of the empire. The evidence collected at Sarajevo and the attitude of the Serbian press seem to have convinced him, however, that the preservation of the Dual Monarchy was dependent on a war to "put an end to the downright intolerable conditions in the south-east."[10] A month after the war began, he would write to his niece: "My conscience is clear. Already the noose had been thrown around our necks with which they would have strangled us at a favorable moment, unless we cut it now. We could not do otherwise, but it agonized me that we had to do as we did."[11] Thus the Austrian decision for a localized war with Serbia, with its risk of a more general conflagration, clearly arose from its leaders' fear that the long-run existence of the state was endangered, combined with their inability to perceive any tolerable way to restore "peace and quiet" except through violence.

The second step was taken by Russia on July 25, in response to the news of the Austrian ultimatum. A Ministerial Council that afternoon ordered the secret implementation of the plans for the "Period Preparatory to War" and approved in principle the drawing up of plans for a partial mobilization against Austria, in order to fulfill its role as a great Slav power. Actual implementation of partial mobilization was ordered on July 29 by Sergei Sazonov and the czar (in response to the Austrian declaration of war and the bombardment of Belgrade) and was followed almost immediately on July 30 by the third step—an order for general mobilization against Germany as well as Austria.

The vision of Russia as the protector of the Slavs and the particular patron of Serbia was initially a self-chosen one and continued to be so for certain elements in Russia's ruling class, in particular the Pan-Slavists and nationalists like the Grand Duke Nicholas. By 1914, however, the role had achieved heavy external credibility. The Serbian government, as well as French Ambassador Maurice Paléologue and Prime Minister Poincaré, for example, consistently made it clear that they expected Russia to involve itself in the affair, while even the British and German spokesmen found Russian interest in the Austrian-Serbian conflict understandable and "normal."

Russian ruling circles, however, were not unified on this matter. Many of the more conservative and reactionary politicians as well as the intimate court of the czar (led by his wife) were strongly pro-German and at least friendly toward the monarchical Hapsburgs. In particular, the two crucial decision makers in this affair (the czar himself and Sazonov, the Foreign Minister) were not enamoured of their assigned role as defenders of the Slavs. Thus Sazonov could confide to the Austrian Ambassador Szápáry on July 27 that

> He had no feelings for the Balkan Slavs. They were actually a heavy burden on Russia and we [Austria] could hardly imagine how much trouble they had already given Russia. Our aims as described by me [self-defense], were perfectly legitimate but he thought the way we had chosen to attain them not the safest.[12]

Similarly, Prince Trubetzkoi of the czar's personal entourage could explain with perfect sincerity to the kaiser's personal representative at the Moscow court that "We do not love the Serbs in the least, but they are our Slavic brothers, and we cannot leave our brethren in the lurch."[13] Caught between the expectation that they would protect Serbia and their own reluctance to do so, the czar and Sazonov initially (on July 25) adopted secret measures to make a display of force possible if it should be necessary, while actively and publicly seeking one-on-one negotiations with the Austrians. They hoped thereby to achieve a peaceful resolution of the situation and eliminate the need for more vigorous action.

Unfortunately, the conversations on July 27 between Sazonov and Szápáry focused on an extraneous issue (the specific form of the ultimatum) and failed to address itself to the real issue: the Hapsburg desire to secure a peaceful future by subverting Serbian sovereignty. Moreover, Vienna deliberately failed to respond to Sazonov's request for further negotiations. Instead, after his facile optimism of July 26–27, Sazonov suddenly found himself faced, on July 28, with the fait accompli of an Austrian declaration of war.

Moreover, while Sazonov was prepared to acknowledge and even sympathize with a punitive retaliation on the part of the Hapsburgs, he was plagued from the beginning with doubts as to the real motives and intentions of Austria (as well as the danger that another diplomatic failure could cost him his ministerial position). Thus his initial response on July 24 was an angry fear that Austria had expansive goals in view and that he would be "forced" to respond militarily to such aggression. (Hence the secret preparations.) When on July 29, during a third interview with Szápáry, he learned of the bombardment of Belgrade, he immediately interpreted the act as an indication of expansive aims. Szápáry reported to Vienna that "He was completely transformed. . . . 'You just want to gain time by negotiations, yet you go ahead and bombard an unprotected city. What more do you want to conquer now you have possession of the capital!' "[14]

Granted this mood, it was unfortunate that a curt note from the German Chancellor, Bethmann-Hollweg, was delivered to him almost on the heels of the news about Belgrade: "Kindly call M. Sazonov's serious attention to the fact that further continuation of Russian mobilization measures would force us to mobilize and in that case European war could scarcely be prevented."[15] Though the Germans intended this simply as a clarifying warning, Sazonov heard it as a threat and exclaimed to one of his aides, "Now I have no doubts as to the true cause of Austrian intransigence."[16] Since the previous winter Sazonov had feared that Germany was aiming to gain control of the Dardanelles, and that fear was now reinforced. It transformed him from a reluctant defender of Serbia into an aggressive defender of Russian interests, since he was convinced that Russia's prestige demanded that the Dardanelles be controlled by either the weak Turks or Russia itself.

This fear of German intent left him particularly susceptible to the military view that partial mobilization was not only almost impossible, but would be extremely dangerous for Russia (because of the inevitable confusion) if German military support of Austria should require general Russian mobilization later. After July 29 Sazonov joined the military in pressuring the czar for general mobilization, as he had come to expect eventual German military intervention in the situation. He assured the czar that war had been "thrust upon Russia and Europe by the ill-will of the enemy, determined to increase their power by enslaving our natural Allies in the Balkans, destroying our influence there and reducing Russia to a pitiful dependence upon the arbitrary will of the Central Powers."[17]

Sazonov's fear that Russia might be facing a deliberate plan to attack her vital interests (as well as a challenge to the rights of a protégé) was critical in the course of events in Russia. As long as he believed a peaceful resolution was probable, he was in the essentially unassailable position of being solidly in agreement with the czar. With Sazonov's change of front, however, Nicholas was isolated as the lone proponent of nonviolence among his military and diplomatic advisors. Backed by the peace-oriented and Germanophile views of his wife and closest intimates, and bolstered by the slightly hectoring appeals of his Imperial cousin "Willie," Nicholas (except for about an hour on the evening of July 29) held out for almost forty-eight hours against the argument that war was inevitable and immediate general mobilization necessary to protect Russia from the dangers inherent in its military arrangements.

Such resistance cannot have been easy for a man who disliked disagreements and was only too inclined to assent to the plans of the last minister who happened to have his ear. At the critical meeting with Sazonov on July 30,

> for almost an hour the Tsar's firm desire to avoid war at all costs made him hesitate. . . . The tenseness of feelings which he lived through in these minutes expressed itself among other ways in the irritability, unusual for him, with which he snubbed General Tatishchev [his personal representative to William II]. The latter, who had taken no part in the conversation, remarked in a moment of silence: "Yes, it is hard to decide." The Tsar replied in a sharp and displeased tone: "I will decide," and gave his decision for an immediate general mobilization.[18]

It is difficult to avoid the conclusion that for the czar personally the decision to mobilize was a way to remove himself from the intolerable pressure of harassment. Having given his assent, he retreated (as on many other occasions) into a mood of religious fatalism and refused to have the discussion reopened. Thus he concluded an unproductive interview with the German ambassador Pourtalès on the morning of July 31 by remarking that "he hoped everything would turn out right in the end. When I answered that I did not think this possible unless Russian mobilization were stopped, the

Tsar pointed upwards with the words: 'Then there is only One who can help.' "[19]

In deciding on general mobilization, the Russian leadership was not motivated by a desire for war. Indeed, they continued to negotiate and to seek a peaceful resolution right up to the afternoon of August 1. But while they sought peace, they feared that Austria and Germany were committed to attacking interests they considered vital to their prestige and long-term national security. They mobilized as a measure of self-defense, on the assumption that their worst fears were true.

The fourth step was the decision taken on July 31 by the German kaiser, William II, his chancellor, war minister, and chief of staff, in response to the news that Russian mobilization had begun secretly on July 25 and general mobilization been formally ordered on July 30. On July 31 they agreed to implement the steps preliminary to general mobilization involved in the order "Threatening Danger of War," and to send Russia and France ultimatums demanding they halt military measures or promise not to mobilize. If the ultimatums were not accepted, the German leaders planned to begin general mobilization on August 1, an act understood by them as being identical with a declaration of war. It was this decision, rather than the earlier (June) approval of Hapsburg action vis-à-vis Serbia, that was decisive for Germany.

When in June Berchtold and Conrad started to plan an attack on Serbia, they were agreed that they must secure at least general German approval for such a move; the Germans, however, were not told the full scope of the Ministerial Council decisions. The Berlin response to Berchtold's request for understanding was more encouraging and generous than even the most sanguine Hapsburg leaders had expected. The kaiser, approaching the situation through the mythic lenses of revenge and honor, excoriated the Serbs in his marginalia (on diplomatic papers and ministerial reports) as "murderers," "regicides," and "bandits," and was immediately convinced that "Matters must be cleared up with the Serbians, and that soon. That's all self-evident and the plain truth."[20]

The Foreign Office, however, took a less romantic view of the situation, and one that coincided (if unflatteringly) with the Hapsburgs' own assessment. Thus Gottlieb Jagow, Secretary of State for Foreign Affairs, wrote on July 18 in a memo intended only for the eyes of Prince K. M. Lichnowsky, the German ambassador in London, that

> Whether we have made a very good bargain in the alliance with that steadily disintegrating agglomeration of states on the Danube may be questioned.... Austria, whose prestige has suffered more and more from her failure to take resolute action, now scarcely counts any longer as a full-sized Great Power....[21]

Alfred Zimmermann, his assistant, was even more brutal in his explanation of events to the Bavarian Legation in Berlin: "Austria-Hungary, thanks to her indecision and her desultoriness, had really become the Sick Man of Europe, as Turkey had once been, upon the partition of which Russians, Italians, Romanians, Serbs and Montenegrins were now waiting."[22] Since they were concerned that the Hapsburgs move quickly (while public opinion was still under the influence of the tragedy and therefore likely to be sympathetic to Austrian punitive action) and since they were essentially dubious about Austria's courage and staying power, they not only offered no checks to the development of Hapsburg plans, but their communications (needlessly) encouraged Austria to act firmly and quickly.

Nonetheless, though the Germans were aware of the danger of European intervention, they were optimistic about keeping the affair "localized," perceiving Russia, France, and England as plagued with internal troubles and England and France as generally peaceably inclined. Thus when at the beginning of July the Imperial Minister of War Erich von Falkenhayn was apprised of the situation by the kaiser, he passed on to Helmuth von Moltke, Chief of the General Staff, the observation "that he had not gained the impression of any warlike developments being imminent, but merely of energetic political actions."[23] Neither held discussions with their Hapsburg counterparts; Falkenhayn went off on his vacation, von Moltke continued his cure at Carlsbad, and neither returned to Berlin until July 26.

When the kaiser saw the Serbian reply (which the Hapsburgs did not take seriously) on July 28, he viewed it as a great moral victory for his allies: "This is more than one could have expected! A great moral success for Vienna; but with it every reason for war drops away.... After such a thing, I should never have ordered mobilization."[24] Indeed, he began to hope that he could secure some diplomatic victories for himself in the situation. Thus he developed the so-called Halt at Belgrade plan, which would, if successful, have provided him with a starring role in the resolution of the crisis. Bethmann-Hollweg seems initially to have shared his ruler's belief that some form of military success for Austria and diplomatic glory for Germany was possible.

By the evening of July 29, however, in the face of escalating pressure from London and St. Petersburg and Viennese intransigence, Bethmann-Hollweg began to lose his optimism and attempted to put the brakes on the Hapsburgs, warning that while "We are, of course, ready to fulfill the obligations of our alliance, [we] ... must decline to be drawn wantonly into a world conflagration by Vienna, without having any regard paid to our counsel."[25] But in these hectic days he never took the step of threatening Vienna with the loss of German military support if German advice was not listened to. Such a radical change in formal policy could only have been undertaken with the kaiser's approval, and there is every indication that William would never have given it.

From July 26 onward, moreover, a swelling stream of reports began reaching the German Foreign Office and the Army and Navy Intelligence Offices concerning military activity on the Russian border across from German territory. Russian explanations to the German military attaché in St. Petersburg were reported to be at best confused and unconvincing. Then on the afternoon of July 29 the Foreign Office learned officially of Russian mobilization against Austria; late that evening a telegram arrived from the German ambassador in London that made it clear that Britain was unlikely to remain neutral if France and Russia went to war with Germany; and finally on the morning of July 30 a telegram from the czar seemed to indicate that mobilization had begun five days earlier (which, in effect, it had, if not formally or in the intent of Nicholas and Sazonov).

The kaiser's reaction was vehement and hysterical. His note at the end of Nicholas's message expresses all of the paranoia, fear, and anger that the overthrowing of his little plan for a cheap success occasioned.

> I no longer have any doubt that England, Russia and France have *agreed* among themselves . . . to use the Austro-Serb conflict as a *pretext* for waging a war of *annihilation* against us. . . . This means we are either basely to betray our ally . . . [or] get set upon and beaten by the Triple Entente in a body, so that their longing to *ruin* us can be finally satisfied. . . . The net has suddenly been closed over our head. . . . Even after his death Edward VII is stronger than I, though I am still alive![26]

As important as the kaiser's shift of mood is the fact that the growing evidence of Russian military measures brought von Moltke and von Falkenhayn onto the policy-making scene.

As late as July 29 the generals had viewed the situation as primarily a matter for the politicians to handle. That morning von Moltke still saw no need to take any significant steps to prepare for mobilization, while at a late-afternoon meeting with the chancellor, the proposal that Germany should mobilize in response to Russia's partial mobilization

> was negatived by the Chancellor against slight, very, very slight opposition from Moltke. . . . [There] can be no interference from military advisers, except where an essential military interest is at stake. This was, however, not the case here, for it was to be assumed that our mobilization, even if two or three days later than that of Russia and Austria, would be more rapid than theirs. . . .[27]

During the morning of July 30, however, von Moltke changed his views and became convinced that an "essential military interest was at stake." At about 1 P.M. he unsuccessfully pressed Bethmann-Hollweg to agree to "Danger of War" measures being implemented, a direct reversal of his position twenty-four hours earlier. Not satisfied by Bethmann-Hollweg's promise of a decision on July 31, he had an interview at 2 P.M. with the Austrian military attaché during which he urged Austria to mobilize immediately against Russia and promised (though he had no power to do so) that Germany would immediately mobilize in support of Russia. Early the next morning he personally telegraphed the same message to Conrad. The decisive factor in this shift from passivity and peaceableness to aggressive action is generally believed to be the impact of the czar's telegram and Kaiser William's marginal reaction to it, information of which seems to have been leaked to von Moltke during the morning of July 30. While the kaiser's shift from mediation to bellicosity was undoubtedly important to a loyal servant of the crown, the seeming confirmation of reports of secret Russian mobilization was probably even more decisive.

Since the Franco-Russian alliance of 1892, the German high command had been convinced that in the case of any general European encounter, Germany would face a two-front war with France and Russia. Because of German inferiority in numbers, the country clearly could not hope to win on both fronts simultaneously. The accepted solution was to stand on the defensive on one front while dealing (it was to be hoped) a knock-out blow on the other. The decision, under the guidance of Chief of Staff Alfred von Schlieffen, to direct the first blow against France was based on certain very concrete military facts, including the slow pace of Russian mobilization. (Schlieffen was also convinced that a long war of attrition would result in a social revolution in Germany; only in France could he see the possibility of a quick "battle of annihilation.")

At the time of Schlieffen's retirement, the mobilization plans involved risking an invasion of eastern Germany in order to mass a decisive force in the west. While a small eastern army fought a delaying offensive battle against the Russians, the heavily strengthened right of the western army was to swing through the northern plains of France in a circling movement that would, it was hoped, trap and crush the major French forces. Such a plan, which accepted the possibility that both Russia and France would occupy portions of German soil, made von Moltke nervous. Thus he deliberately strengthened the left wing at the expense of the right in the west, while in August 1914 he sent two more army corps from the western right wing to help the German forces in Prussia, with unfortunate results for Germany.

In this context it is understandable that the news that Russia was almost a week ahead of Germany in mobilizing was perceived by von

Moltke as a further escalation of the risk and danger confronting his country. From his perspective, every single additional day of delay increased the probability that Germany would find itself invaded, crushed, and defeated in a two-front war. Certainly this fear dominated von Moltke's private conversation on the night of July 30–31 with Major Hans von Haeften, a younger member of the German General Staff.

> Germany can purchase the preservation of peace now only at the price of severe national humiliation, for any treating under the pressure of Russian mobilization is tantamount to national humiliation. Yet if we mobilize, it means war. Should Germany now delay this measure . . . Germany will enter the war in the most unfavourable conditions. We should thereby be allowing our enemies to carry war into German territory. If we linger over mobilization, our military position will become every day more unfavorable and may have the most disastrous consequences for us. . . .[28]

Von Moltke's fright that evening was the desperate anxiety of an insecure man who felt he had been given responsibility for the almost impossible task of protecting Germany should war occur.

On July 30, Bethmann-Hollweg had still been hopeful that Austria might respond favorably to William's "Halt at Belgrade" proposal. By the morning of July 31, though the Austrians had avoided giving any official reply to his inquiries, he had received enough information of an unofficial sort to make success on that score appear unlikely. While he, Falkenhayn, and von Moltke were in conference around noon, a telegram arrived from Moscow confirming that Russian general mobilization had begun. The three men immediately agreed on the necessity of proclaiming "Danger of War" measures; William hurried up to Berlin from Potsdam; and that afternoon about three o'clock ultimatums were dispatched to both Russia and France. At 5 P.M. on the following day, general mobilization orders were signed by the kaiser and put into effect immediately. They were orders, moreover, that required the violation of Luxembourg and Belgian neutrality as necessary strategical steps to achieving a quick, decisive victory over the French army.

Thus having encouraged Austria to take steps against Serbia in the hope that a weak ally would gain strength and prestige from an easy victory over an even weaker state, Germany suddenly perceived itself as forced to choose between a painful diplomatic humiliation and an incredibly frightening military risk. For the German leadership, war, however dangerous, seemed preferable to a diplomatic defeat that would hasten even further the disintegration of its major ally and destroy its self-image of Germany as a world power.

The fifth step was the decision by the French Cabinet on August 1 to begin French general mobilization immediately, while at the same time maintaining the July 30 decision to hold all troops five to ten kilometers behind the French frontier.

There was no hesitation among the men in control of French foreign policy about the necessity of rejecting the German ultimatum. Indeed, despite the deliberate withdrawal of troops from the frontier, the French were so determined to support their Russian ally that the French orders for general mobilization were actually promulgated thirty minutes before the German orders were signed. Moreover, French policy in the summer of 1914 was undoubtedly the most clear-sighted and focused of that of any major power. Its broad outlines were explained by Poincaré in a speech given in 1922. After reaffirming his 1912 pledge that "Even though I were sure in advance that a war would bring us victory I would never take the responsibility of letting it be declared," he went on to explain that

> I was no less determined to do everything in order that, if it broke out in spite of all our endeavours for peace, it should end in victory and the liberation of Alsace-Lorraine. It is this double thought—whatever people may say, there is nothing self-contradictory about it—which for thirty-five years has inspired my whole political life.[29]

While France would not itself initiate a war, if war came it was viewed as a chance to pursue a territorially oriented policy, a policy well within the *realpolitik* tradition of the ancien régime.

In line with this policy, Poincaré seems to have encouraged Russia to pursue "peace combined with strength, honor and dignity,"[30] that is, by assuming its role as protector of the Serbs. Thus

Paléologue, the French ambassador at St. Petersburg, consistently assured Sazonov and the czar of French support in any eventuality. French diplomacy in the final days of peace was, in fact, less concerned with restraining Russia than with insuring that Britain would not remain neutral when war came. The skill and success of French policy in these weeks is undoubtedly the result of the clarity of aim and the general unity of vision among the French ministers and diplomatic staff. The only fear that exercised them was the realistic fear of English noninvolvement. This was dealt with as effectively (and successfully) as possible by quickly pledging respect for Belgian neutrality and by accepting the risk involved in leaving undefended an area immediately behind the frontier, so that Germany would have to fire the first shot.

The sixth and essentially final step was the English Cabinet decision on the evening of August 3 to send to Germany the next day an ultimatum demanding that it respect Belgian neutrality. Refusal of the ultimatum was to be (and was) followed by a declaration of war.

This was an extremely problematical decision, as the ruling circles of England, like those of Russia, were divided on the appropriate policy to pursue vis-à-vis the growing conflict on the continent.

> [There] was on one side a small party which held that, if Germany attacked France, both honour and policy would require us to intervene, and on the other side a small party which was equally clear that in no circumstances ought we to intervene. Between the two, the main body of the Cabinet held that we were under no moral obligation to do so unless we were attacked or until the course of events compelled intervention in our own interests.[31]

The divisions within the Cabinet were also present in the Liberal party and the country as a whole, though the uncompromising "pacifists" were a small proportion of the national leadership and the firm interventionists included the Conservative opposition, the army and the navy, but not the economic elite.

The view of the permanent Foreign Office staff was clearly and unhesitatingly interventionist from the beginning of the crisis.

> The moment has passed when it might have been possible to enlist French support in an effort to hold back Russia. . . . [This was written on July 25!] Whatever we may think of the merits of the Austrian charges against Serbia, France and Russia consider that these are the pretexts, and that the bigger cause of the Triple Alliance versus Triple *Entente* is definitely engaged. . . . The point that now matters is whether Germany is or is not absolutely determined to have this war now. There is still the chance that she can be made to hesitate, if she can be induced to apprehend that the war will find England by the side of France and Russia.[32]

The pessimism of the Foreign Office about German and Entente motivation was not shared, however, by Sir Edward Grey, the Liberal Secretary of State for Foreign Affairs. He was convinced that no British interests were involved in the Balkans, that mediation and peace seeking was the proper role for England, and he was at least hopeful that the conflict could be kept localized.

As his proposals for conferences and negotiations failed to produce an effect, Grey moved closer to the views of his permanent staff. Thus on July 29 he warned the German ambassador, Lichnowsky, about probable British intervention if a European war occurred. This action, which might have worked if the Foreign Office had been correct about German intent, failed because it was seen by the kaiser as a threat rather than a clarification, made him more rather than less belligerent, and indeed redirected his anger from Serbia to the Entente.

The conviction that Britain could not afford to remain neutral in case of a four-power conflict rested ultimately on two bases. On the one hand there was the moral (rather than legal) obligation involved in the close military and naval agreements between England and France. A failure to come to the aid of an ally who had stripped its northern coasts of naval defenses because of those agreements would, in the rather archaic phraseology of Under-Secretary Arthur Nicolson, have rendered England "a by-word among the nations."[33] On the other hand there was a materialistic fear for long-run British political interests. "If we did not help France, the Entente would disappear; and whether victory came to Germany, or to France and Russia, our situation at the end of the war would be very uncomfortable."[34]

However, neither Grey nor the Liberal Prime Minister Asquith believed that they could bring the Cabinet, their party, or the country as a whole to share these aristocratic and *realpolitik* points of view. Therefore, as late as August 2 they were meticulous in refusing to offer France any firm assurance that Britain would declare war in France's defense. On that day, however, Grey did promise, with the consent of a divided Cabinet, that the English fleet would be used to protect the French north coast against attack from the German fleet. The French ambassador left the interview in a euphoric state as he believed, "In truth a great country does not wage war by halves. Once it decided to fight the war at sea it would necessarily be led into fight it on land as well."[35] In fact, Churchill, First Lord of the Admiralty, had mobilized the fleet on his own personal responsibility on August 1, and Sir Henry Wilson, Chief of the General Staff, was busy that day "mobilizing" the Conservatives to put pressure on the Liberal cabinet!

However, by August 2 the attitude of the Cabinet had begun to shift, and the issue on which the undecided majority and even some of the erstwhile pacifists joined the prointerventionists (during a late afternoon meeting) was not the unprotected coast of France or the danger of an attack on England (which no one feared), but the issue of the impending violation of Belgian neutrality. Moreover when the German demand for permission to cross Belgian territory became public, a change in the mood of the country paralleled the shift in the cabinet. As Lloyd George (one of the Cabinet shifters) observed later:

> The war had leapt into popularity between Saturday [August 1] and Monday [August 3]. On Saturday ... the financial and trading interests in the City of London were totally opposed to our intervention in the war. By Monday there was a complete change. The threatened invasion of Belgium had set the nation on fire from sea to sea.[36]

When on August 3 Grey quoted from an 1870 speech by Gladstone, he spoke for the overwhelming majority of his countrymen:

> We have an interest in the independence of Belgium which is wider than that which we may have in the literal operation of the

guarantee. . . . [Could we] quietly stand by and witness the perpetration of the direst crime that ever stained the pages of history, and thus become participators in the sin?

On August 4, after their invasion of Belgium had begun, the Germans were sent an ultimatum demanding withdrawal. The British ambassador was immediately told by Jagow that Germany could not meet the demand. He also had a final and revealing conversation with Bethmann-Hollweg, who argued that

> What we [Britain] had done was unthinkable, it was like striking a man from behind while he was fighting for his life against two assailants. He held Great Britain responsible for all the terrible events that might happen! I [the British ambassador] . . . said that in the same way as he and Herr Jagow wished me to understand that for strategical reasons it was a matter of life and death for Germany to advance through Belgium and violate her neutrality, so I would wish him to understand that it was, so to speak, a matter of "life and death" for the honour of Great Britain that she should keep her solemn engagement to do her utmost to defend Belgium's neutrality if attacked. . . .[37]

Thus in a period of ten days Europe moved from a situation of total, if uneasy, peace to a situation in which five major and two minor powers were preparing to deal with each other violently. The interesting aspect of the drama is the essential similarity of motivation (despite certain nuances of differences) that led four of the five major states to resort to physical force. With the exception of France, in their own perception the initiators of World War I, all took physically aggressive steps for defensive reasons. They perceived the situation as one in which either their very existence (Austria and Germany), their essential national influence and power (Russia, Germany, and England), or their honor and self-righteous image (England, Russia, and Germany) were so seriously endangered that violence (or the threat of it) was necessary. None of them "wanted" a European war, whose unknown and risky quality they all feared. But they were more frightened of what might happen to themselves and their country if they did not act. The "elemental force" controlling men that summer, which Bethmann-Hollweg sensed but could not name, was Fear.

Granted the intensity of their private emotions, it is hardly surprising that, when the leaders faced their respective parliaments, they were able to make a convincing case for their actions and were able to carry their countrymen with them in support of the war effort. Even the Socialist parties, which had for several decades ritually rejected the idea of fighting in a capitalist war, found themselves moved by the cry of "Motherland in danger." Thus the Marxist and Conservative fantasy that there were two nations on one soil, that the proletariat had no homeland, died (or should have) forever. All across Europe young men marched off to fight in defense (they believed) of a land, a way of life, and a sense of pride more important than life itself.

The rapidity with which statesmen in all countries developed territorial and political goals to make the war worthwhile once it had begun, and the seemingly atavistic imperial ambitions of Hitler, Mussolini, and the Japanese in the 1930s, have tended to obscure the defensive, fearful quality of the first democratic war. Yet there are indications that the summer of 1914 was not an isolated or accidental phenomenon. Since 1945, for example, Britain and Israel have attacked Egypt because they feared the destructiveness of unchallenged dictators; the United States has fought in both Korea and Vietnam because it feared Communist expansion; and Russia has invaded both Hungary and Czechoslovakia because it feared the loss of defensive buffers against capitalist aggression. We seem, in fact, to have entered a new period in which human beings wage war primarily because they are afraid.

11
The Rage of Impotence

> For our purpose, only one question concerns us: How can the "terror of history" be tolerated . . . ? Justification of a historical event by the simple fact that it is a historical event, in other words, by the simple fact that it "happened that way," will not go far towards freeing humanity from the terror that the event inspires.
> —*Mircea Eliade*[1]

One of the more illuminating recent studies of the phenomenon of violence is an investigation by Hans Toch of male convicts and policemen who had records of at least one case of assaulting or being assaulted. In the course of the investigation, which focused heavily on the participants' perception of how the violent incident erupted, the researchers discovered that the single incident was always part of a general pattern of violent interaction and that the patterns showed a typology of internal motivation by which the participants could be classified. It also became clear that in about 75 percent of the cases, violence was essentially a self-preserving strategy, intended to defend the individual against physical danger, intolerable pressure, lowered self-esteem, or group denigration. Though such violence-prone individuals generally initiated the actual physical violence, they perceived themselves as doing so in response to an intolerable threat.

In discussing the sources of this violence-prone syndrome, Toch touched on three factors in particular: (1) their early childhood experiences, which had presumably left such men with fragile, weak egos; (2) the (lower-class and ethnic) subcultures that had taught them violence as a proper mode of asserting manhood and solving interpersonal relations; and (3) the dominant culture's attachment to collective violence, particularly war, as an accepted and even idealized mode of international interaction. His concluding comment was:

> Men who press explosive buttons or who sign bloodthirsty orders are entrepreneurs of violence, individuals who coldly plan for inconceivable contingencies, or who produce and disseminate means of destruction. When the roles exercised by such persons have been eliminated from the games societies play, we can attend to our Violent Men with a clearer conscience and a more unambiguous mandate.[2]

Without challenging the connection Toch has drawn between the war maker and the criminal, it is still possible to find his picture of the statesman and soldier oversimplified. Many are undoubtedly greedy or ambitious "entrepreneurs," but there is also evidence that many "warmongers," like their social inferiors in the prisons and the police, are in fact essentially frightened men who lash out in violence because they feel threatened and can perceive no other way to protect themselves and their countries from danger.

Toch and his assistants, for example, divided the self-preserving syndrome into a number of subcategories: self-image promoting, self-image defending, reputation defending, pressure remover. Interestingly, the characterizations provided for these categories also apply to the actions and motivations of major statesmen in 1914. Berchtold, Conrad, and Tisza, for instance, clearly acted like a pressure remover who "feels himself smothered, walled-in, or subject to overwhelming odds. . . ."[3] When the victim fails to heed the warning that he is "crowding beyond the limits of what is bearable," violence erupts as a way to obliterate an intolerable situation. Czar Nicholas and Sazonov, however, had much more in common with the self-image defender "who is extremely sensitive to the implications of other people's actions to his integrity, manliness, or worth."[4] Typically such men let one or two affronts pass, while worrying about their implications, before striking out.

As might be expected from the leaders of a new state, the kaiser and von Moltke acted more like a self-image promoter who "is worried that . . . he will be taken for a weakling or a coward . . . a logical candidate for victimization."[5] Equating manhood with a willingness to fight, self-image promoters tend to involve themselves unnecessarily in the affairs of others and often find themselves taking on more than they can handle, challenging "the wrong man at the wrong time."[6] By contrast, the English Cabinet and Parliament, in going to the defense of France and Belgium, responded like a reluctant reputation defender, "where violence is the fate entailed in a role . . . a matter of 'noblesse oblige,' so to speak. . . . He knows he must champion his people, execute the guilty, and put on a good show."[7] Like Grey, many "rep defenders" find no particular pleasure in their role and try to negotiate a peaceful resolution to the situation. Thus there is reason to think that the "subculture of violence" and the dominant culture have much in common, both ideologically and psychologically.

There is, of course, an enormous difference between the personal styles of the lower classes and the ruling elites of the modern world. The lower-class subculture places a high valuation on the personal use of violence, producing a world in which

> ready access to weapons . . . may become essential for protection against others who respond in similarly violent ways in certain situations. . . . The carrying of knives or other protective devices becomes a common symbol of willingness to participate in violence, to expect violence, and to be ready for its retaliation.[8]

This ethos is so pervasive, moreover, that "even law-abiding members of the local sub-culture may not view various illegal expressions of violence as menacing or immoral."[9] Such a subculture, in fact, reflects and preserves (to some degree self-consciously) an older, aristocratic (warrior) culture, which has become essentially passé as an individual ethic in the world of the bourgeois and bureaucrat.

The ruling classes of the last two centuries have increasingly adopted norms that place a low valuation on personal violence, except in organized sports. The duel has been confined (where it is not banned entirely) to the ritual testing of university students, while personal recourse to fists and knives by adults is deprecated as brawling and socially denigrated as a sign of either immaturity or bad breeding. Even in the military, the actual firing of a gun or thrust of a bayonet is confined to the rank and file and the youngest (lowest) levels of the officers. Indeed by 1914 even the lieutenants and captains in the symbol- and class-conscious British army no longer carried any weapon but a swagger stick when leading men into battle, since by their value system "officers do not kill" or "killing is not gentlemanly."[10] Other upper-class men (managers, bureaucrats, politicians, professionals) are even less likely to resort to personal violence, which can bring them no esteem and is only too likely to hinder their careers.

This upper-class devaluation of spontaneous personal violence is, moreover, accepted by the majority of the population. Indeed, one of the distinct characteristics of urban-industrial civilization is its extreme repression of self-initiated aggression. (Our farming ancestors, of all classes, found it natural to settle disputes by fighting.) Workers crowd city streets, buses, and subways to maximum density without brawling; urban riots become incomprehensible outrages rather than the norm; child and wife abuse is labeled a deviant action and becomes a focus of widespread concern rather than being an unnoticed normality. Not only rape, but simple assault and battery are defined as crimes, their perpetrators are pursued by efficient police (another modern innovation) and penalized by incarceration (which is viewed as more humane, i.e., less violent, than whipping, branding, or public execution). It is a world that is placid and secure beyond the experience or even the imaginings of most civilized people before 1800.

Institutionalized violence carried out by the police and the military has continued, however, to seem appropriate and even necessary. It must be hedged around, of course, by rules and laws, made rational and effective, controlled by constitutional and bureaucratic procedure. (In autocratic Russia in 1914, for example, the order for general mobilization required the signature not just of the Czar, but of the Minister for War, the Navy Minister, and the Minister of the Interior.) In effect, an attempt has been made to "rationalize" violence, to divorce it from the effects of individual personalities, emotions, and chance, and to confine it to "proper" channels. This abstracting of violence is paralleled, moreover, by the increasing impersonality of the actual dispensers of such force. Police ride in squadcars and helicopters; they do not patrol the streets. Warriors in tanks, planes, submarines, and on missile sites fire deadly bombs at enemies they will never see.

While the potential for violence and violence itself on a national or community level has been depersonalized, its importance and destructiveness has been magnified beyond the imaginings of any preindustrial society. Thus in the relatively peaceful decades before 1914, the major European powers spent between 4 and 6 percent of their total gross national product (GNP) on military budgets. Their armies increased in size and deadliness decade by decade until in 1914 the four major continental powers already had over 17 million men available in their standing armies and trained reserves. During the next four years they would mobilize only another 12 million. (A typical Roman army at the height of empire was about 60,000.) Similarly since 1945, though neither has fought a major war, the United States and the U.S.S.R. (and their smaller allies) have spent 6 to 10 percent of their annual GNP on the military and stockpiled a nuclear arsenal equivalent to over 50 billion tons of TNT, enough to annihilate all life on earth several times over. Armies and weapons of that size and costliness represent serious commitments on the part of the community that supports them; their proper use may be hedged with barriers, but a proper condition for their unleashing is unquestionably still accepted as possible.

Obviously some individuals and institutions have personal and greed-based reasons for pursuing such growth. The "military-industrial complex," for example, can pursue expanded career possibilities, greater prestige, and heightened profits in such a situation. But armies, navies, and air forces must be paid for by the society as a whole; they must be "sold" and their appropriateness consented to.

At least since the 1870s in the western world that consent has rested on popular support given through elected parliaments. Even in authoritarian states like the U.S.S.R., it emerges from a bureaucratic debate, no less intense for being secret, in which the interests and needs of the party and the economic managerial bureaucracy each carry weight at least equal to the military's. Nonetheless, no people has ever suggested literal disarmament for themselves.

Two major lines of argument have been presented by politicians and military thinkers to justify the expenditure of resources on military developments. The minimum argument and proposal, associated particularly though not exclusively with the "left," is the need for an instrument of defense against invasion. Even small and nonexpansive nations such as Sweden and Switzerland have adopted this stance, and it has been proposed and worked for in other nations by peace-minded liberals and socialists. Such a position, accepting the instinctual right of defense of self and territory in a war-oriented world, finds a solution in the conception of a citizen militia. As proposed by the French Socialist Jean Jaurès in 1912, for example, it involved a nonstanding army of all (male) citizens, trained for six months and on reserve call for twenty-five to thirty years. Such an army could defend the borders but would have been unavailable for overseas and expansive ventures. For his unsuccessful efforts, Jaurès was vilified (and eventually assassinated) as a pacifist, pro-German, and traitor: all equally false accusations.

No large state has as yet adopted such a purely defensive policy. It does not explain or justify, for example, the naval building programs of Germany or Great Britain in the early twentieth century or the enormous military budgets of the United States and the U.S.S.R. at present. Indeed, as John McNaughton, one of Defense Secretary Robert McNamara's aides at the Defense Department in the early 1960s when its military budget was over 50 billion dollars, observed: "How much do we really need for the *defense* of the United States of America? . . . The maximum for the defense of our shores is one billion dollars. So all the rest of our defense budget relates to what we regard as *our responsibilities as a world power.*"[11]

Since the late nineteenth century the arguments for shouldering the "responsibilities of a world power" have fallen into three consistent and interrelated patterns. First there is the argument that the possession of world power is required by one's inevitable or historic mission, however defined. One has a responsibility or right to spread freedom, self-government, Christianity, Slavic orthodoxy, *Kultur,* racial purity, communism, or to defend the sovereignty of small nations. At its core this is simply a secular version of the old Christian concept of a religious crusade: One has the truth and others do not. In the absence, however, of a cosmic ideology of salvation and hell, the driving motivation for such a sacrificial (in terms of time, goods, and lives) mission is often unclear.

The second argument is economic. The country needs access to other areas (either by agreement or political control) in order to secure necessary raw materials, investments, or markets. The difficulty with such an argument is that it has been impossible to prove that the economic benefits of such imperialism outweigh the costs for the nation as a whole (as opposed to special interest groups). The relative unimportance of economic motivation is, moreover, illustrated by two examples. To avoid an unpleasant political isolation, in the early twentieth century England was willing to compromise its conflicts with its major colonial rivals, France and Russia. Similarly, to maintain ideological purity, the United States was willing in the fifties and sixties to forgo trade relations with the Communist world and would have imposed such an embargo on its allies if it could.

The third argument is even less reasonable, though it explains much of the emotional potency of the other two. This analysis of reality posits violent interaction as "natural" and interprets human experience as a "win/lose" situation. The better adapted (culturally, economically, militarily) win; they establish the Pax Britannica, become another Rome, found a thousand-year Reich, inaugurate the world-wide proletarian utopia. In effect, they gain the accolade of historic immortality. Those who lack the courage, ability, or willpower to win are "unfit," second best, unmanly. Bypassed by history, they will be reduced to insignificance and fail to survive. The alternative to greatness and world power is perceived as historical extinction.

When one looks closely at the arguments for becoming or remaining a world power, what is revealing is the extent to which a common thread of fear is exposed. It emerges as early as 1791 when the French representative Brissot de Warville, in one of his most eloquent speeches for a war against the monarchical powers of Europe, argued that "for a people who had just acquired their liberty after a dozen centuries of slavery, war was necessary in order to establish that liberty on a firm basis, in order to test it, to discover whether people were worthy of it."[12] The success of his argument in molding French policy suggests, at a minimum, that the French middle class was not sure of its own worth and found it necessary to prove its manhood by the test (battle) of the displaced warrior aristocracy. Unfortunately, the French were not the last westerners to be "swayed by out-moded, feudalistic ideas of honor and prestige."[13]

It is not until the 1870s, however, that the fear of extinction becomes a continuous theme, with Benjamin Disraeli opening the growing chorus of imperialism by warning his countrymen:

> The issue is not a mean one. It is whether you will be content to be a comfortable England, modeled and molded upon Continental principles and *meeting in due course an inevitable fate,* or whether you will be a great country, an imperial country....[14]

Twenty years later Joseph Chamberlain argued that if England did not defend its empire, it would be replaced by other nations and in that case, the economic distress of the workers would become chronic because the country would be "entirely unable to support its enormous population."[15] Similarly, Lord Grey was convinced that German domination of the continent would make it "as irresistible as the Roman Empire, with England for the doomed Carthage."[16]

If the British increasingly saw no alternative between imperialism and the "inevitable fate" of distress, defeat, and humiliation, the Germans also began to worry that without more space they were moving toward "a frightful catastrophe," that (in the words of the writer Friedrich Fabri)

> the colonial question has become a matter of life or death for the development of Germany.... A people that has been led to a

> high level of power can maintain its historical position only as long as it understands and proves itself to be a *bearer of a culture-mission*. . . .[17]

They also became convinced that without a navy they were "helpless" against the superior naval power of Great Britain and doomed to economic and political impotence. Thus Gustav Schmoller, one of the champions of the Naval League, warned that if "[we] mean to prevent . . . the division of the earth among the three world powers, which would exclude all other countries and *destroy their trade*. . . . we require today . . . a large fleet."[18]

Granted the presuppositions on both sides, it is understandable that Sir John Fisher, on becoming First Sea Lord in 1904, argued that unless there were substantial reforms and expansion in the British navy, England might as well "pack up and hand over to Germany."[19] Indeed Fisher (and other naval types in Britain) was ready to contemplate "Copenhagening" the infant German fleet, and fears of a British naval attack were widespread in Germany that year. At the same time, Schlieffen, Chief of the German General Staff, wanted to use the opportunity provided by the Russo-Japanese war to initiate a "preventive" war. Otherwise he believed Germany would inevitably be strangled by the growing alliance between England, France, and Russia. In 1904–1905 the civilian leaders were not as frightened as they would be later, and Fisher and Schlieffen were restrained. ("Good God, Fisher," said Edward VII, "you must be mad." He did not, however, suggest that Fisher resign as First Sea Lord.)

The fear of powerlessness that pervades the posturings of Imperial Germany was not assuaged by its defeat (which was not total) and the humiliating peace of 1918. Indeed, it continued as a very real, if concealed, motivation for the acquisitive demands of the Third Reich. Thus when Hermann Rauschning urged moderation in a private conversation with Hitler, he was answered by a hysterical diatribe:

> If Germany is to become a world power, and not merely a continental state (and it must become a world power if it is to survive), then it must achieve complete sovereignty and independence.

... We cannot, like Bismarck, limit ourselves to national aims. We must rule Europe or fall apart as a nation, fall back into the chaos of small states.[20]

Since 1945 few nations have been willing to argue openly for political imperialism. Instead international power is interpreted ideologically and justified as a responsibility to advance peaceful world revolution or to protect freedom and liberty against totalitarianism. Behind the rhetoric of historical inevitability or the rights of man, however, lies a defensive anxiety, such as Lenin's fear that "all events in world politics are necessarily concentrated on one central point, the struggle of the world bourgeoisie against the Russian Soviet Republic. . . ."[21] Thus Russia in the late forties kept almost 3 million men under arms and had plans for sweeping through Europe to the Atlantic, not because the country intended to expand but in the hopes that such a capacity would deter the United States from undertaking a preventive war while the U.S. had a nuclear monopoly. Khrushchev's 1956 speech seems to synthesize adequately the Soviet perception of its dangers during the last three decades:

> Soon after the Second World War ended, the influence of reactionary and militarist groups began to be increasingly evident in the policy of the United States of America, Britain and France. . . . It reflects the aspirations of the most aggressive sections of present-day imperialism to win world supremacy, to suppress the working class and the democratic and national-liberation movements. . . .[22]

Unfortunately the United States also became frightened, once Roosevelt's wartime plans for a new world order based on economic multilateralism that would assure the U.S. "supreme position in world finance, commerce and industry" failed to materialize.[23] Thus in essence the U.S. reverted to the 1904 perspective of Theodore Roosevelt:

> The right of freedom and the responsibility for the exercise of that right cannot be divorced. . . . The eternal vigilance which is the price of liberty must be exercised, sometimes to guard against

outside foes. . . . A great free people owes it to itself and to all mankind not to sink into helplessness before the powers of evil.[24]

With the Truman Doctrine of 1947 this view was given structure in the "domino" theory. The United States was perceived as faced with "a militant minority, exploiting human want and misery . . . able to create political chaos. . . . At the present moment in world history nearly every nation must choose between alternative ways of life."[25] If the U.S. failed to confront and repel each communist attempt at expansion or subversion, the will of other states to resist would decline and the communist belief in the U.S.'s lack of courage would be reinforced. "Should we fail to aid Greece and Turkey [or Korea, Formosa, Vietnam, etc.] in this fateful hour, the effect will be far-reaching to the West as well as to the East. . . ."[26]

At a minimum, such analyses rest on a paranoid perception of others as hostile and threatening and an equally neurotic perception of a large and materially wealthy community as weak and potentially impotent. Like the cosmologies of earlier civilizations, the analysis is essentially a mythopoetic mode of defining reality. The interesting issue is why such a myth (whatever its usefulness to the high priests of the "military-industrial complex") is so readily embraced by the populace as a whole and has such emotional potency.

In analyzing "violent men" Toch and his colleagues found certain psychological and social characteristics common to all of them. They were all men who had "been flooded all [their] life with strong feelings of not being able to be" what they should be, who felt "unsure," weak and insignificant, "helpless," "easily panicked," "precarious," and fearful.[27] While they were deficient in verbal and other social skills, they were distinguishable from others who had the same deficiencies because they feared being mistaken for a coward and victimized, were perpetually on guard against being denigrated and belittled, and were always on the alert for "another danger lurking around a nearby corner."[28] Their violence was, in fact, an expression of an inability to cope; it was a blind rage, a frantic, "desperate, lashing-out," in an effort to obliterate the situation, to destroy the other person. The satisfaction was always "the removal of the irritation," so that life was now (it was to be hoped) "silent and peaceful again."²⁹ What is unwittingly being described is essentially the annihilating aggressiveness of the trapped and frightened animal.

It may be objected that, unlike their social inferiors, diplomatic, military, and political elites are not lacking in verbal and social skills. But the important thing is not the quantifiable degree of skills, but the internal experience of adequacy or inadequacy. Certainly verbal and social skills are relative concepts. A limited but pithily handled vocabulary, for example, may be all that a peasant needs and more than adequate for conveying real wisdom and knowledge within the confines of a farming community. In international circles, on the other hand, where wit, brevity, precision, a wealth of allusions, and facility in several languages may seem necessary for minimum competency, even well-educated individuals may feel limited and awkward by comparison with the demands of their situation. More important, verbal facility that is socially skillful springs, in the last analysis, from a core of personal centeredness that allows one to assess a social scene with a fair degree of realism, to be clear about one's own feelings and goals, and thus to express them with clarity and forcefulness. If such ego-strength is not present, then verbal fluidity may become a sign and a source of weakness (as with William II), confusing others as it both conceals and reveals internal insecurity and fear.

A look at the personalities of the major figures who decided to mobilize or declare war in the summer of 1914 is instructive in this regard. William, Nicholas, and von Moltke were all men who were "not so much false as feeble."³⁰ Heirs to great names and great expectations, they were plagued by an extreme diffidence and lack of self-confidence. All three disliked and avoided verbal confrontations, alternated between an easy optimism and deep pessimism, and were deeply fearful of an imminent social revolution. In William II and von Moltke this emotional nervousness was so severe as to produce physical symptoms and even hysteria in situations of extreme stress.

If these men "inherited" their roles, the foreign ministers seem to have been chosen deliberately for their flexibility. Unfortunately their ability to see both sides of a question arose from weakness and was a sign of an almost mercurial temperamentalness.

Both Berchtold and Sazonov, for example, were hesitant; afraid of responsibility, isolation, and an independent stand; and inclined to go along with others for the sake of peace and quiet. At the same time they disliked the image this fluctuation produced and could easily be goaded into precipitous action, creating a fait accompli in order to prove that they were not simply rubber stamps. Whereas they were overly susceptible to external influences, Lord Grey's indecisiveness was internal in origin. He was "not one man but two who could not see eye to eye, indeed who were at war the one with the other."[31] A love of nature and privacy fought with a strong sense of public duty; a hatred for modern armies and war with a "hard-nosed" belief in empire and power politics. In effect, throughout his adult life he was a conscientious man who personally wanted one thing but acted according to the very different norms of his class and country.

By contrast, Tisza, Conrad, and Churchill were overtly self-confident, arrogant, and domineering. They were, however, likely to see dangerous violence lurking everywhere. Churchill, for example, considered Mahatma Gandhi "tigerish" and assumed striking British workers were bent on revolution. All were inclined as a result to see force as a proper, if not the only, recourse to problems. In 1912 Tisza, for example, had used the police to "purge" the Hungarian parliament of his political opponents, precipitating a fracas in which several men were killed. Though Tisza's Calvinist conscience made him view war as repugnant, there is no doubt that Conrad consciously shared the liking for the excitement of armed conflict Churchill expressed in an early August 1914 letter to his wife: "Everything tends towards catastrophe & collapse. I am interested, geared up & happy. Is it not horrible to be built like that? The preparations have a hideous fascination for me. I pray to God to forgive me for such fearful moods of levity."[32]

One could go on, but this portrait gallery is hardly reassuring as to the personal stability of national leaders. It has been a shibboleth of constitutional theorists that one critical flaw in a monarchical system is that it can place unstable or inadequate individuals in charge of national destinies. But the personae of 1914 suggest that the criteria for bureaucratic or political success can be just as unfortunate in their results, and that a parliamentary regime like Great

Britain was only a little better represented than a monarchy like Germany.

Nor does recent American experience suggest that the phenomenon is strictly European, or that the quality of democratic leaders has improved with time. Lyndon Johnson, for example, has been described as

> a man of endless, restless ambition . . . of stunning force, drive and intelligence, and of equally stunning insecurity. The enormity of his accomplishments never dimmed the hidden fears which had propelled him in the first place. . . . There was in all of this more than a small element of the bully in Johnson. . . .[33]

If insecurity (and the bully is essentially a man who desperately fears fear) marred this son of a provincial elite, Richard Nixon demonstrates that it can also characterize a son of the lower middle class. President of the most powerful nation in the world, about to be reelected by the largest majority ever given a president, Nixon was nontheless haunted by the dangers supposedly inherent in a disarrayed Democratic opposition and a politically and economically weak resistance movement. Since he feared the internal "enemy" more than the external, his actions met no resonating approval from an American public that did not share the intensity of his particular paranoia.

The childhood experiences that produce strong, stable egos or weak, fragile ones thus seem to have little to do with class, relative wealth, or material security, though wealth and position (and the training they can purchase) often mask this lack of internal self-reliance and even allow it to be neurotically handled by the pursuit of power. Indeed, if one considers the price one must normally pay (in terms of energy and time expended on distasteful tasks, subordination of personal inclinations, sacrifice of personal pleasures and family ties) to rise to preeminence in either a bureaucracy such as the army or a competitive democracy, the wonder is that mass societies produce any stable rulers. Certainly the insatiable hunger for power that can (and perhaps must) drive individuals to pursue political or bureaucratic eminence suggests the presence of an equally insatiable interior vacuum and fear. Under great stress or situations of crisis it may reveal itself in a devastatingly destructive manner.

The large military budgets and the wide acceptance of the "fear" myth of failure due to powerlessness also make it clear that insecurity and unconscious anger are not confined to the social and political extremes of industrial civilization. Ironically, a sense of powerlessness and the potential for frightened rage seem to be dominant emotional characteristics of a technological society that began by promising mankind limitless power and security. But the irony is at least understandable when one realizes that, as with the agricultural revolution, so with the industrial: The price of greater control over nature has been the subjection of the individual to greater external social control. The secret of technological abundance has been the division of creative aggression into its minute, discrete parts. The cost has been the subjection of human beings to technological (and commercial) requirements, plus incredible complications of the process of linking desire to fulfillment.

One must beware, of course, of overemphasizing the negative elements in modern life. There is no question but that the majority of the industrialized second generation would choose it over the laborious effort and skimpy rewards of farming; that they come to like the peacefulness, plentitude, pluralism, and seeming freedom of choice it offers and have no desire to return to the life of their forebears. Moreover, if they are at times consciously unhappy, most people nonetheless manage to adjust, marry and raise families, avoid trouble with the law, and create at least islands of pleasure and value.

Nonetheless the inability of such a society to incorporate and tolerate the deviant within its boundaries, the high and rising rates of suicide and mental illness, the angry rebelliousness of the young and the pathetic aloneness of the aged, as well as the widespread fascination with expensive modes of destruction, all point to an underlying and pervasive pathology. The initial source of this pathology must be sought, of course, in the adjustment required by a new phase of civilization, in the techniques of socialization common to industrial people.

Here one observes that although the heavy physical disciplining meted out to peasant children is dropped by the dominant classes, it is replaced during the early stages of industrialization by emphasis on early toilet training and cleanliness. Later pervasive (and often unrecognized) control of the young becomes the norm. Homes become small and obsessively clean; play areas are restricted and generally heavily controlled by "helpful" adults; undomesticated nature is almost inaccessible except in organized groups. School, once the rule only for the mandarin class, becomes the norm for all children between six and sixteen and for the ambitious can stretch on for another ten years. And school means conforming for seven hours a day to the timetable and commands of adults, while repressing physical movement. Males, moreover, are subjected to a double-bind situation since they are simultaneously urged to be active, aggressive, domineering, and able to "take care of themselves"—but only at certain times and in certain situations. Essentially only those who can and will conform to such an externally imposed regime can expect access to the dominant adult society. The others will find themselves shunted into the outer limbo of the underemployed, the criminal, and the insane.

The repression of initiative and spontaneity does not end with school, however. Indeed school is probably the necessary tool of socialization for industrial adulthood where both personal violence and other forms of personal initiative are severely limited. (Indeed, the first, "unschooled" generation of industrial workers in England violently objected to the whole new system, which they found degrading and intolerably regimented.) With rare exceptions (the intellectual, artist, sportsman—all either despised or idolized), industrial life requires of adults rigid timetables, suppression of emotions, no or repetitive physical actions, fragmented production or artificial sociability or both. One does not build one's own house, hunt, raise or cook one's own food, sew one's own clothes, educate one's own children, sing one's own songs, or fight one's own fights. At the same time satisfaction, the sense of pleasure that comes from the successful expenditure of energy to fulfill a felt need, is one of the least common experiences of industrial society. Either the need is so easily fulfilled (one buys a TV dinner or a dress off the rack) that little energy is expended and little sense of achievement experienced, or the path to fulfillment is so indirect (one must work for years at an unrelated job in order to "buy" a home) that the emotional connection is attenuated.

A sense of personal power rests ultimately on the unblocked

internal ability to define one's desires and the experience of releasing and directing one's energies toward the goal of satisfying those desires. Failure per se does not create a feeling of powerlessness. If one has truly exerted all one's strength and failed, there may be sadness and grief, but the very scope of the effort usually broadens one's experienced range of capacity and strength. Once the failure has been assimilated, one at least has learned not only what one can do, but what one can endure and survive (which may explain the relative peaceableness of small countries like Belgium or Holland). The dignity and strength of the aged (and the truly defeated) rests on repeated experiences of just such successes and failures, completed gestalts.

The requirements of industrialization, unfortunately, repeatedly interrupt this process. The spontaneity of one's own gestalts must be replaced constantly (and especially in school and work) by externally formulated demands. To the extent that social norms are simply introjected and not assimilated, one's own desires are repressed, though not destroyed. Life in an advanced industrial society is thus an experience of constant, low-level frustration and incomplete gestalts, providing little experience of the sense of power and competency that comes from large, self-defined achievements. The result is a semiconscious sense of powerlessness, impotence and insecurity, and an unconscious sense of rage and anger.

The introjected social self receives, moreover, little positive support from the culture of the society. The traditional and comforting view that one's particular role or status is divinely ordained and has cosmic significance is abandoned and instead the naked individual is urged, even in socialist regimes, to excel and distinguish him or herself, to be competitive. Reassuring external indicators of one's worth and value are, however, hard to achieve. Since the majority share the same material rewards, wealth loses its symbolic potency as a sign of cosmic approval and social prestige, though a lack of such goods may carry a heavy weight of disapproval and shame. Specialness and distinction (available to almost everyone in a small community) is awarded in a mass society to only the handful recognized by the media. The majority are inevitably unsure of their social worth and angry about their probable insignificance.

The rage and anger is really directed at the introjected social norms and the deprecated self, but it is handled by projecting the despised elements on to "the other" who do not "conform": imperialist dogs, commies, Jews, niggers, honkies, hippies, cosmopolitans, and so forth. They are then consciously available as appropriate objects of both fear and rage. Indeed the myth of national powerlessness makes most sense if it is understood as a myth of the internal psyche. There the spontaneous self competes with the introjected self, no cooperation in a stable ecological niche appears possible, and the stronger aims always to defeat or silence the weaker. The external "enemy" is, moreover, both the spontaneous and the controlling self; hence the anomaly that he or she is always perceived as simultaneously less inhibited by "our" norms and more determined to "control" us. No matter how powerful we may seem externally, the enemy is more threatening because (in the internal drama) he or she has the desire and perhaps the capacity to extinguish a part of us perceived as "essence," essential. The win/loss drama of the internal world is thus projected onto the external world; hence the danger that some external conflict will suddenly be perceived as a threat to the continued existence of the fragmented, fragile self.

For all animals (including the most timid and least predatory), there is one point at which they will fight. This is the point at which they find flight (the normal response to aggression) impossible, so that the "choice" is between accepting destruction passively or fighting in an attempt to avoid death. In that situation the titmouse or the squirrel will turn into a whirlwind of viciousness, lashing out against the threatening predator with tooth and claw. Such aggression is cold and deadly: it seeks to annihilate the danger, to either remove it entirely or make escape possible. In such a situation even the mildest animal is capable of prodigies of violence.

The annihilating aggression of the endangered is broader, more complex, and potentially more easily misdirected than the focused, appetitive aggression connected with hunger for food, sex, or shelter. For one thing, it can involve a functional definition of "self" that extends beyond the actual biological organism to include the dependent offspring. Thus the female of most species (and the male in some) will fight to the death in the defense of endangered young, even in cases where parental flight is possible. The threatened death of the young is responded to "as if" it were the death of the protecting adult.

Equally important is the fact that an animal can perceive aggression in a situation and respond with annihilating rage when in fact no actual threat to its existence is being posed. Defensive aggression, after all, rests on response, often genetically programmed, to certain signs, regardless of the other's intent. Thus human hikers, intending merely to get from one point to another, have often unwittingly endangered their lives by getting too close to a den of lion cubs or by seeming to challenge a bear on a trail too narrow for easy withdrawal. Presence is equated with destructive intent and the animal, dangerously trapped in its own (mis)perception, responds with a deadly ferocity. Wise humans and smaller animals run in such a situation. Those who will not (or cannot) confirm by their continued presence the frightened animal's perception of their destructive intent. The result is then likely to be a fight that may be ended by a "sign of appeasement," but may also result in death.

That humans share such a response with their animal brethren has long been known to military leaders. As early as 500 B.C. Sun Tzu, the great Chinese military theorist, made it explicit in his strategic principle of the "Death Ground," that is, a position from which it is impossible to retreat.

> For it is the nature of soldiers to resist when surrounded; to fight to the death when there is no alternative, and when desperate to follow commands implicitly. . . . Then officers and men together put forth their utmost efforts. In a desperate situation they fear nothing; when there is no way out they stand firm. . . . But throw them into a situation where there is no escape and they will display the immortal courage of Chuan Chu and Ts'ao Kuei.[34]

Unfortunately, the supposedly greater intelligence of humans does not reduce the chances of misperceiving another's intent; instead consciousness (carrying the capacity for projection and fantasy) intensifies the probability of misunderstanding. Indeed, once violence between human beings has come to seem normal or natural in a culture or subculture, the possibility is increased that another human may be perceived as dangerously threatening to one's existence.

Moreover, the human sense of "self" may be broadened by socialization to include a particular self-image (as well as one's tribe, clan, or nation). Thus simple biological survival can be less important than, and may even be sacrificed to, the need to protect the sense of one's self (and group) as powerful, honorable, righteous, and in control of things and events.

12
The Mega-Tantrum

> We give them money—But are they grateful?
> No, they're spiteful and they're hateful
> They don't respect us—so let's surprise them
> We'll drop the big one and pulverize them.
> —*Randy Newman* [1]

In January 1980 President Carter proposed that registration for the draft be reinstated and that American women, for the first time, be required to register. In the uproar that followed his announcement, it quickly became apparent that the registration of women was politically unfeasible. The effective coup de grace was delivered a few days later by "Tip" O'Neill, Massachusetts Democrat and Majority Leader of the House, who summed up his and the general congressional rejection of the proposal with the assertion that "no civilized state drafts women into the army." Behind this resistance to the idea of female draftees lay an assumption about the proper relation between women and war that was potent before civilization developed. Certainly it was already an old established "fact," when

Hector dismissed Andromache, his wife, "to thine house and . . . to thine own tasks, the loom and the distaff, and bid thine handmaidens ply their work; but for war shall men provide and I in chief of all men that dwell in Ilios."[2]

The exclusion of women from both the heroic and regimented armies of the Bronze and Iron ages had some basic justification in sheer physical differences. As long as an effective warrior had to wear thirty to sixty pounds of armor and simultaneously wield swords, lances, or maces weighing five to twenty pounds, women as a sex were at a disadvantage. Their smaller bone structure and lighter muscular development (especially in the upper arms) meant that the average woman (however trained) was inferior as a warrior to the average man, while few (if any) women could hope to aspire to the competency and stamina of the true hero.

But in both tribal and technological warfare, sheer brute strength has been much less important—and, in fact, such societies have often used women on the battlefield in support roles. Thus among the Shasta and Guiana in North America and the Tapuya and Juruas in South America, women traditionally accompanied their husbands to war and acted as "squires" during the battle, while in the sixteenth and seventeenth centuries European armies were normally accompanied by large groups of predominantly female camp followers who provided logistical support and at times even acted as reserve units. In modern armies women have been widely used as clerks, mechanics, gunnery instructors, antiaircraft fighters, ferry pilots, and even (though less commonly) combat infantry. In most of these roles they have withstood the same physical stresses and dangers as their male companions and have displayed comparable efficiency and bravery, though they have seldom been similarly rewarded.

Moreover, the increasing mechanization and use of electronic instruments in war has come close to reversing the relative physical advantages of the sexes in combat. Thus while infantry fighting under jungle conditions remains beyond the capacity of all but a few women, there is substantial evidence to suggest that women do better than men in handling the close confinement and temperature extremes associated with planes, tanks, submarines, and antinuclear personnel carriers. The physiological differences between the sexes thus explains the masculine character of war only during certain technological periods or under particular conditions. The other genetically based arguments seem to have even less justification.

It has been argued, for example, that women are genetically coded to be both less aggressive than men and also more aggressive and uncontrollable when actually angered. However true this may or may not be in civilian interactions, it bears little relation to the evidence provided by military history. In the first place, ideally the aggressiveness of the ordinary soldier is impersonal; it is a response to orders, not to personal desire. Men have to be trained and disciplined to carry out such orders; they do not do so "instinctively." At the same time, elite women who have found themselves in command positions (Margery Paton, for example, supervising the defense of the family castle in the fourteenth century or Isabella of Castile masterminding the expulsion of the Moors), have been proportionately at least as successful as men in both defensive and offensive roles.

This is hardly surprising since indirection, encirclement, entrapment, and at times passivity are as strategically important as "penetration" or "bold assault" in winning wars. The greatest and perennially preferred strategy is, in fact, the one that has been variously labeled "the art of deviation" (Sun Tzu), the indirect approach (Frederick the Great and Liddell Hart), or "maneuver to the rear" (General Hubert Camon's term for the typical Napoleonic strategy). A classic and simple example of this method is afforded by Hannibal at Cannae, when

> he pushed forward the Gauls and Spaniards, who formed the centre of the infantry line, while holding back his African foot, posted at each end of the line. In that way the Gauls and Spaniards formed a natural magnet for the Roman infantry, and were, as intended, forced back—so that *what had been a line bulging outwards became a line sagging inwards.* The Roman legionaries, flushed with their apparent success, *crowded into the opening.* . . . [At] this juncture Hannibal's African veterans wheeled inwards from both sides, thus automatically enveloping the thickly packed Romans.[3]

On the level of tactics, great generals have often been similarly characterized by the willingness to risk passivity and penetration, as with Gustavus Adolphus's remarkably open line of battle, which enemy cavalry could easily penetrate but from which withdrawal was difficult, or Wellington's tendency to hide his infantry behind the brow of a hill until, at the last moment, the "thin red line" could move quickly forward and enclose the confused French column on three sides. Thus the parallels on the physical level between indirect strategy and tactics and traditional female gender roles are clear and instructive, as well as amusing. Moreover, the concern with psychological techniques favored by practitioners of the indirect approach (deception, enticement, surprise, concentration on the enemy's weakness) are also humorously similar to the types of "wiles" generally considered especially feminine.

There may be some relation between strategy and sexuality: that is, between a soldier's sexual self-image and the manner in which he will handle himself and the persons who are extensions of his will on the battlefield. If so, a simpleminded, narrow "masculinity" has never offered the best approach to, much less a guarantee of, victory. Indeed, many of the greatest generals have been either homosexuals or bisexuals (Julius Caesar and Frederick the Great, to name two) or androgynous heterosexuals with strong "mothering" qualities (such as Villars and Eisenhower).

Finally there is the argument that war must remain masculine because the effectiveness of a fighting unit requires the development of a sense of close communion that comes naturally to men, who "instinctively" bond, whereas women do not. The actual failure of many all-male units to develop such cohesion, however, casts considerable doubt on the supposed genetic base of male bonding, while a new generation of female anthropologists are discovering the existence of comparably bonded female groups. Such arguments ignore, moreover, the fact that the most common and enduring form of human bonding has not been unisex groups but rather the mixed-sex family in its many variations. Indeed, some of the most effective fighting units have been modeled on the affectional structure of the family rather than the sadomasochistic hierarchy of the men's house.

For example, the incredible bravery and perseverance of British battalions under the decimating fire of trench warfare in 1914–1918 is usually explained by the parental attitude of the British officer, who combined a feudalistic paternalism toward the lower orders with a maternal concern for their physical well-being.

> The fact was that he had won his way into our affections. We loved him. . . . If anyone had a sore foot he would kneel down . . . and look at it. . . . If a blister had to be lanced, he would very likely lance it himself. . . . There was something almost religious about this care for our feet. It seemed to have a touch of the Christ about it.[4]

It had also, certainly, a touch of the nurturing mother. Similarly, the Ethiopian troops whom S.L.A. Marshall judged to be the most effective platoons fighting in the Korean war were distinguished (among other things) by a deep, familial loyalty to each other.

> [The] Ethiopians alone could boast that they had never lost a prisoner or left a dead comrade on the battlefield. Every wounded man, every shattered body, had been returned to the friendly fold. . . . If there were dead or wounded to be carried, the officer or NCO leader was the first to volunteer. When fog threatened to diffuse a patrol, the Ethiopians moved hand in hand, like children.[5]

Such bonding techniques, based on sibling affections, work as well between the sexes, once they are socially prescribed.

In effect, then, military experience suggests that whether the psychological differences between the sexes are genetically based or socially contrived, they are not ultimately compelling. Instead, many of the qualities traditionally associated with the female gender have also characterized notably effective soldiers and their commanders.

Besides the physiological/psychological arguments, a second set of objections to women as combat soldiers is less susceptible to rational resolution because it rests on emotional attitudes of real potency and great antiquity. First is the assumption that woman's special reproductive role, biologically tied to menstruation, pregnancy, and lactation, incapacitates her for military functions. The relief from reproduction afforded by modern science and the statistical evidence that such "ills" cost the army much less lost time than does the male tendency to get drunk, become drug addicted, or go absent without leave have not alleviated this conviction, and cannot. It is clearly based, like the Neolithic taboos from which it stems, on a perception of the natural female biology as dangerous to the rational objectives of institutionalized warfare.

Second is the assumption that women must stand in a particular relation to men if the family and human existence are to continue or even be worth preserving. In the chivalric or polite version of this attitude, women are portrayed as nurturing mothers who must be protected. If the "mothers" of the race are forced to fight, their lives will be endangered, their availability as child rearers will be diminished, and their nurturing qualities destroyed. Simultaneously, however, women who are not protected by men are viewed as sexual objects; in this role they are simply part of the "booty" of war, to be raped, owned, and used. Typically in male cross-group dialogue, "my" women are good and protected; "your" women are bad and deserve to be raped. In effect, then, there are two male-controlled roles traditionally assigned women: Good Mothers who are protected and Bad Whores who are punished. The strength of these attitudes is believed likely to undermine the strength of any mixed-sex army. Troops will either overprotect the females in their unit at the cost of efficiency, or they will break the cohesiveness of the army by their tendency to harass and rape women perceived as natural booty. And, of course, training substantial numbers of women for armed combat might strengthen their resistance to both roles.

Third is the assumption that war is a specifically male ritual that is essential to male ego-strength and adult identity. Thus General William Westmoreland believed that "no man with gumption wants a woman to fight *his* battles"[6] while Marina Sulzberger, wife of a famous newspaper columnist, could assure American soldiers in Vietnam that "Every man should have his war."[7] Such views reflect the traditional connection between warfare and male initiatory rites. To allow women to participate in these rites will, it is believed, inevitably emasculate them. There is particular resentment of women's refusal to accept the sadistic toughening that has traditionally been a central element in the creation of men and soldiers. For example, the admission of women to Annapolis has been decried because it ended the traditional harassment of first-year men, a system that had previously meant

> I and my classmates were regularly tested and abused inside Bancroft Hall, our living spaces. We were pushed deep inside ourselves for that entire year, punished physically and mentally, stressed to the point that virtually every one of us completely broke down at least once. And when we finished our first year, we carried out the same form of abuse on other entering classes. That was the plebe system. It was harsh and cruel. It was designed to produce a man who would be able to be an effective leader in combat. . . .[8]

At the same time female success in battle is seen as a crippling attack on the fragile sexual identity and individual dignity of the male. Thus Arab soldiers facing sexually mixed Israeli combat units have fought to the death rather than allow themselves to be captured by women.

Clearly these three arguments or social facts are closely interrelated. Woman, defined by her reproductive and sexual biology, is a value that must be protected, a danger that must punished and controlled, and a condition from which the male must isolate himself, because she threatens the very selfhood of men (and, to a lesser extent, other women). This attitude, moreover, is not confined to the military perspective. Rather, the military drama is part of a wider pattern that in every society identifies woman with the flesh, mortality, and nature, focusing on her the awe and fear associated with the mysterious, the powerful, and the magical.

The exclusion of women from military operations is then simply one aspect of the human attempt to come to terms with the contingent nature of mortal existence.

> Alien, dangerous nature, conveniently concentrated near at hand in woman's flesh, can be controlled through ritual segregation, confinement, and avoidance; it can be subdued through conventionalized humiliation and punishment; it can be honored and placated through ceremonial gifts and adornments, through formalized gestures of respect and protectiveness. History and ethnography abundantly illustrate human use of this opportunity.[9]

Whether one seeks to control nature and existence through ritual warfare, the greedy accumulation of wealth and power, or scientific knowledge and technical power, woman is excluded as participant because she is the emotionally potent symbol of that which must be controlled.

Perls, originally trained as a Freudian analyst, never personally addressed the perplexing question of male-female relations—primarily because he believed that the most basic psychic problems of our century had to do with the blocking of aggression rather than sexuality per se.[10] In the 1970s, however, Dorothy Dinnerstein filled this void in gestalt theory. Trained in experimental gestalt psychology and a student of gestalt social psychologist Solomon Asch, she has brought the insights of that tradition to bear on the theoretical work of neo-Freudians such as N. O. Brown and Melanie Klein. She attempts to articulate the effect of our "gender arrangements" in child rearing upon our adult life as culture creators and makers of history. While she does not, in the process, consider the role of the psychological and bodily mechanisms (introjection, retroflection) that lie at the core of Perls's reasoning, there is no basic contradiction between her argument and conclusions and Perls's therapeutic position.

Dinnerstein believes that the psychological roots of our universal identification of women with nature as well as our concomitant strong love-hate relation with both lie in the biological fact of the human neonate's long dependency on adults and the historic fact that until the twentieth century, women's heavy childbearing responsibilities made her the logical child rearer. As a result, woman has provided for both girls and boys their first experience of the pains and delights of the flesh, of hopeless dependency and exhilarating self-sufficiency, of unavoidable submission and successful rebellion. Moreover, she is so experienced when our sense of the self ("I-ness") is least developed, emotions most overwhelming, and the capacity for rationality and competency weakest. As a result "the mother is first experienced by every one of us as an 'It,'" and woman never completely escapes this aura, "this role as half-human 'other.'"[11] Human attitudes toward "otherness" in general and women in particular are then heavily affected by the early, infantile resolutions adopted in dealing with the mixture of pain and pleasure her presence represents.

On the whole humans have been unable to integrate their resentment and gratitude, anger and love. Unable or unwilling to come to terms with the ambivalent, contingent character of reality, they have not only avoided acknowledging woman as a fellow human being but have insisted upon the bifurcated character of Woman/Mother/Nature, opposing the totally Good (whom one wants to own and placate) to the totally Bad (who must be punished or rejected). For men this fantasy is acted out directly as husband, warrior, and ruler; for women the satisfaction is more indirect. As wife, victim, and subject, she identifies with the loved-hated mother and accepts both adoration and denigration, while through identification with "her" male she vicariously acts out her own fantasies of reparation and revenge. The meaning of this human sexual arrangement is particularly clear in war, where man acts symbolically to control and dominate the Bad in the interests of the Good, while woman makes herself available as the protected mother, the punished victim, and the joyful and laudatory recipient of the fruits of victory.

Such a resolution of the basic traumas of mother-reared humanity may be neurotic, but it is, on the whole, an arrangement that has worked for the species until now. Moreover, the military strategy of peasant-based civilizations has been such as to maximize the entire range of the sexual drama while minimizing its destructive aspects. Ideally wars have been fought at the borders or on someone else's territory, so that one's own women and children are protected from real danger. Thus, as in the Trojan war, it remains a male game; women are either left safely at home or protected by the walls of ships and town. Only a Trojan defeat will label any sizable group of women "bad" and therefore suitable and actual victims.

In addition, when defeat looms, it is not uncommon for a society to lift the taboo on women as warriors. Besieged towns, guerrilla bands, and nations subjected (like Russia in World War II) to a massive invasion of the Motherland have regularly incorporated women into their fighting forces. When actual danger strikes too close to hearth and home, so that the game in fact becomes deadly serious, then the rules of the ritual no longer apply. Menstrually bloody females and lactating mothers join in the desperate fight for survival, and male sexual identity somehow survives the shock. Once the crisis is over, the traditional rules and sexual arrangements are reestablished and the role women actually played is likely to be forgotten or denied.

Since the end of World War II, however, military operations have possessed a bifurcated character. On the one hand there have been numerous "small" wars, which have included Afghanistan, Algeria, Angola, Burma, Cambodia, Cameroons, China, Cuba, East Germany, El Salvador, Haiti, Hungary, Indochina, Indonesia, Kashmir, Laos, Morocco, Mongolia, Palestine, Poland, Tibet, and Vietnam. Most have been wars of insurgency in which a guerrilla-type "liberation" army is pitted against either a major industrialized power or a local elite allied to, and provided with weaponry by, such a power. Writing in 1965, Bernard Fall estimated that "these wars, *in toto*, involved as many people as either of the two world wars, and caused as many casualties."[12] In addition, there have been "limited" wars, such as Korea and the several Israeli-Arab conflicts. In these, the great powers have either participated in a direct but deliberately restricted fashion or have been concerned spectators, holding the ring while smaller powers fought.

For the industrialized powers involved, such "limited" or "small" wars have represented a return to the "normality" of earlier civilized wars. They have been fought on someone else's territory in order to secure or defend control over political and economic resources and have involved little disruption of the ongoing civilian life of the industrially developed homelands. In contrast to the increasing involvement of women as both active participants and victims in World Wars I and II, such limited wars have seemed to represent a return to the masculine sanity of limited goals and *realpolitik*. (Typically, the involvement of women in insurgent armies is viewed, as in Vietnam, as evidence of the "uncivilized" and evil nature of the rebels.) Even the substantial antiwar sentiment that developed in France during the Algerian war and in the United States during Vietnam has essentially been dismissed as the temporary result of fighting "the wrong war," rather than as rejection of "the John Wayne image" and the game itself.

The limited nature of these wars has theoretically been made possible by the existence of an unfought but potential war of deterrence centered around the nuclear capabilities of the United States, Russia, and their allies. It is this unfought war that sets a limit to encroachment by either side on the "essential" interests of the other. To cross the boundaries deemed critical to survival can, and presumably will, provoke a nuclear attack, while an irresponsible preemptive attack is prevented by the fact that neither side can hope to wipe out the nuclear resources of the other. Thus the civilian populations of both NATO and Warsaw Pact countries are vulnerable to a devastating second-strike counterattack. The SALT disarmament negotiations have attempted to limit the escalating destructiveness (and costliness) of this strategy but have accepted its logic as the unavoidable parameters of any serious discussions.

Thus limited wars are made possible, and major wars prevented, by a strategy whose rules are clearly understood by the leaders of both sides. For the deterrence strategy to work both sides must believe in the ability and willingness of the other to deliver, under provocation, both a first- and second-strike response.

> Indeed, it is now an essential element of global stability that each superpower in effect bare the breast of its people to a nuclear attack or counterattack by its adversary; otherwise, deterrence, which depends on the vulnerability of each side to a reprisal by the other, would break down. . . . Once, military forces were deployed to protect the civilian population, but now the civilian population is deployed to protect the military forces. . . .[13]

Thus in 1962 millions of unarmed Russian and American women and children were the hostages whose endangered existence made the intricate power plays and ploys of the Cuban Missile Crisis both possible and presumably necessary.

Granted the character of the deterrence policy, it is difficult to believe that the contemporary refusal to use women as fighters stems from chivalric and loving motives. Though both Russia and the United States are theoretically committed to sexual equality, their actual policy affirms that women, weak enough to die as hostages, cannot as a group be armed or allowed access to the top levels of decision making and command. The implications of this strategy become even clearer if one follows out the logic of a nuclear policy that has failed to deter—a possibility inherent in the assumptions on which the strategy rests. (If humans are so aggressive and greedy that only fear keeps them peaceful, they are also irrational enough to make mistakes in calculation or to lash out in fear sometime within at least the next fifty to one hundred years.)

It is, of course, impossible to predict the course of any future war. Nonetheless, a nuclear war is likely to be short enough, and its logic has been pondered long enough by the strategists, for its main outlines and a series of probable conclusions to be broadly discernible. Unquestionably the primary target in any first strike would be the nuclear delivery resources of the opposition (the missile systems, long-range bomber bases, aircraft carriers, submarines, etc.) in an attempt to eliminate or reduce counterattack capabilities. The dispersal of such resources into rural or wilderness areas (Minuteman fixed silos, for example, currently occupy 9,000 square miles scattered over seven states) will reduce the losses in the civilian population but increase the general contamination of the environment. (In the early sixties Hermann Kahn estimated that even in a "small" nuclear war, the area around Strategic Air Command headquarters would be rendered uninhabitable for at least a century.) As such sites are heavily protected and most of their missiles and planes would be evacuated in counterattack response before the sites themselves were actually hit, it is unlikely that such strictly military targets would be the sole focus of any first strike strategy.

The next most obvious targets would be the military and political headquarters and the transportation, energy, and storage centers of the other country. As all tend to be located in major population centers, some large cities would be logical targets in even the most militarily conservative, rational first-strike planning. For the United States, for example, a minimum list might be expected to include Washington, New York, Chicago, Atlanta, Dallas, Los Angeles, and San Francisco. It will make military sense, moreover, to reserve the smaller 355 kiloton nuclear warheads for the more pinpointed military targets, while getting the maximum results from 20 megaton thermonuclear bombs by dropping them on the population centers. "Such a large thermonuclear device exploded in midtown Manhattan, for example, would probably kill 6,000,000 out of New York

City's 8,000,000 inhabitants, and produce an additional 1,000,000 or more deaths beyond the city limits."[14]

In the absence of an immediate surrender, civilian targets would escalate in importance, because the remaining military targets are likely to be too small and dispersed for attacks to be cost effective. Instead both sides are likely to adopt a strategy of old-fashioned attrition or "blackmail," in the conviction that though a nation "might be willing to fight to the last man . . . there are *almost no circumstances that are likely to occur* in which it should be willing to fight to the last woman and child."[15]

The costs of such a war are more difficult to predict than its strategic scenario, as both the potential nuclear armory and the military defense system has increased with each decade. If the figures given by American and Russian leaders in the early sixties are accurate (and they may have been exaggerated for rhetorical effect), then 150 to 300 million will die in the first eighteen hours of the war and 700 to 800 million before it is over. The long-term effects of radiation on the natural environment would be equally severe, resulting in the "almost total destruction of Europe, the Soviet Union, and North America."[16] On the other hand, RAND theorists such as Hermann Kahn have argued that with adequate civilian defense and thoughtful leaders, a nuclear war could and *would* be fought in a more limited and rational fashion. In that case the cost could be held to a "tolerable" limit of 20 million for the United States and an overall total of 70 to 80 million. However, such civilian defense costs have not been shouldered, while Kahn's optimism about political and military leaders is unconvincing. As the men who precipitate a nuclear war are all too likely to be fearfully angry, to expect them to be calmly rational and restrained once the war begins is to ignore what we know of the history of human behavior.

While recognizing that total devastation is a technical and political possibility, let us assume that the war is brought to a halt after a few days when the death toll reaches the 200 to 300 million level. This would mean that roughly one third of the population of Russia, the United States, and Europe had been killed and accords with Kahn's finding that most of his acquaintances in the scientific and political community *on reflection* considered such a loss justified if it was the only way in which the United States could meet its treaty obligations to Europe. In that case, regardless of who "wins" or who "surrenders," all major participants will face a similar "post-attack environment" without the possibility of receiving any substantial outside aid. Aside from the enormous loss of life, there will be concomitant psychic dislocations, long-range and as yet unpredictable genetic costs, the contamination of large portions of the environment, and the likelihood of serious epidemics and eventual ecological disasters.

At the same time the surviving population of each country is likely to be confronted with a serious breakdown in existing political and economic structures. As S. G. Winter, Jr., an analyst with RAND Corporation, testified in a Civil Defense hearing in 1961,

> a complete failure in the recovery effort might occur . . . [in] a situation where the effectiveness of the Federal Government and many State governments is greatly diminished, the banking system disrupted, most surviving firms are bankrupt, electric power and water supply systems are severely damaged, and the transportation network broken in many places, and where few survivors have the responsibility, authority, and plans to do anything about it.[17]

Since most of the conditions he lists are precisely the kinds of situations that logical military planning would attempt to produce in the first forty-eight hours of attack, this is not just a possible but a highly probable result of nuclear war. Moreover, the breakdown of the economy will be accentuated by the well-documented tendency of adults in such a catastrophe situation to seek out, and concentrate their attention on, the survival of their own immediate family.

Under these conditions it is very likely that, as in Hiroshima and Nagasaki,

> when people are unable to meet their minimum needs by the usual and socially desirable means of participating in the production process, they are likely to turn to unusual and socially undesirable means, such as foraging, plunder, and sterile trading in household goods.[18]

In addition, as the survivors flee cities or rural areas that have become uninhabitable, this mentality will go with them and be met by an equally antisocial response. Thus in the early 1960s, as a reaction to Civil Defense planning, local officials in Nevada

> considered creating a five-thousand man militia to repulse potential refugees fleeing bombed areas in Southern California. . . . Another official advised Las Vegas residents to build bomb shelters in their backyards, and then went on to say, "If the builder takes a shotgun into the shelter with him as I advocate to protect his family, the head of the family must be prepared to repel invaders—even those who come from across the street."[19]

(Of course, if the MX missile track had been installed as planned, Nevada and Utah would have been subject to devastation in the first minutes of the war.) The result of such social dislocation, Winter believes, will be "a much lower level of economic life" and the eventual re-creation of minimum social organizations "at the level of self-sufficient families, communities, or regions."[20]

There is one group of survivors who might have both the authority and power to eventually impose "law and order" at a wider level of coordination: the predominantly male army. Substantial elements of this organization are likely to survive the war intact and armed, though its immediate effectiveness will be undermined by the tendency of some men to go absent without leave in order to find their families. However, if enough economic resources remain centralized to support these military groups, unattached men (including the widowed) will remain with their unit and others will join or return to these fighting hierarchies (and the camp followers they will attract). As the interests of the self-sufficient familial communities and the parasitic, centralized military will generally be opposed, conflicts are likely to develop along the lines of a sheep-goat dichotomy: that is, between those men who are bonded with women and those who have bonded with other men. The "post-attack environment" may thus produce hundreds of little Trojan wars before some kind of stability is reached.

Most nuclear futurists have been men. It is understandable that in their predictions they have ignored the probable changes in sexual arrangements that these conditions will produce. From a female perspective, however, it is clear that, whether the family or the army proves to be the most enduring and powerful organizational group, the primary victims will be women and the small gains we have made toward more independence and greater equality. Lacking arms and training in their use, women in the "post-attack environment" will be forced to seek for themselves and their children the protection of weapon-bearing and therefore more powerful men. Once again we will all be either barefoot and pregnant in the fallout shelter or servants and prostitutes in the baggage train. In either case we will be docile and appropriately grateful, weeping (like the handmaidens of Patroklus) for our own fate when a man who has been kind to us dies.

In effect, then, nuclear strategy temporarily protects the women of industrial nations from war; when it fails to deter, however, the women of all industrial nations will become the primary victims. An actual nuclear war thus abandons the traditional dualistic (placate and punish) approach to mother/nature and casts the feminine strictly in the role of conquered victim. That shift alone is enough to indicate that the potential and probable major war of the future will have a symbolic and emotional meaning that differentiates it from the military rituals of the past. Though the reenslavement of women and the destruction of nature are not conscious goals of our nuclear stance, the language of our bodies, our postures, and our acts is a critical clue to our unexamined motives and desires.

Early in his book *On Thermonuclear War*, Kahn tells a story about himself that provides a rare autobiographical glimpse of the man. In the late fifties he was giving a public lecture in which he explained that if every survivor of a nuclear war had received about 250 roentgens, about 1 percent of the next generation who could have been healthy would now be born defective and that this burden would continue in diminishing degrees for another twenty to forty generations. He added that he could imagine conditions in which both American and Russian statesmen would accept this risk as the necessary cost of important political goals.

> At this point in the lecture a lady in the audience got up and said in a very accusing voice, "I don't want to live in your world in which 1 percent of the children are born defective." My answer

was rather brutal, I fear. "It is not *my* world," I observed, and I then pointed out if she did not want to live in a world in which 1 percent of the children were born defective she had a real problem, since 4 percent of the children are born defective *now*.[21]

The point of the story for him is that, though "war is a terrible thing . . . so is peace."

> And it is proper, with the kind of calculations we are making today, to compare the horror of war and the horror of peace and see how much worse it is.
> I do not believe it will help us . . . to discuss the problems of war and peace on an emotional rather than a factual basis. . . . In the complicated and dangerous world in which we are going to live, it will only increase the chance of tragedy if we refuse to make and discuss objectively whatever quantitative estimates can be made.[22]

Kahn's response was, in fact, typically masculine in that he deliberately avoided the emotional content of the woman's remarks in order to respond to its factual content in a way that dismissed her "to thine house . . . and to thine own tasks" as an ignorant, silly, and sentimental woman. His own general comments are even more instructive, reflecting as they do a rejection of the human condition ("it is not *my* world") that in its tragic aspects he clearly finds terrifying and horrible. Despite his theoretical assumption that there is no circumstance under which a nation *should* fight to the last woman and child, his response to an actual woman and to the realities of human reproduction (defined by him as a female problem "which only pregnant women worry about") reflects a distaste and disgust that is not far from destructive rage. Moreover, he can repeat the story unself-consciously because he is in fact unaware of his own emotions, perceiving himself only as the instrumental social scientist, concerned with the facts and dedicated to discussing "objectively whatever quantitative estimates can be made."

Kahn's moment of self-revelation is not important for what it reveals about him as a lone individual, but rather as an example of the scientific mentality, quantitative methodology, and technical experimentation that produced the atomic and thermonuclear bombs and informs current strategic thought. He is merely one of the many "decent" men and women who are heirs to that cultural tradition, exceptional only in his outspoken courage. The stress on "objectivity" and the quantitative approach as a guarantee of truth, as well as the relegation of emotions to a peripheral and unconscious existence, has carried from its beginning in the seventeenth century the burden of an essential hostility to the body, the feminine, and the natural environment.

Both the literature and the law courts of the late sixteenth century document the existence in European society of a growing fear of the female, experienced both as "wild and uncontrollable nature that could render violence, storms, droughts, and general chaos" and as human witch who "raised storms, caused illness, destroyed crops, obstructed generation, and killed infants."[23] This perception of nature and women as angry and hostile rested on an element of reality (as well as projection). On the one hand the commercial activities of the previous century were producing ecological disasters as northern forests were denuded to build ships, southern rivers were contaminated by mining wastes, and the air made unhealthy by coal-burning fires. At the same time the attempt to substitute the ethics of an economically aggressive nuclear family for the communitarian supportiveness of village and guild was creating strife at the most basic level of human existence. In particular, older women grumbled and cursed when denied traditional charities, while younger women increasingly joined rebellious and socially egalitarian millennarian groups. If the commercial revolution were to proceed unchecked, both nature and women had to be controlled.

In the realm of sexual politics, the male-dominated institutions of church and state responded by organizing a witch hunt that sent at least 100,000 women to the stake after subjecting them to ferocious torture. The ruling elite thus acted very directly to undermine any female tendency to rebel, while simultaneously attacking as heretical the old animist tradition that had provided women with a direct, nonhierarchical access to power. In addition, the torture chamber and law court provided models for the new experimental approach to nature. For example,

> Bacon stated that the method by which nature's secrets might be discovered consisted in investigating the secrets of witchcraft by inquisition... [from which] "a useful light may be gained not only for a true judgment of the offenses of persons charged with such practices, *but likewise for the further disclosing of the secrets of nature. Neither ought a man to make scruple of entering and penetrating into these holes and corners, when the inquisition of truth is his whole object....*"[24]

The efficacy of either approach was theoretically and psychologically in danger, however, as long as the old vitalist conception of nature possessed emotional strength. Women who wanted to be "good" might willingly accept passive dependency and confinement to the narrowing walls of the private home, but witchcraft still offered a powerful option for the angrily independent. Nature also was inevitably ever present and inconceivably more powerful. As long as nature was perceived as living and holy, attacks on her body such as Bacon suggested would smack of blasphemy and arouse sensations of fear and anxiety. Thus Edmund Spenser, a contemporary of Bacon, repeated the warnings of Pliny, Ovid, and Seneca and denounced human mining operations, since

> Then gan a cursed hand the quiet wombe
> Of his great Grandmother with steele to wound,
> And the hid treasures in her sacred tombe
> With Sacrilege to dig....[25]

Such ancient cosmologies, in fact, demanded a conscious acceptance of some limits upon human enterprise, including at least a partial recognition of "how vulnerable, how isolated and finite, it—the living body—is."[26]

In the seventeenth century, however, western European thought deliberately broke with that tradition and sought to avoid that recognition. Carolyn Merchant has traced how, instead, the classical image of nature as mother was transformed first into the vision of nature as welcoming rape and eventually into the idea of nature as machine. Merchant correctly labels this intellectual transition the (symbolic) death of nature. There was, however, a psychological side to this transformation that she does not address. The primal human perception of nature as living was, in fact, not just accidental. It was rather the result of the human psychic structure and particularly of the role normally played by our emotions in human existence.

Emotions are a basic, important, and early developed part of the human cognitive capacity. They are

> our way of representing to ourselves the fate of our goals . . . a direct consequence of the understanding of our situation . . . [a] direct response to the realization of our dependence on the surroundings and the necessity of choosing and deciding . . . the concrete expression of our involvement.[27]

Arising as a result of the interaction between the body and its environment, they are both felt in, and expressed through, the flesh itself. Indeed, "emotions and expression are integral parts of the same process; both are the organ's response to given conditions. The expressive part of emotions is usually the visible form of the emotional experience, mirroring its content and dynamics."[28] Thus emotions are the tie between our environment, bodies, and thoughts, the cognitive boundary between the self and the field with which it is involved. Their absence is no guarantee of truth; indeed to deny expression or consciousness of emotions in a situation of real involvement requires the retroflection of enormous energy against the body itself and therefore a loss of clarity and vitality.

As long as the emotional boundary remains active and aware, however, the world appears

> neither inanimate nor empty but redundant with life; and life has individuality, in man and beast and plant, and in every phenomenon which confronts man. . . . Any phenomenon may at any time face him, not as "It," but as "Thou." "Thou" is not contemplated with intellectual detachment; it is experienced as life confronting life, involving every faculty of man in a reciprocal relationship. Thoughts, no less than acts and feelings, are subordinated to this experience.[29]

Such emotional awareness can and has coexisted with both an instrumental approach to nature and the speculative philosophy of classical and Christian thought. But the awareness of the universe as sharing with humans both life and sentience has also acted as a limit on human manipulation and greed.

Thus "objectivity" as an attempt to block any emotional response to nature was a prerequisite both for unlimited exploitation of nature and for any widespread adoption of the mechanistic model of reality. In that sense the symbolic death of nature required the burial by retroflection of human emotionality, while the anger, fear, and greed rampant in the seventeenth century provided the energy for that retroflection. In psychological terms, such a retroflection and the accompanying projection upon nature of the myth of the machine were simply a new and extreme extension of the very ancient human attempt to

> deny the loss of omnipotent infant unity with the first parent—to deny, that is, our dependence on what we cannot control—by ignoring the (fluid and permeable, but never wholly breachable) borders that imprison the weak self in its separateness . . . to maintain a fantasy of being safer and more self-sufficient—because less limited and distinct—than we would know ourselves to be if we kept full emotional contact with the needy, imperilled flesh.[30]

Since human beings make machines, nature as machine is ultimately the creation of human will grown godlike. But the illusion of omnipotence is purchased at the cost of a radical deadening of the body itself, since the neutrality of the environment can be purchased only through a socialization process (such as that discussed in chapter 11) that inhibits "spontaneous pleasure, playfulness, anger, indignation and fear."[31]

It also requires a social structure that radically separates home and family (as the enclosed and truncated sphere of the despised flesh and its emotions) from the public world where rationality, objectivity, and technology can reign supreme and unchallenged. All societies have traditionally institutionalized some separation of men and women in terms of occupation and assigned gender personality. The public sphere, moreover, has usually been seen as appropriately male. But modern technological society is unusual in the radical degree to which it has physically separated women and children from adult males and from the realms of economic production and artistic endeavor as well as those of political ritual and decision making.

As a result, infancy and early childhood have become almost totally dominated by women, while men and the young are segregated and alienated from each other in a way they have not been in hunting and gathering or even farming communities. Moreover, if the male child has not by personal choice begun to devalue the body and its emotions during infancy, he will soon learn that the price for admission to the modern male realm of enterprise and command is the repression (retroflection) of all the tenderer emotions and sensibilities. (This has not always been true: for example, Achilles could cry noisily and openly with no loss of prestige among his peers. When Ed Muskie wept a few tears in public, however, he found he had disqualified himself as a presidential candidate.) But though love, fear, and sorrow can be repressed, they cannot be annihilated. They remain a continuing, troubling element in the psyche, the source of a vague sense of anxiety and powerlessness, calling for continuing retroflection of anger and judgmentalness against the self. But that deadening or numbing of emotional sensibility is the price required if power-oriented objectivity and the ability to view nature as inanimate matter is to be maintained in the public sphere.

The movement of women into the public workforce in recent decades has not changed this situation. Not only has there been no balancing countermovement of men into the child-rearing role, but most female workers have been channeled into low-status and unorganized service jobs that are simply extensions of the despised family and without significant impact on the realm of culture and decision making. Those isolated women who have battled their way into the "male" professions and positions of power have usually done so only by paying the male price: by being tough, competitive, and (above all) nonemotional and objective. As a result, they are often (like British Prime Minister Margaret Thatcher and U.S. Ambassador to the United Nations Jeane Kirkpatrick) more "masculine" than their male peers.

The men and women who in the sixteenth century began the series of discrete and multitudinous choices that we today label the scientific, technological, and industrial revolutions were not consciously choosing death and disaster. Like their remote ancestors, they were risking the unknown in an attempt to create a better life —for themselves, their families, and even for humanity as a whole. (Thus Bacon hoped that the benefits of his discoveries would extend "to the whole race of man . . . through all time."[32]) What none of our enterprising forebears could have predicted, however, was the size of the psychic costs (and the physical risks) imposed by their decisions. None grasped the full implication of Bacon's aphorism that "Nature to be commanded must be obeyed."[33] Thus again and again western society has blithely chosen abundance of "having" in preference to abundant "being."

Nor did our predecessors intend to eliminate entirely the world of the flesh and the emotions, to destroy the realm of the female and the infantile. Instead the hope has been that these could be preserved within the private walls of the nuclear family as a retreat from, and an antidote to, the harsh and scarifying demands of the public realm. Indeed, the hope still buoys many and is one element in the desperate resistance to the women's liberation movement that goes beyond the issue of male versus female power. If women also enter the public sphere and become "as men," if they too become warriors dedicated to power and death, then the last refuge of the body with its sensitivities and needs seems threatened with extinction. For most men and women this is a frightening and undesired possibility.

What such resistance avoids recognizing is that the home, procreation, and the ongoing life of the species was already in danger by the end of the 1950s and at the height of the feminine mystique and female domesticity. The experiment in radically separating the male world of enterprise from the female world of emotions has not worked for either realm. The shrunken world of the isolated family has turned out to be an inadequate (and crazy-making) channel for the energies and enterprising needs of most women, while male enterprise, separated entirely from the emotional life of the flesh, has been committed primarily to the building of more and greater (dead) machines. Whatever our initial intentions and hopes, we have chosen a way of life that now threatens the very procreativity of the species and of nature herself.

Fortunately, our modern technology makes other alternatives possible. We could, if we would, end the radical segregation both of men and women and of reason and the emotions. If we can find, as our ancestors did, the courage to risk and dare new ways and new cultural forms, we can reintegrate our personal and social psyches and our ways of life. Admitting women and their emotions to the public sphere and men into the child-rearing family (with all that implies in terms of reallocation of national wealth and time) can be a means of reenlivening and increasing the truly imaginative fertility of both realms. Our cultural norms may then be less "objective" and harsh, but they will also be more realistic and more truly in love with being itself.

13
Boundaries of Power

All animals, including Homo sapiens, possess aggressive capacities—invaluable as instruments for furthering the survival and growth of the individual and the species. Humans, moreover, because of their long childhood and their genetically based drive to create and transmit culture, are capable of separating this aggressive capacity from the satisfaction of simple physiological needs. Indeed, all human societies impose taboos on some aspects of eating, sexual relations, and the distribution of goods, thus essentially inhibiting total physical spontaneity of adults. At the same time societies create culturally defined gestalts that direct aggressive capacity into symbolic and utilitarian channels perceived as useful to the community as a whole. Because the human infant is genetically coded to learn, and indeed gains great satisfaction from experiences of (imitative) competency, our tendency to assimilate both taboos and culturally defined goals as a part of our basic psychic structure is a normal part of our species' survival capacity. Even if aggressive energy channeled into building a dam or constraining oneself to conform to an ascetic ideal is individually harmful, it is functional for the group. Interestingly, most societies have considered battle and war to be just such socially constructive, if individually risky, enterprises.

This judgment about warfare seems to be based on two psychological characteristics of the human species. In the first place, the human consciousness is predisposed to create, out of the multifarious sense data of daily life, patterns that impose order or structure (meaning) upon the chaos of experienced reality. Dreams, rites, symbols, language, and myth (including art, literature, music, and scientific theory) all attest to the power of this need and the beautiful and useful purposes it has served. War appears to be not only one of the most elaborate and widely shared of these gestalt-creating and satisfying acts, but also one by which humans have addressed most specifically the basic terror and disequilibrium created by unexpected death and disaster. From its Neolithic beginnings war has clearly been perceived by human beings as a critical ritual for establishing appropriate (ordered) relations between the nonhuman environment and the human community. In a world in which, as individuals and societies, humans are buffeted by painful events that seem to have no pattern or meaning, war has been a gallant attempt to establish a humanly defined pattern by returning the blow. Thus the potentially incomplete, lopsided, and chaotic character of actual experience is given symmetry, completeness, and balance. Death and destruction may not be eliminated, but they are forced into an ordered gestalt that human consciousness can encompass because it is commensurate with human limits and meanings.

At the same time human socialization patterns often create emotional needs that are essentially compulsive and unsatisfiable. Thus we are distinctive among animals in our socially induced desire for revenge, our greediness, our guilt and resentment-laden need for the confluence of punishment, and our anxious and paranoid sense of powerlessness. Such psychic rigidities are not only individually stunting; when too widely shared within a culture, they are disruptive of any kind of stable community bonding. Among the many creative ways in which humans have attempted to deal with such disruptive tendencies, war has seemingly been one of the more successful. Rather than allow such potentially destructive and angry aggressiveness free reign to disturb social cohesiveness, our cultures have directed such energy into the safe channels and external goals provided by the ritual of warfare. Of course, the prescribed "enemy" is seldom if ever the true (though unconscious) object of the original and uncompleted gestalts that feed such compulsive aggressiveness, fear, and anger. Thus the energy mobilized for war is neurotically misdirected. But the ritual functionality of war at least insures that such energy will be socially useful. If humans are or have become neurotic animals, we are at least adaptively imaginative and creative in the uses we make of our neuroses.

Such an analysis, however, raises serious questions. In particular, "by what criteria does one prefer to regard 'human nature' as what is actual in the spontaneity of children" and other animals?[2] After all, neurosis (like symbol making) is an ancient and omnipresent human tendency. To what extent and by what standards is human aggressiveness, however rigidly controlled and repetitive, any more unnatural than that of other animals? The answer, I think, must be sought in biology and ecology. From the perspective of biology, the capacity for aggression serves the purpose of life: One destructures food in order to assimilate it and create the energy for continued existence. Thus aggression is simply one of the instrumentalities whereby the cycle of life and death is made possible. As long as destructive aggression is balanced by re-creation it must be viewed as natural and ecologically sound.

There is, however, evidence that in certain individuals this balance between creativity and destructiveness is lost, so that instead of creating or defending life, aggression becomes sterile. Nowhere, for example, is such deadened aggressiveness more noticeable than on the battlefield, where one of the enduring appeals of combat for certain individuals rests on a sinister "delight in destruction." Of this phenomena, Glenn Gray has observed:

> We sense in it always the Mephistophelean cry that all created things deserve to be destroyed. . . . The utter absence of love in this inverted kind of creation makes the delight essentially sterile.

... Soldier-killers usually experience an ineffable sameness and boredom in their lives. The restlessness of such men in rest areas behind the front is notorious.[3]

Gray goes on to ask whether Empedocles and Freud were right in imagining that Strife and Thanatos were as strong and recurrent as Love and Eros. Biologically speaking, the answer is yes. But what Gray has been describing is not a balanced psyche. Rather, the soldier-killer exhibits a personality structure in which the capacity for aggression and destruction has gained control and overthrown the capacity for union and creativity.

In gestalt terms the aggressive impulses of such soldier-killers have been so retroflected against the self as to inhibit the capacity for, and any delight in, spontaneity, affection, or union. Such men, in effect, want to be beaten. The desire to destroy "all created things" is simply an unconscious magnification of what is at bottom self-hatred. When Ernest Juenger, speaking of his experience in World War I as a storm trooper, emphasizes the "monstrous desire for annihilation" that hovered over the battlefield, he inadvertently gives the show away: The projected desire was his own. The berserker soldier is a suicidal man who has been unable to develop an adequate sense of the boundaries that separate the self from its environment. Thus his self-hatred and anomie produce a raging desire to obliterate all of creation.

Just as individuals can become suicidal, so can societies. It is at this point, when social aggression threatens to overbalance social creativity, that human neurosis clearly ceases to be a form of adaptive adjustment and becomes potentially deadly vicious and without redeeming social or biological value. We do not know exactly how many human societies have maneuvered themselves into such deadly dilemmas in the past, but the evidence is clear that it has happened. Unfortunately, our technological society seems to have developed just such a suicidal tendency at the same time that our destructive capacity is so great that we may eliminate not only mankind but all other forms of life on earth—an ecological disaster.

All the rituals of war that we have analyzed have involved an attempt, either unconsciously or in full awareness, to control nature in the interest of human happiness and survival. Thus our Neolithic ancestors believed that through battle they could reestablish the orderly potency of the original dream time and thereby force death to remain within its proper/desired channels. Similarly, both rulers and ruled in civilized empires perceived war as a divinely ordained ritual for establishing the proper relation both within the human sphere and between the human and the divine. The result, symbolized in the golden booty of war and the gold-encrusted ritual of court and temple, would be life and prosperity for all. Even the more socially selfish understanding of the heroic warrior valued battle because it induced a sense of vitality and self-forgetfulness that made it seem an appropriate yoga or sacrament for union with the ultimate source of life. Thus existence in the present was set at risk in pursuit of the haunting promise of immortality or nirvana.

Modern mythology has in many ways continued the more materialistic, this-worldly understanding of traditional civilizations. As a society (if not as individuals) we have been as convinced as our remote forebears that (if we could just find the proper gesture) war would be a means of eliminating external dangers and establishing the good life. Increasingly since the seventeenth century we have devoted an enormous amount of our time, energy, material wealth, and blood to this pursuit. At the same time, however, we have lost or rejected some of the mythic beliefs that made traditional understandings of war tenable and even functional.

Traditional cultures clearly understood war as a form of discourse between the human and "the other." As a result they accepted that the conversation must conform to certain syntactical rules and limits if the communication was to be effective. Moreover, they also hypothesized that war, like any other valued dialogue, was ongoing, continuous, and cyclical. The natural environment and the human enemy must, in some degree, be protected and preserved, if only as necessary elements for continuing the divine-human drama. Such conventions not only insured that battle followed cosily familiar patterns, but they also insisted upon a recognition of boundaries, on the distinction between the actor and the play, the figure and the background. An infantile desire to control reality may have been acted out through the ritual, but the rite also demanded that the original infantile sense of omnipotence and omnipresence be renounced. The existence of a will different from, or contrary to, the human (individual or social) will was insisted upon and the solipsism of childhood denied reality. Thus even as Achilles hoped for the obliteration of his world, the mythology of that world forced him to recognize that only "the gods" could grant his wish and they were unlikely to do so.

Since the seventeenth century, however, humans have slowly but thoroughly abandoned, in theory and act, any sense of life as a dialogue between the human and the divine. Initially this decision was made out of pride and will, as nonhuman nature was denied living reality and intent and the cosmic drama was reduced to the anthropomorphic stage of History. The rules of engineering—mass times velocity—became the new syntax of war, and war itself became a testing ground (an underwriters' laboratory) in which a people were either certified as safe or rejected as malfunctioning mistakes. Since World War I, however, any facile belief in the progressive character of History has become intellectually and emotionally untenable. But if no inherent pattern in History insures progress, no dialogue with History is possible: Its answers come always too late.

In and of itself, such a situation is pregnant with the possibility for growth, creativity, and maturity. Our inability to believe any longer in a mystic "otherness" is also potentially the occasion for reclaiming religious projections as parts of our own being. The recognition that there are no externally given rules implies an opportunity to abandon introjections and retroflections and accept our own response-ability, that is, our ability to respond to reality, to give meaning and structure to our lives. And, finally, this creative void provides an opportunity for establishing contact with the actual living environment that surrounds us.

Unfortunately, the collapse of any mythic dialogue was accompanied by a loss of any sense of boundaries and therefore of any sense of the reality of our surroundings. Thus Samuel Beckett perceives man as waiting endlessly upon an empty stage; neither human artifacts nor the vibrant cosmos any longer truly exist. Additionally, the symbolic mechanization of nature and the actual mechanization of human life has been paralleled in both capitalist and communist societies by a fearful rejection of differences. But if the earlier mythic conceptions of a divine "other" were human projections, our contemporary solipsism is simply a delusion. The search for uninterrupted confluence is no less infantile for being buttressed with electronic gadgets, nuclear arsenals, and test tubes of DNA.

In actual physiological terms there are, of course, always both boundaries and interpenetrations between an organism and its environment. The individual is at once both an entity with distinct physical limits and a pulsating process that takes in sensations, air, and nourishment and gives back sensations, air, and excrement. Without both structure and interpenetration, life as such is impossible, while it is also at these boundary points of contact that we are most fully alive and aware. This is where gestalts form, emotions arise, and energy is mobilized as excitement—and where pain, loss, and frustration first affect us.

All adults experience sporadically and sharply moments of confluence in which the awareness of contact boundaries disappear in the ecstasy of orgasm, extreme concentration, or effective ritual. But only newborn infants live in a seemingly continuous confluence broken by the sporadic and sharply felt experience of hunger, cold, and wetness. Moreover, only in that original confluence can we be passive and successfully dependent, without any need to mobilize our own capacities for self-support beyond a few cries and the simple act of latching onto and sucking at a breast perceived as part of our own being.

For humans the gradual loss of that early sense of confluence should normally be compensated for by a growing delight in our own independence and self-sufficiency. If, however, we refuse to take the step toward maturity, our only alternative (since physically we must grow up or die) is to deaden our awareness of the contact boundaries in an attempt to preserve that original infantile paradise. All neurotic processes are an attempt, to some degree, to interrupt some part of the normal functioning of these contact boundaries (by introjection, projection, etc.) in order to avoid pain in and to manipulate the external world. In certain individuals, however, all contact boundaries are deliberately denied awareness in a search for permanent confluence.

> He cannot experience himself because he has lost all sense of himself. . . . He does not know where he leaves off and others

begin. As he is unaware of the boundary between himself and others, he cannot make good contact with them. Nor can he withdraw from them. Indeed, he cannot even make contact with himself.[4]

In bodily terms such a personality structure expresses itself through the hanging-on bite of the suckling or the alcoholic; socially it involves a babylike attempt to remain dependent, in a liking for big government, big corporations, big father figures. Moreover, such "muscular paralysis and desensitization" tend to find release only in the random spontaneity of uncontrolled hysteria.

Unfortunately, such a neurotic defense against loss seems to have become a characteristic of technological society as a whole. One clue to its pervasiveness in our culture is our common attitude toward death, which is the symbolic adult equivalent of that original infantile loss. As the French historian Philip Ariès has convincingly demonstrated, death has become *the* taboo subject and grief *the* interdicted behavior of the mid-twentieth century. Our mourning rituals attempt to deny (via embalming in the United States, for example) the reality of death, while conventions prohibit both the display and the experience of grief and loss.

> Thus during the wakes or farewell "visitations" which have been preserved, the visitors come without shame or repugnance. This is because in reality they are not visiting a dead person, as they traditionally have, but an almost living one who, thanks to embalming, is still present, as if he were awaiting you. . . . The definitive nature of the rupture has been blurred. Sadness and mourning have been banished from this calming reunion.[5]

As a result, the most final and limiting boundary of organic existence is avoided. "And surprise! Our life is not as a result gladdened." Ariès goes on to pose the possibility that there is a fundamental relationship between one's idea of death and one's vision of the living self. "If this is the case, must we take for granted . . . contemporary man's recoil from the desire to exist?"[6]

Indeed, the attempt to maintain the experience of confluence exacts a deadly price, since the illusion is not reality. At a minimum, we are still physically in contact with our environment; desires and pains can be retroflected or pushed from awareness, but not eliminated. They remain an unexplainable part of our experience, sources of restlessness, boredom, and the insatiable pursuit of fun. Since we refuse to recognize the existence of our surroundings, we also have no external focus for our anger and no recognition that desiring conflict might be a source of new possibilities and joy: hence our unconscious self-hatred and our suicidal-homicidal rage. In the end, our unsuccessful attempt to avoid both the pains and joys of organic life means that we are more than half in love with "easeful death."

By the late 1960s, if not before, it was clear that the strategy of scientific domination, mechanical functionality, and rational objectivity had not worked. Nature, like any human mother, has her own designs, very real limits to her abundance, and enough mortality to die. Humans have been equally resistant to the process of mechanization and control: Women have refused to be completely passive and the "lesser races and classes" are rebellious. Patriarchal nuclear families and industrial empires alike are disintegrating as the limits to human power become increasingly clear-cut. As good scientific materialists (whether communists or capitalists), we have held our breath until we are blue in the face and still the cosmos has refused to conform to our desires. We seem faced, at last, with the desperate choice of either throwing a tantrum or growing up.

If gestalt therapists and my historical analysis are correct, however, an angry, moralistic demand for immediate nuclear disarmament is likely to be counterproductive. The men and women who built and support those nuclear arsenals are deeply frightened individuals seeking security in a defensive armor. The more they feel attacked, the more likely they are to cling to their imagined defense against the frightening fantasy of disintegration and meaninglessness. But if we cannot hope to secure immediately a dismantling of our nuclear warheads, we can at least attempt to reorganize our army in a manner that would allow such fears to be tackled more realistically and perhaps satisfyingly. In particular, universal conscription of men and women might dramatize the full meaning of our military policy, inhibit imperialistic adventures, and provide a sense of defensive preparedness more satisfying than the ghostly presence of nuclear submarines and missile sites. The inclusion of women within the ranks of the military would, moreover, force awareness of the new symbolic and practical meaning of our existing nuclear policy.

I am tentative about this suggestion, however, since I believe that survival requires us eventually to move away from the ritual of war entirely. Splitting the atom was like opening Pandora's box. Since the secret is out, there is no way in which we can free ourselves, in a future war, from the temptation to use it. Indeed, the only valid justification for our current policy of nuclear deterrence is that it clarifies conspicuously the fact that any future war between major powers will in fact be a nuclear war. But how can we hope to dismantle the military institutions and ideologies so deeply embedded in our culture and psyches?

The very act of writing a book like this is in itself an expression of optimism and hope, a demonstration of faith that awareness and knowledge are sources of health and healing. Certainly I am aware of the danger in which we stand and of the fact that we may not have much time left in which to abandon our current folly. Nonetheless I am also sustained by the knowledge that in the past human societies have been capable of making momentous adjustments in the service of life and have sometimes made such adjustments in a very short period of time. There is at least the possibility, then, that once again we can exercise our capacity to create, rather than simply repeat, cultural forms.

One of the unfortunate distortions imposed by a historical approach such as I have adopted is that it suggests a causal determinism that, in fact, does not exist. For example, when one focuses on socialization processes as the catalyst to social neuroses, there is an implication that adults cause infantile responses. But, in fact, human infants always choose (at least from within a fairly broad cultural range) the way in which they will react; we are intrinsically and fully response-able for ourselves. Similarly, whatever the past context of those early choices, we have always the present possibility to choose anew. We can cling to our old, unconscious but familiar defenses or we can bring them to loving awareness as once useful tools for survival, and then abandon them as no longer necessary or functional. We can, as individuals and nations, make such a choice now.

Modern industrialized society is not as monolithic as my analysis has suggested. Beneath the dominant modality controlling our policy and mythology, a substantial counterculture has emerged in every part of the world that continuously struggles to reverse or modify the life-threatening elements in our social and cultural complex. Within the United States alone, ecologists, pacifists, socialist-anarchists, the human growth movement, and feminists all direct attention to aspects of our malaise—and do so with an increasingly realistic sense of the interconnectedness and interdependence of their concerns and efforts. There are also countless individuals and families within the population of every continent who not only live life to the fullest, but value and would preserve it.

The answer to the problem posed by our current neurotic dependency on war lies, I believe, in fostering every possible change that increases our sense of individual empowerment and response-ability as well as our contact with, and our tolerance for, a diverse and conflictful environment. Though all of the evidence suggests that the major root of war lies in our human sense of fraility and anxiety, the opposite is also true.

> *"Rendering oneself unarmed when one has been the best armed,*
> *out of a height of feeling—that is the means to real peace of mind;*
> *whereas the so-called armed peace, as it now exists in all countries,*
> *is the absence of peace of mind. . . ."* Nietzsche rightly sees that
> . . . peace will never occur as a consequence of weakness, exhaustion, or fear.[7]

We can only let go of the need for battle when we can find other ways in which to experience our ability to survive and support ourselves. Moreover, as long as Eros balances Thanatos, even if precariously, there is reason for hope. Of course, we have no guarantee that a hopeful vision of the future will be fulfilled: The unknown is always a risk. What seems sure, however, is that a complete absence of hope is only too likely to be a self-fulfilling prophecy.

14
Of Machines, Bureaucrats and Outlaws

> Despite the propaganda, there are no monsters, or none that can be finally buried. Finish one off and circumstances and the radio create another.
> — *Margaret Atwood*[1]

Guerrilla warfare is one of the oldest of all modes of war. It is also a widespread and entrenched characteristic of modern life. Even as the nuclear threat has restrained super-power confrontations, guerrilla wars have escalated. Revolutionary fighters in Asia, urban terrorists in South America, Ireland and the Middle East, tribal guerrillas in Afghanistan, Africa and Kurdish Iraq have become a continuing part of the international military scene. Moreover, the nationalist violence which has erupted with the lifting of party control in Russia and Eastern Europe suggest that those areas may also spawn guerrilla activities in the near future. Indeed, guerilla operations may be *the* war of the post-atomic era.

Assassinations, arson and bombings, ambushes, hit-and-run raids — all are the tactics of rebels unable even to confront successfully the organized violence of an established state. Such tactics aimed at the enemy are paralleled, moreover, by propaganda, selective terror and organization-building intended to ensure popular support and a hidden, logistical base. At the same time, strategic aid from external foes of the regime under attack — solicited by David from the Philistines, by the Vietnamese from their hereditary Chinese enemies — is accepted as a necessary if distasteful resource.

Mao Tse-tung and Ho Chi Minh may have been particularly successful practitioners of guerrilla strategy, but they did not invent it. A careful reading of I Samuel, for example, makes it clear that, almost thirty centuries earlier, David used similar tactics against Saul. Indeed, only two developments clearly separate modern guerrilla tactics from more ancient ones: the self-conscious organization of peasant villages as a political as well as a logistical tool, plus the increasing importance of terrorism as the tactic of urban guerrillas.

Theoretical justifications for guerrilla operations, however, have varied widely. Where Mao and Ho appealed to the land-hunger of peasants in the name of a dialectically determined egalitarian utopia, David appealed to the "oppressed, in debt, and discontented"[2] in the name of religious purity and "the will of Yahweh." Some — like the Vendée in eighteenth-century France or the Southern guerrillas in Civil War Missouri — have been essentially conservative, defending a previous mode of religious or social organization. Other groups — like those led by Garibaldi or Castro — have been overtly revolutionary, attacking existing regimes in the name of cultural nationalism or social justice. Whether conservative or progressive, however, the guerrilla cause is always identified with an ideal believed to be grounded in (and assured success by) divine or historical necessity.

In addition, guerrillas typically identify themselves with a "correct" attitude towards women. Even as they encourage individual women to support their operations, guerrillas envision themselves, and thereby assert their civilizing mission, as protectors and upholders of an idealized gender relationship. What is considered "correct" will, of course, depend on broader cultural norms. During the American Civil War, for example, it entailed a chivalric politeness for Southern fighters; for the Vietcong it was an idealization of women's self-sacrificing resourcefulness. Thus, it is no accident that Irish-American leaders who wished to undermine Irish-American financial support for the IRA did so by emphasizing the extent to which their terrorist campaigns harmed "helpless women and children."

The propaganda war is important, moreover, since guerrilla operations cannot be sustained unless there exists a sizeable pool of public support for, and approval of, such rebellious activity. The IRA, for example, has been unable to move beyond the urban-guerrilla level of bombings and other acts of "illegal" terrorism to the level of a guerrilla militia. However, their capacity to sustain even that level of warfare over more than two decades points to the high degree of legitimacy they have achieved among the Catholics of Northern Ireland.

Popularity remains one of the most lasting legacies of a guerrilla band. If successful, the memory of how they actually achieved power tends to be glossed over, tidied up and consigned in offical texts to a hallowed but supposedly unrepeatable past. Even such a cleaned-up, Whiggish version of history can be dangerous, however, if the state created by revolutionary fervor becomes in time the object of new rebellious attacks. Thus Castro deliberately and explicitly identified his cause and his strategy with the memory of the nineteenth-century guerrilla nationalist, José Martí. Similarly, the Viet Minh and NLF leaders drew on Vietnam's long nationalistic tradition of resistance against colonial powers as a source of both inspiration and tactics, while Algerian rebels in the 1950s drew on the tactics of French partisans during World War II.

Even unsuccessful guerrillas, such as Robin Hood and Jesse James, live on as part of popular culture. Idealized as heroic figures despite their later descent into banditry, they become the icons of children's literature and adolescent movies.

> He was soft. His heart was with the little people, to whom he reputedly gave money and kindness so generously. He was hard. He destroyed and exploited the exploiters. As had Robin Hood, he reveled in blood revenge, which also gave deep pleasure to those honoring his legend.[3]

If one omits the reference to Robin Hood, the words could refer to the legendary Le Loi, a fifteenth-century Vietnamese guerrilla, just as well as to the American Jesse James. The mythic status such men acquire suggests, moreover, that the real institutionalization of guerilla warfare may be cultural — a product of folk memory. It also reveals a deep-seated human desire for a "savior" who will right injustice and succor the down-trodden.

Thus, the similarity of guerrilla tactics and mythic representations makes their shared nature and goals clear. Guerrilla warfare is the war of the relatively powerless against the powerful. It is the response, sporadic but persistent, of the governed and the dependent to political, economic or religious structures perceived as unjust and oppressive. It is the active side of the resentment discussed in chapter six.

If guerrilla-type warfare is becoming a widespread characteristic of the post-atomic world, one would expect to find indications of its impact on the military operations of ruling states. At first glance, however, this does not seem to be happening. The military forces of industrialized countries like Britain, the United States and the Soviet Union, as well as those of their protégé states, seem unchanged in essence from their nineteenth-century predecessors. They are tightly disciplined, highly trained and enamored of high-tech weaponry. Their preferred enemy — as indicated by their tactical organization and established doctrines — is another conventional army. The Falkland Islands and the Persian Gulf wars remain the epitomes of their visions of "a good war." (After the power display in the Gulf, however, they may find "sparring partners" hard to come by.)

At the same time, such wars increasingly display a slightly Gilbert and Sullivan-ish quality. The disparity in power typically gives them a stagey, melodramatic quality. Did we really watch the British fleet steam across the Atlantic to save a rock-strewn island of shepherds — or was that a late-night movie? Did we really adopt the visual perspective of a "smart bomb" as it zeroed in on an Iraqi headquarters — or was that part of the latest sci-fi film? It's all a little nostalgia-laden and surreal.

Moreover, governments, since at least the 1940s, have moved towards the adoption of terroristic tactics as well as alliances with guerrilla organisations. Indeed, though they are quick to decry the behavior of guerrillas whose goals they find unacceptable, many contemporary governments simultaneously support other guerrillas whose goals seem linked to their own national interests. Thus the Russians engaged in a long-drawn-out war against Islamic guerrillas in Afghanistan, while they were supportive of the equally Islamic Palestinian guerrillas. Similarly, the United States was hostile to guerrilla operations in El Salvador, while providing the primary support for Contra guerrillas in Nicaragua.

Conventional armies have also themselves broken down the distinction between civilians and the military which was characteristic of traditional warfare. In particular, the strategic bombing of enemy civilians which characterized World War II in both Europe and the Pacific was a critical development. Justified then and since as an attempt to break the morale and loyalty of ordinary citizens, such operations are difficult to distinguish, except in terms of their overtness and sheer firepower, from guerrilla bombings and assassinations aimed at the same objective.

In fact, the very word "terror" has increasingly lost any distinctive meaning, becoming simply a pejorative condemnation of enemy tactics. Thus when General Schwarzkopf characterized Iraq's setting Kuwaiti oil wells on fire as "terrorism," he seems to have meant primarily that he did not see any military purpose to the action. On the other hand, he would undoubtedly characterize Allied bombings of Baghdad and other Iraqi towns, including the "collateral damage" of at least 100,000 civilian dead plus water and sewage systems destroyed, as an unfortunate, but legitimate military necessity.

But such bombing raids, as well as the SCUD attacks on Israel, the destruction of Dresden and the Christmas bombing of Hanoi, struck terror into the hearts of the civilians subjected to them. And most were intended to do so. (That the air raids and SCUD-Patriot duels of the Gulf War also "terrorized" many of the American children who watched some of the attacks on their families' television screens was, presumably, just another instance of "collateral damage.") By contrast, IRA or PLO terrorism is clearly small-scale — and relatively ineffective!

However, all armies have been at least temporarily impacted by the number of counter-guerrilla operations they have had to sustain. Inevitably, the more successful the guerrillas are in their attack, the more the armies of defending states are drawn into similar types of unconventional and small-scale operations. The French use of torture to break the battle of Algiers as well as the American use of search-and-destroy tactics and the counter-terrorism of the Phoenix program in Vietnam are clear examples of such a tendency.

Writing about Union army policy and practice in the Missouri guerrilla conflict during the first modern war (the American Civil War), Michael Fellman concluded:

> The knowledge that their guerrilla enemies generally took no prisoners and warred on civilians all the time weakened local Union commanders' demands for good conduct from their subordinates. If the Union army failed to respond in kind, it would risk destruction at the hands of the enemy. It was also contrary to their sense of equitable justice to obey an honorable set of rules disregarded by the other side...[4]

Thus, even in a war in which racial and social disparities between opposing warriors were minimal, "the guerrillas set the actual policy to which enraged local Union units responded in kind,"[5] producing a state of brutal anarchy. My Lai incidents are, in fact, a commonplace in counter-guerrilla operations.

Understandably, the commanding generals of industrialized states are deeply ambivalent about such developments. On the one hand they want to win; on the other hand, they despise the breakdown of discipline and the violation of traditional codes of honor involved in such tactics. Political leaders also fear the possible impact of such counter-guerrillas on the social order they are supposedly defending. Nor is this fear unrealistic. Massive conflicts with guerrillas in the 1950s and 60s, for example, produced in both Peru and France military commands which came to admire their opponents. Having lost confidence in the state they were ostensibly serving, both armies resorted to coups and attempted coups.

Nonetheless, as the discontent of the oppressed and second-class citizens has grown in recent decades, established states have resorted more and more actively to tolerated, if illegal, brutalization of suspect groups by police and paramilitary forces. Rather than modify their social policies, they resort to terrorism. Anonymous kidnappings in the night, the use of torture (sometimes as an end in itself), the growth of concentration camps and the "disappearance" of suspects were characterized in the 1930s as cancerous anomalies of "totalitarian" regimes. In recent decades, however, they have become commonplace, even in the absence of overt guerrilla activities, in South America, the Near East and South-East Asia.

Nor are liberal democracies immune. In America, for example, home video cameras have finally made visible and incontrovertible to the majority, what minorities have long known: that police regularly engage in random brutalization of Blacks and Chicanos. Reflecting on this pattern of "exemplary terrorism," Alexander Cockburn commented:

> Talking to blacks and other minorities in Los Angeles about the cops reminds me vividly of similar conversations with Catholics in Northern Ireland 25 years ago about the "B Specials." ... Catholics driving down a road in Ulster knew somewhere in the backs of their minds that the headlights suddenly appearing behind them might belong to a car full of Specials, and that these Specials might stop them, beat them, frame them, maybe kill them.

Just as the B Specials "were part of the apparatus created by the Ulster elites to keep the Catholics down...," so security forces in Guatemala, El Salvador or Brazil routinely leave mutilated bodies by the roadside as a reminder that the system "can strike you down without justice and with impunity." [6]

Ironically the footsoldiers for both guerrilla and counter-guerrilla styles of political violence come from the same disadvantaged classes. Both forms of violence seem, moreover, intimately tied to the development of an international and heavily technological mode of organizing economic and political life.

Contemporary conservatives, of course, tend to depict guerrilla leaders as immature, psychopathic, unrealistic and addicted to violence. Yet these qualities are not evident in those terrorist and guerrilla leaders who have come to power: Samuel Adams in the United States, Eamon de Valera in Ireland, Josip Tito in Yugoslavia, Menachem Begin in Israel, Chou En-lai in China, Houari Boumedienne in Algeria, to name a few. Rather, these men seem to be distinguished from other political leaders mainly by their efficiency and a high level of self-confidence.

Moreover, not all guerrillas continue to be involved in military or political activities once they have won. Paul Revere went back to work as a silversmith. Saadi Yacef, who directed the terrorist campaign in Algiers, became a successful movie producer. Aohra Drif, one of the women who planted bombs for him, was later a lawyer and secretary-general of the Algerian National School of Administration. These are not professions associated with psychological disorders or immaturity. At most one can say that guerrilla leaders are impatient and unwilling to adjust to the status quo.

What produces such rebellious men and women? The answer seems to lie in a combination of normal socialization patterns, specific historical developments and individual psychology.

Ordinarily, parents try to socialize their children in ways which will enable them to survive and prosper. In particular, they teach them techniques of prudence, including obedience to the powerful and the authoritative. At the same time, they socialize them to identify with their own group — their religion, social class, nation, race or culture. Children are taught a language (including its poetry and songs), specific social and religious rituals, a historical tradition. Such a cultural heritage is valued both for its prudential effectiveness and for the sense of self-esteem and dignity it can engender.

Such a self-identity, fulfilling one's needs and enhancing one's sense of power, creates very strong group loyalties. Under ideal situations — when a person is a member of a majority group in power, for example — prudence and group loyalty work hand in hand, providing both the survival techniques and the sense of security needed for a workable, productive life. But there are times when prudence and loyalty come into conflict. At the moment of a foreign conquest, or when a political or economic revolution produces radical change, a very real psychological conflict is created. Prudence dictates obedience to the new rules, while loyalty to the norms of one's original group demands resistance.

Some groups resolve the conflict between prudence and loyalty by resisting change. This is particularly likely to occur — and most easily understood — when the differences between the social norms and organizations of the defeated and the conqueror are very great.

OF MACHINES, BUREAUCRATS AND OUTLAWS 251

Thus the Montagnards of South East Asia and the Indians of North America fought valiant, if unsuccessful, guerrilla wars in an attempt to preserve a tribal way of life against the encroachment of Vietnamese peasants and American farmers and traders, respectively. Disparities in power usually condemn such resistance to failure or to peripheralization in relatively unproductive regions.

When such resistance fails, the defeated group can still maintain its sense of self-identity by means of "internalized resistance." Thus conquered ethnic and religious groups like the Basques, the Kurds and the Irish Catholics have maintained, over the centuries, a tradition of both prudent adjustment and an ongoing, resentful sense of "us" versus "them." The conflict they felt when first conquered is passed on to succeeding generations through customs, stories and songs — and is expressed from time to time in guerrilla operations.

At the same time, a prudential desire to survive will lead many individuals and groups to obey and even cooperate with the new rulers, especially when the conquering group shares cultural values with the conquered élite. Indeed, conquerors have traditionally counted on and encouraged such a prudent response in order to simplify the task of governing new territories. This was particularly marked, for example, in the Roman Empire, where "citizenship" was offered to those of the wealthy and the educated classes who would serve Rome. Such assimilation was also attempted by many of the Indian upper-classes who learned to speak English, wore European clothing and sent their children to school in England.

But the technique of "assimilation," however successful as a response to the growth of the Roman Empire, has not secured a very high pay-off in the modern world. Unlike the Romans, Western imperialists (at least since the nineteenth century) have carried with them a sense of racial superiority which has placed a very clear limit on the capacity of even the most educated and wealthy to assimilate successfully. In the words of Jules Roy, a Frenchman born and raised in Algeria:

> One thing I knew, because it was told me so often, was that the Arabs belonged to a different race, one inferior to my own ...
> Yes, their happiness was elsewhere, rather if you please, like the

happiness of cattle... Who suffers seeing oxen sleep on straw or eating grass?[7]

Thus Gandhi, educated as a British lawyer, found himself subject to consistent humiliation as an Indian whom even the lowliest British worker could despise.

As a result, both rejected assimilationists and the children of families committed to internalized resistance have reason to attack foreign rulers in the twentieth century. Even indigenous regimes, such as those in South America or the Middle East which are overly dependent on foreign economic and political power, can appear threatening to one's personal dignity and safety as traditionally defined. Under these conditions, many impatient, self-confident young men and women will set out, through revolutionary agitation or guerrilla operations, to achieve independence and exemplary status for their people and for themselves. In the process, they will seek to channel the anger of the masses into political action.

Just as modern racism has undermined the assimilationist tendencies of conquered élites, so the impact of modern economic practice undermines the passive acquiescence to hierarchic rule which has traditionally characterized the peasantry and urban poor.

Both peasant-based civilizations and feudal societies eased their task of governing and taxing their subjects by two tactics. On the one hand, they kept intervention in the ongoing life of peasant villages to a minimum. Within fairly loose limits, a self-governing "little society" was allowed to develop its own economic, social and even political structures. As a result, rulers seemed both distant and "natural." They became an accepted problem, like the drought, to be overcome or avoided, but essentially peripheral to the real center of human life, the village itself.

At the same time, all major world religions preached a justification of the existing order of reality. One's place in the social hierarchy was defined as part of the divine order. The good life was identified (among other things) with recognizing and fulfilling the obligations of one's inherited position. To rebel against earthly rulers was to challenge the divine rule — a personally dangerous act and one certain to result in defeat. Hence, pre-modern rebels tended to define their goals in terms of "restoration," attributing change (and therefore violation of the divine norm) to the ruling class.

The industrialized, capitalistic, rational culture developed by Europeans and exported to other countries by both conquest and economic penetration inevitably undermined both of these pillars of traditional governance. As a result, it has spawned the seeds of mass unrest, the potential clientele of guerrilla activists.

A money-based economy, individualized property laws, and competition from manufactured goods gradually undermined peasant cultures — first in Europe itself and then on other continents. Relations based on face-to-face interaction tempered by traditional social rules are now being replaced by abstract, monetary considerations. Simultaneously, modern technology provides both the means and the necessity for governmental intervention. Tax-collectors and policemen, an obligatory and unitary educational system, the development of economic infrastructures and social welfare systems make the role of the state impossible to ignore.

For the bureaucrats and intellectuals identified with such regimes, individuals become bare statistics: quantifiable, interchangeable and ultimately disposable, Thus *The Ecomonist* could observe of the potato famine which cost Ireland approximately 2,500,000 inhabitants (out of 9,000,000) that "the departure of the redundant part of the population of Ireland and Scotland is an indispensable preliminary to every kind of improvement."[8] Moreover, the British government's callous complicity in the "natural disaster" was only an early example of the dehumanizing tendency inherent in "the triumph of an attitude of value-neutral, calculating rationality as the predominant mode of problem-solving in practical affairs."[9]

Finally, such economic and political penetration of the countryside is typically accompanied by massive urbanization. The impact of such a process, as Europeans have known since the nineteenth century, is to create an alienated, impersonal, society. Moreover, though cities continue to be envisioned as locales of opportunity, they become, like the countryside itself, overpopulated, having little use for the unskilled, under-employed masses who huddle in their *bidonvilles* and ghettos.

Under these conditions, impatience born of frustrated hopes and rage born of injured pride can make violence seem a powerful and necessary choice. Some turn their anger against themselves and their own group. In that case, the anger that one is afraid to direct against the ruling class

> finds outlet regularly in bloodthirsty explosions — in tribal warfare, in feuds between sects, and in quarrels between individuals... By throwing himself with all his force into the vendetta, the native tries to persuade himself that colonialism does not exist... It is as if plunging into a fraternal blood-bath allows them to ignore the [real] obstacle...[10]

Fanon, of course, was talking about areas which had been politically colonized by Europeans, but his analysis has a much wider relevancy. It offers at least a partial explanation of the teenage gangs, drug wars and random violence prevalent among the poverty-stricken everywhere.

Modernization also undermines the second pillar of traditional governments: the world religions with their assumptions about a static social order. Thus a religious/cultural crisis accompanies and deepens the broader socio-economic crisis. In particular, the intelligentsia is forced to confront the problem of adapting the core value of their traditional culture — whether expressed in the Analects of Confucius, the Koran, or Catholic theology — to a new, changing situation. Typically, successful adaptations (such as those achieved by Ho Chi Minh) combine traditional symbols with a progressive sense of social justice and the promise of a more "brotherly" communal structure. They offer both reassurance and the possibility of meaningful change to the increasingly disillusioned and disoriented rural and urban masses.

The result has been the rise of such ideologies as Asian Marxism, Nasserism and liberation theology, as well as the continued strength of divisive regionalism and nationalism in Europe, India and the USSR. All are attempts to combine some aspect of traditional values and beliefs (and therefore one source of group self-esteem) with a more humane accomodation to modern economic forces. Moreover, all are open to being used as justifications for both mass revolutionary action, military adventurism or guerilla-type violence.

Over the centuries, men and women have developed just three basic ways of naming or envisioning "the enemy:" the heroic, the objectified and the demonic. The heroic vision, which creates an enemy who is one's mirror image, an admirable human being able to test and confirm one's prestige and glory, is long lost to the modern world. In its place we have established objectification, turning the enemy into an abstraction or a thing to be controlled and mastered by one's greater competency and power.

Initially military leaders objectified both the enemy and their own forces as part of the technical, calculating rationality which came to dominate Western culture in the seventeenth century. Just as in civilian life the craftsman was replaced by the factory hand, so on the battlefield the individual soldier became a mere appendage of his weaponry, a musket or a pike. Human beings were simply quantifiable commodities or animate tools to be used by capitalists, bureaucrats and commanding generals to achieve economic, political and military goals.

Such objectification, however, has spread in recent decades from the military hierarchy to the public in general, and become specifically equated with "the enemy."

> The American is the Pershing Missile; the Soviet is the SS20. In portraying what we both call "*the* threat," both the United States and the Soviets picture each others' military hardware... It is as if people had vanished from the scene and we expected the next war to be fought between weapons systems that were directed by preprogrammed computer scenarios.[11]

And, indeed, the televised version of the Gulf War came close to fulfilling this expectation. We saw numerous shots of weapons in action, both our own and the enemy's, and were delighted when our weapons proved smarter than theirs. Human fighters on either side were practically invisible until the battle was over.

Parallel to this modern vision of the objectified enemy, however, an older vision of the enemy as demonic has persisted, particularly in the iconography of guerrilla warfare. In that context, the enemy is depicted primarily as a criminal or an outlaw. To take one example of this tendency, President Reagan called "terrorist states" like Iran, Libya, North Korea, Cuba and Nicaragua, "outlaw states,...run by the strangest collection of misfits, 'Looney Tunes' and squalid criminals since the advent of the Third Reich." Simultaneously, Nicaraguan posters depicted the United States as a criminal, "Wanted: The Enemy of Humanity. Reward: Peace, Sobriety and Justice."[12]

Although both the objectified and the demonic vision of the enemy are partly the product of propaganda, the fact remains that to be effective propaganda must tap into existing reservoirs of anxiety or anger. The question then arises as to what our vision of the enemy as either a machine or an individual demon tells us about modern society. What is the dark side of the human psyche or the human condition which is being dealt with through this imagery — and this ritual?

Analyzing one's own self or times is always tricky; moreover as a Euro-American academic I can claim neither involvement in, distance from, nor expertise concerning Third World cultures. Fortunately, a cinematic trilogy, the "Rambo" movies produced by Sylvester Stallone, provides a Western source for investigating the meaning of both the guerrilla and "the enemy" as machine and outlaw. Like *The Iliad,* the films manage to maintain a basic ambiguity about the value of violence, while their international popularity suggests that they speak of a widely shared experience.

Within both America and the international community in general, of course, the "Rambo" series has typically been seen, by intellectuals and critics, as a symbol of the Reagan/Thatcher era — an attempt to erase the "Vietnam/welfare syndrome" and to assert the validity of traditional "macho" and patriotic values. Such an analysis, though it has some validity, is overly simplistic. It ignores, for example, the fact that Rambo is not just a Vietnam veteran who wants to reverse the outcome of that war. He is also explicitly part Indian. Thus he is a representative of a "natural" way of life which was essentially destroyed in the nineteenth century, the victim of the very forces of individualism, "progress" and industrialization idealized by conservative "hawks." As an Indian, moreover, he speaks for all communities trapped in a similar losing battle, while as a veteran he speaks for the expendable footsoldiers of both sides.

At the same time, the plot structure of all three films is derived from the western — an American genre which has evoked substantial international resonance. Specifically, as the lone hero who rights a wrong and then moves on, Rambo plays a role whose historical roots lie in a very short period of American frontier history *and* in the mythic role ascribed by popular culture to Jesse James and other Missouri guerrillas.

In this symbolic context, [the guerrilla-outlaw figure] was both a gritty social bandit and an anarchic superhuman figure — striking out against the very social forces [the eastern banks, railroads, absentee landlords] which... had continued to wear down American farmers and small-town residents after the war...[13]

Stallone simply takes the myth-making process in a complete circle and presents Rambo, in each of the films, as either essentially or explicitly a guerrilla fighter.

At the same time, Rambo is also a heroic symbol for the marginalized in general. Physically potent but verbally inarticulate, Rambo is fated in civilian life to be a gas-station attendant or a hard-time convict — part of the lumpenproletariat. Colonel Samuel Trautman, his commanding officer in the Green Berets and the only person Rambo still trusts, comments in *First Blood* that "God didn't make Rambo. I made Rambo," and refers to him as a machine which has blown a gasket. Thus Rambo is one of the objectified and expendable. As such he speaks for the many who fear that, in a highly technical world, they are doomed to be stand-ins for machines rather than their manipulators. Such men and women, obviously, do not exist only in America.

Understandably, Rambo is also a fearfully angry man who feels that his very selfhood is endangered. What is not clear to him, however, is *who* exactly is the enemy: American civilians who won't love him, foreign Communists, or military technocrats. His diffused anger is paralleled, moreover, by a false nostalgia. In a world of high-tech weaponry, for example, Rambo is portrayed as a veritable Geronimo (or Robin Hood), fighting with relatively simple, hand-held weapons — a knife, a rope, bows and arrows. Such *passé* instruments of violence are clearly symbols of a time when individual prowess and bravery were important.

Rambo's enemies are also portrayed as technologically unsophisticated. Thus the Russian officer in *Rambo II* relies on a rusty bedspring and an out-of-date electric generator as his instruments of torture. Himself the product of a working-class environment, Stallone understands that Rambo needs such enemies. They may attack him physically, but they at least take him seriously. In *First Blood*, faced with Trautman's uninvolved attitude towards Rambo, the sheriff who wants to kill him finally explodes: "Jesus Christ! Where do you people come from?" Obviously he is more emotionally involved with Rambo than the career officer. Thus Stallone produces a demonic vision of the enemy because it both allows him to avoid the irrelevance of individual physical prowess in modern life and grants Rambo (and the viewers who identify with him) psychic importance.

Stallone's vision of reality, however, is not confined to the traditional simplicities of the "noble outlaw/guerrilla" myth. For all of his identification with the needs and values of Rambo, he places him in a recognizably post-modern reality. In the process, he deprives the western genre of two of its normal characteristics: its optimism and moral clarity.

Typically in the western, the distinction between good and evil is quite clear. This is not, however, the case in the first two films in the trilogy. The community which the western hero would normally save, turns out in *First Blood* to be itself essentially evil. Intolerant of differences and non-conformists, it has created a police force which practices "exemplary terrorism." In *Rambo II*, the American political bureaucracy, interested only in creating good PR copy, is as much Rambo's enemy as the Communists.

Ironically, his "worst enemy" in both movies may actually be Colonel Trautman — the establishment "bad" father who does not return his love, but who certainly knows how to control and use him! But Rambo never recognizes this — which may be part of his appeal to the Reagans and the Thatchers of the world. Conservatives, however, can hardly be enamored of the fact that Rambo ends the first film by terrorizing a small American town and the second one by blowing an American computer center to pieces.

Indeed, the endings stand in stark contradiction to the typical western's optimistic vision of reality. Removed from the frontier to the modern world, individual violence is depicted as essentially impotent. Rambo cannot "save" small-town America. He can blow up a single computer center, but he cannot inflict significant damage on a military-industrial complex which has computers in abundance. Although Rambo can save the American P.O.W.s from the Vietnamese Communists and rescue Colonel Trautman from a Russian dungeon, he cannot, like "The Magnificent Seven" or "The Seven Samurai," rescue the peasants from "the outlaws." Instead, he is essentially dependent on them (and American technocrats) for help in accomplishing his own "mission."

Also, for all of his "macho" characteristics, Rambo fails in one of the most basic of traditional masculine roles: the protector of women. There are only two women in the Rambo films. One is an African-American mother whose son has died from cancer as a result of his exposure to Agent Orange — surely a meaningful symbol for millions of Third World mothers. The other is a beautiful, brave, resourceful and ultimately wistful young Vietnamese guerrilla fighter. Both are accorded respect and dignity, but Rambo can offer them neither help nor protection. The complete absence of women from the third film in the trilogy conveys a bleak sense that there is no room for women or the womanly side of human nature in the devastating and chaotic world Rambo attacks — or in the passive celibacy of monasticism to which he retreats! For Stallone, seemingly, the day of the lone, chivalric hero is past. (Of course, in fact, the communally organized guerrillas in Afghanistan went on to victory.)

The current attraction of guerrilla action for Third World and minority groups, as well as the Northern Hemisphere's horrified fascination with "the terrorist" and "noble outlaw" films like *Rambo*, have similar roots. Most contemporary populations have an ambiguous attitude towards "the machine." One part of us wants to embrace industrialization for the material abundance and sense of power such instruments provide. But we also fear the world of machines and bureaucrats because it conveys a personally scarifying vision of reality: one is expendable. And so we project, onto "the enemy" as machine, the threatening side of industrial capacity.

Guerrillas act out that fear, asserting by their acts the possibility that there is still a historic role for the individual warrior. They also point to the injustice encapsulated in industrialized and bureaucratic orderliness, while projecting onto it the "outlaw" aspects of their own actions. Simultaneously, conforming citizens watching the "Rambo" films or reading about terrorists in their morning papers can act out in fantasy the rebellious element in their own psyche, while righteously projecting those criminal tendencies onto the guerrilla.

Despite the level of social approval it engenders, however, guerrilla warfare as an ongoing rebellious atttack on injustice and mechanistic control produces primarily insecurity and escalating brutality. It cannot by its very nature be routinized or made the basis of security and material well-being. Mao's attempt to achieve such an institutionalization of anti-hierarchical rebellion durung the 1960s is, in fact, the exception which proves the rule. The ensuing dislocations of society have made the Cultural Revolution anathema to Chinese of all persuasions.

Instead, successful guerrilla leaders normally abandon their original strategy and adopt established modes of politico-military organization and strategy, usually on the way to victory itself. They also become the "founding fathers" of fairly conventional states — with all the elements of oppression and control such institutions entail. The results of successful modern movements — as in China, Vietnam, Algeria, etc. — suggests, moreover, that the task of combining industrial abundance with personally validating forms of social organization is extremely difficult. Nor does the resort to small-sized, ethnically defined states seem more likely to suceed. The increasing power of multinational corporations, combined with television-induced greed for greater material wealth, is likely to turn such states into hollow shells. At the same time, the continued existence, in all modern states, of groups and individuals who perceive themselves as relatively oppressed — culturally, economically or politically — seems likely to produce ongoing generations of guerrilla fighters.

The conception of communal justice and the desire for a recognition of one's humanity which fuel guerrilla activities in all centuries are not neurotic goals. They are needs intrinsic to humans as members of a social species. What is neurotic is the belief that violence can achieve such ends, that a small group of noble fighters can restore us to an orderly world in which we can effortlessly control our own destinies. It is, moreover, a disfunctional belief nourished both by our cultural addiction to the rites of war and by the international ruling classes' reliance on the technology of violence to exploit and control, but not to eliminate, the Rambos — and the Saddam Husseins — of this world.

Source Notes

Preface ☐

1. "Why Blunder Back Into Quicksand?" *Los Angeles Times*, 4 April 1991, B7.
2. *Times Literary Supplement*, 14-20 Sept. 1990.

Chapter 1 ☐ WAR AND HUMAN NATURE

1. Benedict, *Patterns of Culture*, pp. 234–235.
2. While it is true that a few women have been soldiers, war has always been institutionalized as a male activity. In this book, I acknowledge this fact by using masculine nouns and pronouns in discussing both warriors and political leaders. (Some of the reasons for this socially created sexual dimorphism are discussed in chapter 12.) When paraphrasing thinkers who used the word "man" as a symbol for humanity, I have retained their traditional (and revealing) usage.
3. Lorenz, *On Aggression*, p. 261.
4. MacDonald, *Company Commander*, p. 16.
5. Ibid., p. 212.
6. Ibid., p. 213.
7. Wilson, *On Human Nature*, p. 114.
8. Marshall, *Men Against Fire*, p. 78.
9. Ibid., p. 81.
10. This book is based especially upon the theories developed by gestalt therapists and social psychologists. The literature of gestalt therapy is not large, but the most comprehensive statement of its theoretical foundation is to be found in the third part of Perls, Hefferline, and Goodman, *Gestalt Therapy*. (Goodman was the actual author of this section.) The initial formulation is Perls, *Ego, Hunger and Aggression*, while the most readable introduction is Perls, *Gestalt Therapy Verbatim*. Asch's work, *Social Psychology*, carefully establishes the connection between the discrete discoveries of the experimental gestaltists and a generalized theory of social organization.

11. Wallen, "Gestalt Therapy and Gestalt Psychology," in Fagan and Shepherd, eds., *Gestalt Therapy Now*, p. 12.
12. See Carpenter, *Naturalistic Behavior of Non-Human Primates* and "The Contribution of Primate Studies to the Understanding of War" in Fried et al. (eds.), *War: The Anthropology of Armed Conflict and Aggression*, pp. 49–58.
13. See Harlow et al., "The Sad Ones: Studies in Depression," *Psychology Today*, 4(12):60–63. May, 1971.
14. Perls, Hefferline, and Goodman, *Gestalt Therapy*, p. 345.

Chapter 2 □ THE RITES OF WAR

1. Martindale, *Social Life and Cultural Change*, p. 54.
2. Hocart, *Kings and Councillors*, p. 41.
3. Compare, for example, Lee and de Vore (eds.), *Man, the Hunter*, with Chagnon and Irons (eds.), *Evolutionary Biology and Human Social Organization*.
4. See, for example, Chagnon, *Yanomamo: The Fierce People*, and Rappaport, *Pigs for the Ancestors*.
5. Turney-High, *Primitive War: Its Practice and Concepts*, p. 23.
6. Ibid., p. 21.
7. Ibid., pp. 46–47.
8. Ibid., p. 47.
9. See, for example, Otterbein, *The Evolution of War*, as well as Turney-High, *Primitive War*.
10. See Krige, *The Social System of the Zulus*, and Ritter, *Shaka Zulu*.
11. Middelkoop, *Head Hunting in Timor*, pp. 111–112.
12. See Chagnon, *Yanomamo: The Fierce People*.
13. See Rappaport, *Pigs for the Ancestors*.
14. See Turney-High, *Primitive War: Its Practice and Concepts*, p. 161.
15. See Williams, *Orokaiva Society*.
16. See Underhill, *Singing for Power: The Song Magic of the Papago Indians*.
17. See Rappaport, *Pigs for the Ancestors*.
18. See Harner, *The Jivaro: People of the Sacred Waterfalls*.
19. Lowie, *Indians of the Plains*, and Gardner and Heider, *Gardens of War*.
20. Underhill, *Singing for Power*, p. 64.
21. See, in particular, the work of Susan Langer: *Mind: An Essay on Human Feeling*, vol. 2, and *Philosophy in a New Key*.
22. Lifton, *Home From the War*, p. 13. This section draws heavily on

Lifton's interpretation of the My Lai incident, which was based on extensive interviews with the soldiers of Charlie company.
23. Perls, Hefferline, and Goodman, *Gestalt Therapy*, pp. 263–264.
24. Ibid., p. 261.
25. Ibid., pp. 264–265.
26. Lifton, *Home From the War*, p. 53.
27. Ibid., p. 47.
28. See Clark and Piggott, *Prehistoric Societies* and Coulborn, *The Origin of Civilized Societies*.
29. Dumézil, *The Destiny of the Warrior*, p. 134.
30. Perls, Hefferline, and Goodman, *Gestalt Therapy*, p. 362; italics added.

Chapter 3 ☐ THE NEOLITHIC REVENGE

1. Benedict, *The Chrysanthemum and the Sword*, p. 146.
2. See Meek, *Law and Authority in a Nigerian Tribe*, and Gardner and Heider, *Gardens of War*.

Chapter 4 ☐ THE DESTRUCTION OF CHAOS

1. Langer, *Philosophy in a New Key*, p. 185.
2. Chagnon, *Yanomamo: The Fierce People*, pp. 41–48.
3. Ibid., p. 48.
4. See Schapera, *The Khoisan Peoples of South Africa*.
5. See Basso and Opler (eds.), *Apachean Culture, History and Ethnology;* Goodwin, *The Social Organization of the Western Apache;* and Opler, *An Apache Life-way*.
6. See Underhill, *Singing for Power*.
7. See Chagnon, *Yanomamo: The Fierce People;* and Krige, *The Social System of the Zulus*.
8. See Lévi-Strauss, *The Savage Mind*.
9. See Eliade, *The Myth of the Eternal Return*.
10. See Frankfort, *Before Philosophy*, and Jacobsen, *The Treasures of Darkness*.
11. See Loewe, *Imperial China*.
12. Stobart, *The Grandeur That Was Rome*, and Taylor, *The Divinity of the Roman Emperor*.
13. See Vaux, *Ancient Israel: Its Life and Institutions*, vol. I.
14. See Frankfort, *Before Philosophy*.

15. See Bergaigne, *Vedic Religion*, vols. 2 and 3, and Griswold, *The Religion of the Rigveda*.
16. See Dumézil, *The Destiny of the Warrior*.
17. Ibid.
18. Virgil, *The Aeneid*, p. 169.

Chapter 5 ☐ CULTURES OF GREED

1. Tacitus, *The Histories*, p. 102.
2. Hsun Tzu as quoted in Creel, *Chinese Thought from Confucius to Mao Tse-Tung*, p. 102.
3. Horney, *The Neurotic Personality of Our Time* p. 100.
4. See, for example, Speier, who observes in *Social Order and the Risk of War* that "The one who pays honor expects the bearer to conduct his life in accordance with certain rules, which constitute the code of honor. . . . In this way or that honor sets up boundaries; it disciplines life" (pp. 42–43).
5. Mills, *An Essay on Government*, p. 58.

Chapter 6 ☐ THE SATISFACTION OF GUILT

1. Camus, *The Stranger*, p. 134.
2. Gray, *The Warriors: Reflections on Men in Battle*, p. 45.
3. Pritchard (ed.), *The Ancient Near East*, vol. 1, p. 206.
4. Stover, *The Cultural Ecology of Chinese Civilization*, p. 184.
5. Ibid., p. 205.
6. Mote, *Intellectual Foundations of China*, p. 44.
7. Brown, *The White Umbrella*, p. 29.
8. Ibid.
9. Loewe, *Imperial China*, p. 248.
10. Edwards, *The Hammurabic Code and the Sinaitic Legislation*, p. 11.
11. Thorpe (ed.), *Ancient Laws and Institutes of England*, p. 267.
12. Livy, *The Early History of Rome*, p. 399.
13. Loewe, *Imperial China*, p. 84.
14. Perls, Hefferline, and Goodman, *Gestalt Therapy*, p. 123.
15. Jacobsen, *The Treasures of Darkness*, p. 154.
16. Josephus, *The Jewish War*, pp. 372–373.
17. Durkheim, *The Division of Labor in Society*, p. 102.
18. Perls, Hefferline, and Goodman, *Gestalt Therapy*, p. 363.

19. Horney, *The Neurotic Personality of Our Time*, pp. 232, 280.
20. Shakespeare, *Henry V*, IV, iii, ll. 60–64.
21. Gray, *The Warriors*, p. 45.
22. Carroll, *Puritanism and the Wilderness*, p. 212.

Chapter 7 □ HONOR AND GLORY

1. Janowitz, *The Professional Soldier*, p. 216.
2. Froissart, *Chronicles of England, France, Spain, and the Adjoining Countries from the Latter Part of the Reign of Edward II to the Coronation of Henry IV*, vol. 2, p. 349.
3. Homer, *The Iliad*, pp. 155–156.
4. Ibid., p. 292.
5. Ibid., p. 456.
6. Ibid., p. 401.
7. *The Ramayana and the Mahabharata*, pp. 302–303.
8. Ibid., p. 310.
9. Homer, *The Iliad*, p. 456.
10. Ibid., p. 105.
11. Ibid., p. 442.
12. Ibid., p. 158.
13. *The Bhagavad Gita*, chapter 1, paragraphs 31–35.
14. Ibid., chapter 2, paragraph 19.
15. Ibid., chapter 3, paragraphs 37, 43.
16. Ibid., chapter 18, paragraphs 26, 54.
17. Ibid., chapter 10, paragraph 12.
18. Ibid., paragraph 19.
19. Ibid., chapter 11, paragraph 13.
20. Ibid., paragraphs 24, 27, 30.
21. Ibid., paragraphs 32–33.
22. Ibid., chapter 18, paragraphs 43, 46.
23. Teilhard de Chardin, *The Making of a Mind*, p. 205; italics in original.
24. Homer, *The Iliad*, p. 382.
25. See, for example, Perls, Hefferline, and Goodman, *Gestalt Therapy*, pp. 255–289.
26. Ibid., p. 377.
27. Ibid.
28. Janowitz, *The Professional Soldier*, p. 34.
29. Ibid., p. 22.
30. *Last Letters from Stalingrad*, pp. 54–57.
31. Ibid., pp. 36–38.

Chapter 8 ☐ HARROWING HELL

1. Tillich, *The Courage to Be*, p. 50.
2. There is, of course, a tension between this mythic stance and the institutional church's tolerance during the Middle Ages of clerical involvement in and sanctification of trials by battle or ordeal. Between A.D. 400 and 1200, however, the church was concerned primarily with strengthening any institutions that could prevent bloodshed and preserve order in a warlike and disintegrating social situation. Granted the cultural assumptions of the primarily Germanic populations (and therefore of the relatively uneducated local priests), trial by battle or ordeal seemed preferable to unchecked blood feuds. The costs of this compromise, however, was a deterioration of the Christian theoretical position comparable to the church's increasing involvement in war itself (which is discussed later in this chapter).
3. Soelle, *Suffering*, p. 107.
4. Ibid., pp. 102–103.
5. St. Augustine, *City of God*, p. 327.
6. Ibid., p. 46.
7. Ibid., p. 47.
8. Ibid., pp. 327–328.
9. Sayers, *The Song of Roland*, s. 110.
10. Ibid., s. 277.
11. Ibid., s. 115.
12. Dante, *The Comedy of Dante Alighieri, Paradise*, Canto XIV, ll. 124–126.
13. Soelle, *Suffering*, p. 23.
14. Brown, *Life Against Death*, p. 215.
15. Carroll, *Puritanism and the Wilderness*, p. 11.
16. Ibid., p. 77.
17. Ibid., p. 213.

Chapter 9 ☐ THE CADENCE OF TIME

1. Heller, *Catch-22*, p. 40.
2. Britten, *War Requiem*, Opus 66; lyrics from poem by Wilfred Owen.
3. Clapham, *The Causes of the War of 1792*, p. 106.
4. Quoted from *Patriote Français* in Ellery, *Brissot de Warville*, p. 233.

5. Goethe, *Miscellaneous: Travels of J. W. Goethe*, p. 118.
6. Quoted in Wohl, *The Generation of 1914*, p. 217.
7. J. Guibert, quoted in Quimby, *The Background of Napoleonic Warfare*, p. 124.
8. Lamb, *Memoirs of His Own Life*, pp. 44–45; italics added. For a fuller discussion of the relation between aesthetic considerations, tactics, and strategy, see Mansfield, "War and Aesthetic Sensibility" in *Soundings*, Fall 1968, pp. 308–326.
9. *The Memoirs of Major M'Gauran*, vol. 2, 189–90.
10. Montross, *War Through the Ages*, pp. 448–449.
11. Quimby, *The Background of Napoleonic Warfare*, pp. 110–111.
12. Long, ed., *Personal Memoirs of U. S. Grant*, pp. 555–556.
13. Foch, quoting Clausewitz, in *Principles of War*, p. 44; italics in original.
14. Liddell Hart, *The Second World War*, p. 37; italics added.
15. Henderson, *The Science of War*, p. 15.
16. Keegan, *The Face of Battle*, p. 325.
17. Ellis, *Eye-Deep in Hell*, p. 63; italics added.
18. Manning, *Her Privates We*, p. 240.
19. Chapman, *A Passionate Prodigality*, pp. 133–134.
20. Gray, *The Warriors*, pp. 35–37. At least one of the sources of the disintegration and loss of morale among American soldiers in Vietnam may have been the fact that guerrilla warfare in a tropical jungle provided so few opportunities for the visual experience of functional sublimity. Instead, as Philip Caputo remembers of a search-and-destroy mission, "Being Americans, we were comfortable with machines, but with the aircraft gone we were struck by the utter strangeness of this rank and rotted wilderness. . . . It was the inability to see that vexed us most. In that lies the jungle's power to cause fear: it blinds . . ." (*A Rumor of War*, pp. 53–55). Ten months later he remembers that "staring at the jungle and the ruined temple, hatred welled up in me; a hatred for this green, moldy, alien world in which we fought and died" (p. 315).
21. Ropp, *War in the Modern World*, p. 203.
22. Hackett, *The Third World War*, p. 198; italics in original.
23. Truscott, "Franz Schubert," in *The Symphony, I. Haydn to Dvorak*, pp. 197, 191.
24. Twentieth-century composers have created a new world vision that has much in common with Heisenberg's "principle of uncertainty." Beginning with Debussy's impressionistic *L'Apres-midi d'un Faun*, they have buried "the tradition of 500 years of musical evolution and clean-

cut divisive rhythm with its neat 4/4, 3/4, 6/8 pace" in favor of music that "actually does not move. It has no growth, no action, no driving force or will" (Sachs, *Rhythm and Tempo*, pp. 370, 360). They have also turned to atonality, electronic irrationality, and, above all, to the tattered time and improvisational freedom of black jazz. Their experimentation had led by 1968 to Stockhausen's *Stimmung*, seventy-five minutes of sound built on a single chord. "Time has stopped," the composer wrote, adding that the work should be "a speedy aircraft making for the Cosmos and the divine." Since the interaction between music and warfare runs both ways, many of the musical avant-garde, living in a world of mushroom clouds and six-minute warnings, have retreated into compositional silence.

Chapter 10 ☐ THE DANGER OF FEAR

1. Bruce Springsteen, "The Promised Land," in *Darkness on the Edge of Town*, Columbia Records (1978), side 1.
2. Kant, *Perpetual Peace*, p. 2.
3. Albertini, *The Origins of the War of 1914*, vol. 3, p. 702.
4. Montgelas and Shucking, eds., *Outbreak of the World War*, p. 631.
5. See Perls, *Ego, Hunger and Aggression*, for the fullest discussion of this characteristic. In effect, gestalt theory argues that the failure or inability of a strong and coherent figure to emerge from the background is the result of blocks and interruptions created by introjections, retroflections, and projections. Thus neurotic individuals have poor contact with the external world and with the body itself; they will not look or listen or feel, so there are voids or blank spots in their body and in their gestalt formations. "Where something should be, there is nothing. Many people have no soul. Others have no genitals. Some have no heart; all their energy goes into computing, thinking. Others have no legs to stand on. . . . These are missing parts that he has alienated and given up to the world" (Perls, *Gestalt Therapy Verbatim*, pp. 39–40).
6. See, in particular, Toch, *Violent Men*.
7. Fay, *The Origins of the World War*, vol. 2, pp. 24–25; italics in original.
8. Ibid., pp. 185–186; italics in original.
9. *Austrian Red Book*, vol. 1, 1.
10. Fay, *The Origins of the World War*, vol. 2, p. 242.
11. Ibid., p. 241.

12. Albertini, *The Origins of the War of 1914*, vol. 2, p. 405.
13. Montgelas and Shucking, *Outbreak of the World War*, p. 298.
14. *Austrian Red Book*, vol. 3, p. 19.
15. Schilling, *How the War Began in 1914*, p. 48.
16. Ibid.
17. Sazonov, *Fateful Years, 1909–1914*, p. 201.
18. Fay, *The Origins of the World War*, vol. 2, p. 472.
19. Albertini, *The Origins of the War of 1914*, vol. 2, p. 574.
20. Montgelas and Shucking, *Outbreak of the World War*, p. 61.
21. Albertini, *The Origins of the War of 1914*, vol. 2, p. 157.
22. Montgelas and Shucking, *Outbreak of the World War*, p. 617.
23. Goerlitz, *History of the German General Staff, 1657–1945*, p. 151.
24. Montgelas and Shucking, *Outbreak of the World War*, p. 254.
25. Ibid., pp. 345–346.
26. Quoted in Balfour, *The Kaiser and His Times*, pp. 351–353; italics in original.
27. Albertini, *The Origins of the War of 1914*, vol. 2, p. 502.
28. Ibid., vol. 3, p. 25.
29. Ibid., p. 81.
30. Schilling, *How the War Began in 1914*, p. 32.
31. Spender, *Life of Herbert Henry Asquith, Lord Oxford and Asquith*, vol. 2, p. 94.
32. Gooch and Temperley, *British Documents on the Origins of the War*, vol. 11, p. 101.
33. Nicolson, *Sir Arthur Nicolson*, p. 419.
34. Gooch and Temperley, *British Documents on the Origins of the War*, vol. 11, p. 447.
35. Albertini, *The Origins of the War of 1914*, vol. 3, p. 407.
36. Lloyd George, *War Memoirs*, vol. 1, pp. 65–66.
37. Gooch and Temperley, *British Documents on the Origins of the War*, vol. 11, p. 671.

Chapter 11 ☐ THE RAGE OF IMPOTENCE

1. Eliade, *The Myth of the Eternal Return*, p. 150.
2. Toch, *Violent Men*, p. 248.
3. Ibid., p. 153.
4. Ibid., p. 148.
5. Ibid., p. 137.

6. Ibid., p. 141.
7. Ibid., p. 149.
8. Wolfgang and Ferracuti, *The Subculture of Violence*, p. 159.
9. Ibid., p. 161.
10. Keegan, *The Face of Battle*, p. 316.
11. Halberstam, *The Best and the Brightest*, p. 444; italics added.
12. Ellery, *Brissot de Warville*, pp. 232–233.
13. Langer, "A Critique of Imperialism," *Foreign Affairs* 14 (October 1935), p. 114.
14. Monypenny and Buckle, *The Life of Benjamin Disraeli*, vol. 3, p. 536; italics added.
15. Chamberlain, *Foreign and Colonial Speeches*, p. 135.
16. Trevelyan, *Lord Grey of Fallodon*, p. 288.
17. Quoted in Snyder, *The Imperialism Reader*, p. 116.
18. Barker, *Modern Germany*, p. 95; italics added.
19. Balfour, *The Kaiser and His Times*, p. 250.
20. Rauschning, *Hitler Speaks*, pp. 125–126.
21. Degras, *The Communist International, 1919–1943*, vol. 1, p. 141.
22. *Report of the Central Committee of the Communist Party of the Soviet Union to the 20th Party Congress*, Part 1.
23. Freeland, *The Truman Doctrine and the Origins of McCarthyism*, p. 18.
24. Richardson, ed., *Messages and Papers of the Presidents, 1798–1908*, vol. 10, pp. 834–836.
25. Truman, *Public Papers*, p. 176.
26. Ibid., p. 188.
27. Toch, *Violent Men*, p. 138 et passim.
28. Ibid., p. 164.
29. Ibid., p. 158.
30. Balfour, *The Kaiser and His Times*, p. 148.
31. Albertini, *The Origins of the War of 1914*, vol. 3, p. 368.
32. Pelling, *Winston Churchill*, p. 177.
33. Halberstam, *The Best and the Brightest*, pp. 522, 530.
34. Sun Tzu, *The Art of War*, chapter 11, sections 23, 33, 37.

Chapter 12 ☐ THE MEGA-TANTRUM

1. Newman, "Political Science" on *Sail Away*, Warner Bros., side 2.
2. Homer, *The Iliad*, p. 114.

3. Liddell Hart, *Strategy*, p. 48; italics added.
4. Quoted in Keegan, *The Face of Battle*, p. 276.
5. Marshall, *Pork Chop Hill*, pp. 234–235.
6. Quoted in Fialka, "U. S. Widening Women's Role as Warriors," *Washington Star*, 9 Jan. 1980, p. 1; italics added.
7. Emerson, *Winners and Losers*, p. 328.
8. Webb, "Women Can't Fight," *Washingtonian*, November 1979, p. 146.
9. Dinnerstein, *The Mermaid and the Minotaur*, p. 125.
10. See Perls, *Ego, Hunger and Aggression*.
11. Dinnerstein, *The Mermaid and the Minotaur*, pp. 106–107.
12. Fall, *Last Reflections on a War*, p. 209.
13. "Notes and Comments," in *New Yorker*, 25 Feb. 1980, p. 31.
14. Stonier, *Nuclear Disaster*, p. 24.
15. Kahn, *On Thermonuclear War*, p. 169; italics in original.
16. Harkabi, *Nuclear War and Nuclear Peace*, p. 181.
17. Quoted in Stonier, *Nuclear Disaster*, p. 91.
18. Ibid.
19. Ibid., p. 95.
20. Ibid., p. 91.
21. Kahn, *On Thermonuclear War*, p. 46; italics in original.
22. Ibid., p. 47n.
23. Merchant, *The Death of Nature*, pp. 2, 127.
24. Ibid., p. 168; italics added by Merchant.
25. Quoted in Merchant, *The Death of Nature*, pp. 38–39.
26. Dinnerstein, *The Mermaid and the Minotaur*, p. 136.
27. Asch, *Social Psychology*, p. 110.
28. Ibid., p. 187.
29. Frankfort et al., *Before Philosophy*, p. 14.
30. Dinnerstein, *The Mermaid and the Minotaur*, p. 136.
31. Perls, Hefferline, and Goodman, *Gestalt Therapy*, p. 233.
32. Bacon, *New Organon*, Book I, section cxxix.
33. Ibid., Book I, section iii.

Chapter 13 ☐ BOUNDARIES OF POWER

1. *Tumbleweed* by Tiki Ryan © Field Enterprises Inc. 1981.
2. Perls, Hefferline, and Goodman, *Gestalt Therapy*, p. 319.
3. Gray, *The Warriors*, pp. 52–57.

4. Perls, *The Gestalt Approach and Eye-witness to Therapy*, p. 38.
5. Ariès, *Western Attitudes toward Death: From the Middle Ages to the Present*, pp. 101–102.
6. Ibid., pp. 106–107.
7. Gray, *The Warriors*, pp. 225–226.

Chapter 14 ☐ OF MACHINES, BUREAUCRATS AND OUTLAWS

1. "The Loneliness of the Military Historian," *Times Literary Supplement*, 14-20 Sept. 1990.
2. I Samuel 22:2.
3. Michael Fellman, *Inside War. The Guerrilla Conflict in Missouri During the American Civil War* p. 263.
4. Ibid. p. 117.
5. Ibid. p. 131.
6. "Policing by Exemplary Terror," *Los Angeles Times*, 25 March 1991, B5.
7. Quoted in A. Horne, *A Savage War of Peace*, p. 55.
8. "Effect of Emigration of Production and Consumption," *The Economist*, 12 February 1853, Vol. 11, No. 494, p. 168 quoted in Richard Rubenstein, *The Age of Triage*, p. 122.
9. Rubenstein, *op. cit.*, p. 1.
10. Franz Fanon, *The Wretched of The Earth*, p. 54.
11. Sam Keen, *Faces of the Enemy*, p. 85.
12. Ibid. pp. 52, 74.
13. Fellman, *op. cit.*, 263.

Bibliography

Albertini, L. *The Origins of the War of 1914,* trans. and ed. I. M. Massey. 3 vols. London: Oxford University Press, 1952–57.
Anderson, R. T. *Traditional Europe: A Study in Anthropology and History.* Belmont, Calif.: Wadsworth, 1971.
Ardant du Picq, C. J., *Battle Studies; ancient and modern battles.* Harrisburg: Military Service Publishing Co., 1947.
Ariès, P. *Western Attitudes toward Death: From the Middle Ages to the Present,* trans. P. M. Ranum. Baltimore: Johns Hopkins University Press, 1974.
Asch, S. *Social Psychology.* New York: Prentice-Hall, 1952.
St. Augustine. *City of God,* trans. and ed. V. J. Bourke. Garden City: Doubleday, 1958.
Austrian Red Book. 3 vols. London: G. Allen & Unwin, 1920.
Bacon, F. *New Organon,* ed. F. H. Anderson. Indianapolis: Bobbs-Merrill, 1960.
Balazs, E. *Chinese Civilization and Bureaucracy: Variations on a Theme,* trans. H. M. Wright, ed. A. F. Wright. New Haven: Yale University Press, 1964.
Balfour, M. *The Kaiser and His Times.* New York: Norton, 1972.
Barker, J. E. *Modern Germany; Its rise, growth, downfall and future.* New York: E. P. Dutton, 1919.
Barry, H., I. Child, and M. K. Bacon. "The relation of child training to subsistence economy," *American Anthropologist* (1959) 61:51
Basso, K. H., and M. E. Opler, eds. *Apachean Culture, History and Ethnology.* Tucson: University of Arizona Press, 1971.
Benedict, R. *Patterns of Culture.* Boston: Houghton Mifflin, 1946.
———. *The Chrysanthemum and the Sword: Patterns of Japanese Culture.* Boston: Houghton Mifflin, 1974.
Beauvoir, S. de. *The Second Sex,* trans. and ed. H. M. Parshley. New York: Knopf, 1953.
Bergaigne, A. *Vedic Religion. According to the Hymns of Rigveda,* 3 vols. trans. V. Paranjpe. Poona, India: Arya Sanskriti Prakashan, 1971–73.

Berkowitz, L. *Aggression: A Social Psychological Analysis.* New York: McGraw-Hill, 1962.
The Bhagavad Gita, trans. J. Mascaro. Baltimore, Md.: Penguin Books, 1962.
Bohannan, P., ed. *Law and Warfare: Studies in the Anthropology of Conflict.* Austin: University of Texas Press, 1967.
Boodman, S. G. "Women GIs Cite Sexual Harassment at Army Bases," *Washington Post,* 29 January 1980, p. 6.
Breuil, H. *Four Hundred Centuries of Cave Art,* trans. M. E. Boyle. Montignac, France: Centre d'études et de documentation préhistoriques, 1952.
Britten, B. *War Requiem,* Opus 66. New York: Boosey and Hawkes, 1962.
Brown, D. M. *The White Umbrella: Indian Political Thought from Manu to Gandhi.* Berkeley: University of California Press, 1964.
Brown, N. O. *Life Against Death: The Psychoanalytical Meaning of History.* Middletown, Conn.: Wesleyan University Press, 1953.
———. *Love's Body.* New York: Random House, 1966.
Buss, A. H. *The Psychology of Aggression.* New York: Wiley, 1961.
Camus, A. *The Stranger,* trans. S. Gilbert. New York: Vintage Books, 1946.
Cannon, W. B. *Bodily Changes in Pain, Hunger, Fear and Rage.* New York: D. Appleton & Co., 1929.
Caputo, P. *A Rumor of War.* New York: Holt, Rinehart and Winston, 1978.
Carpenter, C. R. *Naturalistic Behavior of Non-Human Primates.* University Park: Pennsylvania State University Press, 1964.
Carrigar, S. *Wild Heritage.* Boston: Houghton Mifflin, 1965.
Carroll, P. N. *Puritanism and the Wilderness: The Intellectual Significance of the New England Frontier.* New York: Columbia University Press, 1969.
Carthy, J. D., and F. J. Ebling, eds. *The Natural History of Aggression.* New York: Academic Press, 1964.
Chagnon, N. A. *Yanomamo: The Fierce People.* New York: Holt, 1968.
———, and W. Irons, eds. *Evolutionary Biology and Human Social Organization: An Anthropological Perspective.* North Scituate, Mass.: Duxbury Press. 1979.
Chamberlain, J. *Foreign and Colonial Speeches.* London: G. Routledge and Sons, 1897.
Chandler, D. G. *The Campaigns of Napoleon.* New York: Macmillan, 1966.
Chang, K. C. *The Archaeology of Ancient China.* New Haven: Yale University Press, 1968.

Chapman, G. *A Passionate Prodigality.* New York: Holt, 1966.
Churchill, W.L.S. *Marlborough: His Life and Times.* New York: Scribner's, 1968.
Clapham, J. H. *The Causes of the War of 1792.* New York: Octagon, 1969.
Clark, J.G.D. *The Stone Age Hunter.* New York: McGraw, 1967.
———, and S. Piggett. *Prehistoric Societies.* Harmondsworth: Penguin, 1965.
Clausewitz, K. von. *War, Politics and Power,* ed. and trans. E. M. Collins. Chicago: Henry Regnery, 1962.
Collingwood, R. G. *The Idea of History.* Oxford: Clarendon Press, 1957.
Coon, C. S. *The Hunting Peoples.* Boston: Little, Brown, 1971.
Coulborn, R. *The Origin of Civilized Societies.* Princeton: Princeton University Press, 1969.
Craig, G. A. *The Politics of the Prussian Army, 1640–1945.* Oxford: Clarendon Press, 1955.
Creel, H. G. *Chinese Thought from Confucius to Mao Tse-Tung.* Chicago: University of Chicago Press, 1953.
Dante, A. *The Comedy of Dante Alighieri, Paradise,* trans. D. Sayers and B. Reynolds. Aylesbury: Penguin, 1975.
Degras, J. ed. *The Communist International, 1919–1943. Documents, vol. 1. 1919–1922.* London: Oxford University Press, 1956.
de Mause, L., ed. *The History of Childhood.* New York: Psychohistory Press, 1974.
de Pauw, L. D. "Our Women Have Always Been in Combat," *Washington Post,* 6 April 1980, p. E1.
Dinnerstein, D. *The Mermaid and the Minotaur: Sexual Arrangements and Human Malaise.* New York: Harper & Row, 1976.
Dumézil, G. *The Destiny of the Warrior,* trans. A. Hiltebeitel. Chicago: University of Chicago Press, 1970.
Durkheim, E. *The Division of Labor in Society,* trans. G. Simpson. New York: Free Press, 1964.
Earle, E. M., ed. *Makers of Modern Strategy: Military Thought from Machiavelli to Hitler.* Princeton: Princeton University Press, 1966.
Edwards, C., ed. *The Hammurabic Code and the Sinaitic Legislation.* London: Watts 1921.
Eibl-Eibesfeldt, I. *Love and Hate: The Natural History of Behavior Patterns.* New York: Holt, 1972.
Eliade, M. *The Myth of the Eternal Return or, Cosmos and History,* trans. W. R. Trask. Princeton, Princeton University Press, 1974.
Ellery, E. *Brissot de Warville: A Study in the History of the French Revolution.* Boston: Houghton Mifflin, 1915.

Ellis, J. *Eye-Deep in Hell: Trench Warfare in World War I.* New York: Pantheon Books, 1976.
Emerson, G. *Winners and Losers: Battles, Retreats, Gains, Losses, and Ruins from a Long War.* New York: Random House, 1976.
Erikson, K. T. *Wayward Puritans: A Study in the Sociology of Deviance.* New York: Wiley, 1976.
Esposito, V. J. *A Concise History of World War I.* New York: Praeger, 1964.
Fagan, J., and I. L. Shepherd, eds. *Gestalt Therapy Now: Theory, Techniques, Applications.* Palo Alto, Calif.: Science and Behavior Books, 1970.
Fall, B. B. *Last Reflections on a War.* Garden City, N.Y.: Doubleday, 1972.
Farmer, H. G. *The Rise and Development of Military Music.* London: Reeves, 1912.
Farrar, L. L. *The Short-War Illusion: German Policy, Strategy & Domestic Affairs, August–December 1914.* Santa Barbara, Calif.: ABC-Clio, 1973.
Fay, S. B. *The Origins of the World War,* 2 vols. New York: Macmillan, 1930.
Fialka, J. "U. S. Widening Women's Role as Warriors," *Washington Star.* 9 January 1980, p. 1.
Finley, M. *The World of Odysseus.* New York: Viking, 1965.
Foch, F. *Principles of War,* trans. H. Belloc. New York: H. Holt, 1920.
Forster, R., and O. Ranum, ed. *Family and Society,* trans. E. Forster and P. M. Ranum. Baltimore: Johns Hopkins University Press, 1976.
Fortune, R. F. *Sorcerers of Dobu: The Social Anthropology of the Dobu Islanders of the Western Pacific.* New York: Dutton, 1963.
Frankfort, H., et al. *Before Philosophy: The Intellectual Adventure of Ancient Man.* Baltimore: Penguin, 1973.
Frazer, Sir J. *The Golden Bough: A Study in Magic and Religion.* New York: Macmillan, 1963.
Freeland, R. M. *The Truman Doctrine and the Origins of McCarthyism.* New York: Knopf, 1972.
Fried, M., M. Harris, and R. Murphy, eds. *War: The Anthropology of Armed Conflict and Aggression.* New York: Natural History Press, 1968.
Friedl, E. *Vasilika, A Village in Modern Greece.* New York: Holt, 1962.
Froissart, J. *Chronicles of England, France, Spain, and the Adjoining Countries from the Latter Part of the Reign of Edward II to the Coronation of Henry IV,* trans. T. Johnes. New York: The Colonial Press, 1901.
Gardner, R., and K. G. Heider. *Gardens of War.* New York: Random House, 1968.

Gaulle, C. de. *France and Her Army*, trans. F. L. Dash. London: Hutchinson, 1945.
Goerlitz, W. *History of the German General Staff, 1657–1945.* New York: Praeger, 1959.
Goethe, J. W. *Miscellaneous: Travels of J. W. Goethe*, trans. and ed. L. D. Schmitz. London: George Bell and Sons, 1884.
Goldich, R., ed. *Women in the Armed Forces.* Proceedings of the CRS Seminar Held on November 2, 1979, and Selected Readings. 1980.
Gooch, G. P. *Frederick the Great.* London: Longmans, Green, 1947.
———, and Temperley, H. eds. *British Documents on the Origins of the War.* 1898–1914. London: 1926–38.
Goodwin, G. *Western Apache Raiding and Warfare.* Tucson: University of Arizona Press, 1971.
———. *The Social Organization of the Western Apache.* Chicago: University of Chicago Press, 1973.
Gray, J. G. *The Warriors: Reflections on Men in Battle.* New York: Harper & Row, 1967.
Griswold, H. D. *The Religion of the Rigveda.* London: Oxford University Press, 1923.
Guibert, J.A.H. *Essai général de tactique, précédé d'un discours sur l'état actuel de la politique et de la science militaire en Europe.* Liege: Chez C. Plomteux, 1773.
Hackett, J. *The Third World War, August 1985.* New York: Macmillan, 1978.
Halberstam, D. *The Best and the Brightest.* New York: Random House, 1972.
Hall, A. R. *Ballistics in the Seventeenth Century.* Cambridge: University Press, 1952
Hanson, P. *The Dawn of Apocalyptic.* Philadelphia: Fortress Press, 1975.
Harkabi, Y., *Nuclear War and Nuclear Peace,* trans. L. Shenkman. Jerusalem: Israel Program for Scientific Translations, 1966.
Harlow, H., et al. "The Sad Ones: Studies in Depression," *Psychology Today.* 4(12):60–63. May, 1971.
Harner, M. J. *The Jivaro: People of the Sacred Waterfalls.* Garden City, N.Y.: Doubleday, 1972.
Harrison, J. E. *Prolegomena to the Study of Greek Religion.* London: Merlin, 1961.
Harvey, F. *Air War: Vietnam.* New York: Bantam, 1967.
Hays, H. R. *The Dangerous Sex: The Myth of Feminine Evil.* New York: Putnam, 1964.
Heller, J. *Catch-22.* New York: Simon and Schuster, 1961.

Henderson, G.F.R. *The Science of War.* London: Longmans, Green, 1906.
Hocart, A. M. *Kings and Councillors: An Essay in the Comparative Anatomy of Human Society.* Chicago: University of Chicago Press, 1970.
Holborn, H. "Moltke and Schlieffen," in *Makers of Modern Strategy: Military Thought from Machiavelli to Hitler,* ed. E. M. Earle. Princeton, N.J.: Princeton University Press, 1943.
Homer. *The Iliad,* trans. A. Lang, W. Leaf, and E. Meyers, ed. G. Highet. New York: Modern Library, 1950.
Horney, K. *The Neurotic Personality of Our Time.* New York: Norton, 1964.
———. *Neurosis and Human Growth: The Struggle Toward Self-Realization.* New York: Norton, 1950.
Hunt, D. *Parents and Children in History: The Psychology of Family Life in Early Modern France.* New York: Basic Books, 1970.
Hunt, G. T. *The Wars of the Iroquois: A Study in Intertribal Trade Relations.* Madison: University of Wisconsin Press, 1940.
Huxley, F. *Affable Savages: An Anthropologist Among the Urubu Indians of Brazil.* New York: Viking Press, 1956.
Jacobsen, T. *The Treasures of Darkness: A History of Mesopotamian Religion.* New Haven: Yale University Press, 1976.
Janowitz, M. *The Professional Soldier, A Social and Political Portrait.* Glencoe, Ill.: Free Press, 1960.
Jenkins, E. *Elizabeth the Great. A Biography.* New York: Capricorn, 1967.
Johnson, R. N. *Aggression in Man and Animals.* Philadelphia: W. B. Saunders Co., 1972.
Josephus, F. *The Jewish War,* trans. G. A. Williamson. Harmondsworth: Penguin, 1970.
Kahn, H. *On Thermonuclear War.* New York: Free Press, 1960.
Kant, I. *Perpetual Peace.* Indianapolis: Library of Liberal Arts, Bobbs-Merrill, 1957.
Kaufman, H. *Aggression and Altruism. A Psychological Analysis.* New York: Holt Rinehart, 1970.
Keegan, J. *The Face of Battle.* New York: Viking Press, 1976.
Kelly, A. *Eleanor of Aquitaine and the Four Kings.* Cambridge: Harvard University Press, 1950.
Kissinger, H. A. *Nuclear Weapons and Foreign Policy.* New York: Norton, 1969.
Krige, E. J. *The Social System of the Zulus.* Pietermaritzburg: Shuter and Shooter, 1957.

LaFontaine, J. S. *The Gisu of Uganda.* London: International African Institute, 1959.
Lamb, R. Sergeant *Memoirs of His Own Life.* Dublin: J. Jones, 1811.
Lang, P. H. *Music in Western Civilization.* New York: W.W. Norton, 1941.
Langer, S. K. *Mind: An Essay on Human Feeling,* vol. 2. Baltimore: Johns Hopkins University Press, 1972.
———. *Philosophy in a New Key: A Study in the Symbolism of Reason, Rite, and Art.* Cambridge: Harvard University Press, 1978.
Langer, W. L. "A Critique of Imperialism," *Foreign Affairs* 14:1 (October, 1935) pp. 102–119.
Last Letters from Stalingrad, trans. F. Schneider and C. Gullans. New York: Signet, 1965.
Lee, R. B., and I. de Vore, eds. *Man, the Hunter.* Chicago: Aldine, 1968.
Lévi-Strauss, C. *The Savage Mind.* Chicago: University of Chicago Press, 1966.
Liddell Hart, B. H. *History of The Second World War.* New York: Putnam, 1971.
———. *Strategy.* New York: Praeger, 1961.
Lifton, R. J. *Home From the War: Vietnam Veterans: Neither Victims nor Executioners.* New York: Simon and Schuster, 1973.
Livy, T. *The Early History of Rome,* trans. A. de Selincourt. Harmondsworth: Penguin, 1971.
Lloyd George, D. *War Memoirs.* 6 vols. Boston: Little, Brown, 1933–37.
Loewe, M. *Imperial China. The Historical Background to the Modern Age.* New York: Praeger, 1969.
Long, E. B., ed. *Personal Memoirs of U. S. Grant.* Cleveland: World Publishing, 1952.
Lorenz, K. *On Aggression,* trans. M. K. Wilson. New York: Harcourt, 1966.
Lowen, A. *The Betrayal of the Body.* New York: Macmillan, 1967.
Lowie, R. H. *Indians of the Plains.* Garden City, N.Y.: Natural History Press. 1954.
MacDonald, C. B. *Company Commander.* Washington: Infantry Journal Press, 1947.
M'Gauran, E. *The Memoirs of Major Edward M'Gauran.* 2 vols. London: The author, 1786.
Manning, F. *Her Privates We.* London: P. Davies, 1964.
Mansfield, S. "War and Aesthetic Sensibility, An Essay in Cultural History." *Soundings.* Fall 1968, pp. 308–326. "Warfare and Sexual Politics," *Soundings.* Winter 1971, pp. 345–356.

Marshall, S.L.A. *Men Against Fire. The Problem of Battle Command in Future War*. New York: William Morrow, 1947.

———. *Pork Chop Hill; The American Fighting Man in Action; Korea*. New York: Morrow, 1956.

Martindale, D. *Social Life and Cultural Change*. Princeton: D. Van Nostrand, 1962.

Matthiessen, P. *Under the Mountain Wall: A Chronicle of Two Seasons in the Stone Age*. New York: Ballantine Books, 1962.

Meek, C. K. *Law and Authority in a Nigerian Tribe: A Study in Indirect Rule*. New York: Oxford University Press, 1937.

Megargee, E. I., and J. E. Hokanson, eds. *The Dynamics of Aggression: Individual, Group, and International Analyses*. New York: Harper & Row, 1970.

Merchant, C. *The Death of Nature: Women, Ecology, and the Scientific Revolution*. San Francisco: Harper & Row, 1980.

Meyer, L. B. *Emotion and Meaning in Music*. Chicago: University of Chicago Press, 1956.

Middelkoop, P. *Head Hunting in Timor and Its Historical Implications*. Sydney: University of Sydney Press, 1963.

Mills, J. *An Essay on Government*. Indianapolis: Bobbs-Merrill, 1953.

Montagu, A. *Touching: The Human Significance of the Skin*. New York: Columbia University Press, 1971.

———, ed. *Man and Aggression*. New York: Oxford University Press, 1968.

Montgelas, M. and W. Shucking, eds. *Outbreak of the World War: German Documents Collected by Karl Kautsky*. New York: Oxford University Press, 1924.

Montross, L. *War Through the Ages*. New York: Harper & Brothers, 1946.

Monypenny, W. F. & G. E. Buckle. *The Life of Benjamin Disraeli*. 3 vols. New York: Macmillan, 1929.

Mote, F. W. *Intellectual Foundations of China*. New York: Knopf, 1971.

Mumford, L. *Technics and Civilization*. New York: Harcourt, 1963.

———. *The Myth of the Machine: The Pentagon of Power*. New York: Harcourt, 1970.

Munshi, K. M. *Krishnavarata*. Bombay: Bharatiya Vidya Bharan, 1963–68.

Nef, J. U. *Western Civilization Since the Renaissance: Peace, War, Industry and the Arts*. New York: Harper & Row, 1963.

Newman, R. "Political Science," on *Sail Away*. Burbank: Warner Bros. Records, 1972.

New Yorker. "Notes and Comments," 25 February 1980, p. 31.

Nicolson, H. G. *Portrait of a Diplomatist, Sir Arthur Nicolson, Bart., First Lord Carnock; A Study in the Old Diplomacy.* New York: Harcourt, Brace, 1939.
North, C. *The Suffering Servant in Deutero-Isaiah. An Historical and Critical Study.* London: Oxford University Press, 1956.
Oman, C.W.C. *The Art of War in the Middle Ages,* A.D. *378–1515,* rev. and ed. J. H. Beeler. Ithaca: Cornell University Press, 1953.
Opler, M. E. *An Apache Life-way: The Economic, Social, and Religious Institutions of the Chiricahua Indians.* New York: Cooper Square Publishers, 1965.
Otterbein, K. F. *The Evolution of War: A Cross-Cultural Study.* N.p.: HRAF Press, 1970.
Pelling, H. *Winston Churchill.* New York: Dutton, 1974.
Perls, F. S. *Ego, Hunger and Aggression: A Revision of Freud's Theory and Method.* London: G. Allen & Unwin, 1947.
———. *The Gestalt Approach and Eye-witness to Therapy.* Ben Lomond, Calif.: Science & Behavior Books, 1973.
———. *Gestalt Therapy Verbatim,* ed. J. O. Stevens. Lafayette, Calif.: Real People Press, 1969.
———, R. Hefferline, and P. Goodman. *Gestalt Therapy: Excitement and Growth in the Human Personality.* New York: Julian Press, 1951.
Piggott, S. *Prehistoric India to 1000* B.C. Baltimore: Penguin Books, 1961.
Pledge, H. T. *Science Since 1500: A Short History of Mathematics, Physics, Chemistry, Biology.* New York: Harper, 1959.
Pospisil, L. *The Kapanku Papuans of Western New Guinea.* New York: Holt, 1963.
Pratt, E. A. *The Rise of Rail-Power in War and Conquest, 1833–1914.* London: P. S. King & Son, 1915.
Prescott, J. "Body Pleasure and the Origins of Violence," *Bulletin of the Atomic Scientists,* 31:9, pp. 10–20. Nov. 1975.
Pritchard, J. B., ed. *The Ancient Near East: An Anthology of Texts and Pictures,* vol. 1. Princeton, N.J.: Princeton University Press, 1958.
Quimby, R. S. *The Background of Napoleonic Warfare: The Theory of Military Tactics in Eighteenth-Century France.* New York: Columbia University Press, 1957.
The Ramayana and the Mahabharata, trans. R. C. Dutt. New York: E. P. Dutton, 1915.
Raper, M. K. "A Survey of the Evidence for Intra-human Killing in the Pleistocene," *Current Anthropology,* (1969) 10:427.
Rappaport, R. A. *Pigs for the Ancestors: Ritual in the Ecology of a New Guinea People.* New Haven: Yale University Press, 1968.

Rauschning, H. *Hitler Speaks*. London: Thornton Butterworth Ltd., 1939.
Report of the Central Committee of the Communist Party of the Soviet Union to the 20th Party Congress. Moscow: Foreign Languages Publishing House, 1956.
Richardson, J. D., ed. *A Compilation of the Messages and Papers of the Presidents, 1798–1908*. 10 vols. New York: Bureau of National Art and Literature, 1907.
Ritter, E. A. *Shaka Zulu: The Rise of the Zulu Empire*. London: Longmans, Green, 1955.
Ritzenthaler, R. E. and P. *The Woodland Indians of the Western Great Lakes*. Garden City, N. Y.: Natural History Press, 1970.
Roberts, M. *The Military Revolution, 1560–1660*. Belfast: University of Belfast, 1956.
Rogers, R. W. *A History of Babylonia and Assyria*. 2 vols. New York: Abington Press, 1915.
Ropp, T. *War in the Modern World*. New York: Collier Books, 1962.
Ruppenthal, R. G. "Logistics and the Broad Front Strategy (1944)" in *Command Decision*, ed. K. R. Greenfield. Washington: U.S. Dept. of the Army, Office of Military History, 1960.
Russell, J. B. *A History of Medieval Christianity: Prophecy and Order*. New York: Crowell, 1968.
Sachs, C. *Rhythm and Tempo: A Study in Music History*. New York: Norton, 1953.
Sayers, D., trans. and ed. *The Song of Roland*. Harmondsworth, Eng.: Penguin Books, 1957.
Sazonov, S. D. *Fateful Years, 1909–1916: The Reminiscences of Serge Sazonov*. London: J. Cape, 1928.
Schapera, I. *The Khoisan Peoples of South Africa: Bushmen and Hottentots*. London: G. Routledge & Sons, 1951.
Schilling, M. F. *How the War Began in 1914: Being the Diary of the Russian Foreign Office*. London: G. Allen & Unwin Ltd., 1925.
Scott, J. P. *Aggression*. Chicago: University of Chicago Press, 1958.
Shakespeare, W., *The Life of Henry the Fifth*, New York: Penguin, 1976.
Shepard, P. *The Tender Carnivore and the Sacred Game*. New York: Scribner's, 1973.
Sivard, R. L. *World Military and Social Expenditures*. Leesburg, Va.: WMSE Publications, 1977.
Smail, R. C. *Crusading Warfare, 1097–1193*. Cambridge, Eng.: University Press. 1956.
Snyder, L. L. *The Imperialism Reader: Documents and Readings on Modern Expansionism*. Princeton: Van Nostrand, 1962.

Soelle, D. *Suffering.* Philadelphia: Fortress Press, 1975.
Speier, H. *Social Order and the Risks of War: Papers in Political Science.* New York: G. W. Stewart, 1952.
Spender, J. A., and C. Asquith. *Life of Herbert Henry Asquith, Lord Oxford and Asquith.* 2 vols. London: Hutchinson & Co., 1932.
Springsteen, B. "The Promised Land" in *Darkness on the Edge of Town.* Columbia Records, 1978.
Stearns, F. R. *Anger: Psychology, Physiology, Pathology.* Springfield, Ill.: Thomas, 1972.
Steed, G. T. "Personality Formation in a Hindu Village in Gujarat," in *Village India: Studies in the Little Community,* ed. M. Marriott. Chicago: University of Chicago Press, 1969.
Stobart, J. C. *The Grandeur That Was Rome.* New York: Praeger, 1961.
Stonier, T. *Nuclear Disaster.* Cleveland: World Publishing Co., 1964.
Storr, A. *Human Aggression.* New York: Athenaeum, 1968.
Stover, L. E. *The Cultural Ecology of Chinese Civilization: Peasants and Elites in the Last of the Agrarian States.* New York: Pica Press, 1974.
Sun Tzu. *The Art of War,* trans. S. B. Griffith. Oxford: Oxford University Press, 1963.
Tacitus, C. *The Histories,* trans. and ed. K. Wellesley. Harmondsworth: Penguin, 1964.
Tarn, W. W. *Alexander the Great.* London: Cambridge University Press, 1948-1950.
Taylor, A.J.P. *The Struggle for Mastery in Europe, 1848-1918.* Oxford: Clarendon Press, 1954.
Taylor, L. R. *The Divinity of the Roman Emperor.* Middletown, Conn.: American Philosophical Assn., 1931.
Teilhard de Chardin, P. *The Making of a Mind: Letters from a Soldier-Priest, 1914-1919.* Trans. R. Hague. New York: Harper & Row, 1965.
Thorpe, B., ed. *Ancient Laws and Institutes of England.* London: G. E. Eyre and A. Spottiswode, 1840.
Tillich, P. *The Courage to Be.* New Haven: Yale University Press, 1964.
Toch, H. *Violent Men: An Inquiry into the Psychology of Violence.* Chicago: Aldine, 1969.
Trevelyan, G. M. *Grey of Fallodon. The Life and Letters of Sir Edward Grey.* Boston: Houghton Mifflin, 1937.
Truman, H. *Public Papers.* Washington, D.C.: USGPO, 1945-1951.
Truscott, H. "Franz Schubert," in *The Symphony, I. Haydn to Dvorak,* ed. R. Simpson. Aylesbury: Penguin, 1966.
Turney-High, H. H. *Primitive War: Its Practice and Concepts.* Columbia: University of South Carolina Press, 1971.

Underhill, R. M. *Singing for Power: The Song Magic of the Papago Indians of Southern Arizona.* New York: Ballantine, 1973.
U.S. Arms Control & Disarmament Agency. *World Military Expenditure and Arms Trade, 1963–1973.* Washington, D.C.: U.S. Arms Control Disarmament Agency or USGPO, 1975.
Vaux, R. de. *Ancient Israel: Its Life and Institutions.* Vol. I, *Social Institutions.* trans. J. McHugh. New York: McGraw-Hill, 1961.
Virgil, P. *The Aeneid,* trans. C. D. Lewis. Garden City: Doubleday, 1953.
Webb, J. "Women Can't Fight," *Washingtonian,* November 1979, pp. 144–48, 273, 275, 278, 280, 282.
Wedgwood, C. V. *The Thirty Years War.* Garden City: Doubleday, 1961.
Williams, F. E. *Orokaiva Society.* London: Oxford University Press, 1930.
Williams, T. R. *A Borneo Childhood: Enculturation in Dusun Society.* New York: Holt, 1969.
Willoya, W., and V. Brown. *Warriors of the Rainbow.* Healdsburg: Naturegraph, 1962.
Wilson, E. O. *On Human Nature.* Cambridge: Harvard University Press, 1978.
Winter, E. H. *Bwamba: A Structural-Functional Analysis of a Patrilineal Society.* Cambridge, Eng.: W. Heffer, 1956.
Wohl, R. *The Generation of 1914.* Cambridge: Harvard University Press, 1979.
Wolfgang, M. E., and F. Ferracuti. *The Subculture of Violence: Towards an Integrated Theory in Criminology.* London: Tavistock, 1967.
Wright, Q. *The Study of War.* Chicago: University of Chicago Press, 1965.
Yang, M. C. *A Chinese Village: Taitou, Shantung Province.* New York: Columbia University Press, 1945.

Index

Adams, Henry 161
Adams, Samuel 249-50
Aeneid (Virgil) 69, 138
Afghanistan 217, 243, 247, 259
Africa 243
aggression 3, 6, 9-17
   of a chaotic force 55-64
   of children 44-5, 47-8, 49, 50
   Christian holy war 133-42, 194
   definition 9-10
   and genetic code 10, 232
   horticultural societies 46-7, 48, 52
   and learned behavior patterns 10
   as self-defense 9, 14
   theory of natural aggression 1, 3-4
agrarian societies *See* horticultural societies; peasant-based societies
Akhadians 96
Albania 170
Albertini, L. 169
Albigensians 141
Alexander the Great 86
Algerian war 9, 217, 245, 248
anger 6, 8-9, 12
   and revenge, desire for 44-53
      See also revenge
   violent outlets of poor 253-4
Angola 217
Apaches 57-8, 60, 61, 62, 64
Arab-Israeli conflicts 187, 214, 217
Arabs 251-2
Ardant du Picq, C.J. 12
Ariès, Philip 239
Asch, Solomon 215
Asia 243
Asquith, Henry Herbert 185
assimilation: of conquered people 251-2
Atwood, Margaret xv, 243
Augustine, St 131-3, 136, 139
aural effects 6, 19, 158-9

dance and song of primitive people 26, 29, 30, 32, 36-7, 73
Austerlitz, battle of 155
Austria-Hungary 8, 151, 200
   France and Russia, alliance 151
   World War I 168, 170-4 *passim*, 176-82 *passim*, 186-7, 89
Aztecs 58

B Specials 249
Babylonians 65-6, 66-7, 89-90, 91-2, 99
Bacon, Francis 145-6, 152, 226, 230
Basques 251
Beckett, Samuel 237
Beethoven, Ludwig von 154-5, 165
Begin, Menachem 249-50
Belgium 204
   World War I 181, 183, 185-6, 190
Benedict, Ruth 1, 41
Berchtold, Leopold 171, 176, 189, 200
Bethmann-Hollweg, Theobald von 169-70, 174, 178, 179, 181, 186-7
Bhagavad Gita 118-21
Bible 67-8, 92, 100, 101, 128-30, 131, 134-5, 138, 244
Biringuccio, Vannoccio 146
Bismarck, Prince Otto von 162, 197
Boumedienne, Houari 249-50
Bourbons 85, 86
Bourcet, Pierre de 152
Brazil 249
Brissot de Warville, Jacques Pierre 195
Britten, Benjamin 14
Brown N.O. 215
Bruckner, Anton 165, 166
Bulgaria 170
Burma 217
Bush, George xiii-xiv

Caesar, Julius 211

285

Calvin, John 142
Cambodia 217
Cameroons 217
Camon, General Hubert 210
Camus, Albert 89
Carnot, Lazare 146
Carpenter, C.R. 15
Carter, Jimmy 208
Castro, Fidel 244, 245
Catholic church 104, 254
    Albigensians 141
    See also Christianity
Chamberlain, Joseph 195
chaos myth 55-65
Chapman, Guy 160-1
Charlemagne, Emperor: *The Song of Roland* 136-7, 138-9
Charles V, Emperor 85
children/child rearing:
    death of parent 32, 48-9, 50, 51
    female infanticide 25
    and growth of guilt 94-5
    horticultural societies 44-5, 47-52 *passim*, 79, 229
    hunting and gathering tribes 48, 229
    modern era 202-3, 229
    Neolithic people 25
    peasant-based societies 79-85, 94-5, 202
    socializing effect 250
China (ancient and medieval) 65, 66, 75, 90, 91, 93, 124
China (modern) 143, 217, 260
Chiricahua Apaches 57-8, 60, 61, 62, 64
Chou En-lai 249-50
Christianity:
    acceptance of suffering 130-1, 136
    and the Enlightenment 150-1, 168
    holy wars and religious crusades 133-42, 194
    Jews persecuted 141
    Reformation 142
    women burned as witches 225
    See also Bible; religion
Churchill, Sir Winston 185, 200
civil war (England) 5
Civil War (U.S.) 156, 158, 244, 248
Clausewitz, Karl von 17, 24-5, 156-7
Cockburn, Alexander 249
Code of Hammurabi 91-2

Code of Manu 91
Cold War xiii
Confucius 91, 93, 124, 254
Conrad von Hötzendorf, Count Franz 171, 176, 189, 200
Crécy, battle of 107
Crimean war: charge of the Light Brigade 6
Crow 29
Cuba 217, 218, 255
Cumberland, Duke of 6
Cyrus, King 89-90, 129
Czechoslovakia 187

dance and song (primitive people) 26, 29, 30, 32, 36-7, 73
Dani 32, 43
Dante Aligheri: *Divine Comedy*, "Paradiso" 141-2
de Valera, Eamon 249-50
death:
    female infanticide 25
    martyrdom in holy war 142
    minimum of killing 3
    parental 32, 48-9, 50, 51
    primitive people and ritual 27-31, 38, 42, 43, 49
    sacrifice 54, 56, 60
    ritual of mourning 38, 239
    World War I statistics 168
decoration and dress 75, 148, 155, 158, 160
    gold, use of 87
    primitive people 26, 30, 73, 74
Desargues, Girard 146
Descartes, René 146
Dinnerstein, Dorothy 215
Disraeli, Benjamin 195
Dresden 247
Drif, Aohra 250

Eckhart, Meister 131
Economist 253
economy (and war):
    as goal 19, 70-105, 194, 195
    lack of economic goal 18, 25
    strain on 4
    World War I 4, 168
Edgar, King 92

Edward II, King 107
Edward VII, King 179, 196
Edward VIII, King 85
Egypt (ancient) 65-6, 68, 87, 90, 96
Egypt (modern) 187
Eisenhower, Dwight 211
El Salvador 217, 247, 249
Eliade, Mircea 188
Eliot, John 105
Elizabeth the Great 85
Empedocles 235
England 92
    civil war 5
    France, war with 107, 108
    See also Great Britain
Enlightenment 150-1, 168
Errard 146
Eskimos: song duels 46
Ethiopians 212
Europe: nationalism 243, 254

Fabri, Friedrich 195-6
Falkenhayn, Erich von 177, 179, 181
Falkland Islands war 246
Fall, Bernard 217
Fanon, Franz 254
Fellman, Michael 248
feudal elite: warfare 3, 5, 106-26, 136-43
feudal societies: government, tactics of 252
Fisher, Sir John 196
Foch, Marshal Ferdinand 156-7
Fontanelle 146
food:
    and chaos myth 56, 57, 61, 62
    as means of affection 80
    need for 72, 73
    sources defended 21, 22
    taboos 26, 30, 31, 61, 232
    See also horticultural societies; hunting and gathering tribes
fortifications and defences 21-2, 107, 146
France 166, 193, 195, 244
    Algerian war 9, 217, 248
    Austria and Russia, alliance 151
    Austria, Russia, and Prussia, war on 144-5
    England and Russia, alliance 194, 196
    England, war with 107, 108
    monarchy 85, 90

Napoleon and Napoleonic wars 93, 145, 152-27 *passim*, 163, 164, 165, 210
World War I 172, 176-87 *passim*, 190
World War II 245
Franz Ferdinand, Archduke 170, 171
Frederick the Great, King 3, 8, 86, 151, 154, 210, 211
Frederick William I, King 151
Freud, Sigmund 12, 235
Froissart, Sir John 107

Galileo Galilei 146
Gandhi, Mahatma 9, 200, 252
gang wars 2-3, 254
Garibaldi, Giuseppe 244
Germany 193, 195-6
    Third Reich 187, 196-7
    World War I 105, 168, 171-85 *passim*, 190, 196, 199-200, 201
    World War II 39, 124-5, 143, 162
    See also World War I; World War II
Gibbon, Edward 150
Gladstone, William 185
goals and objectives:
    economic 19, 70-105, 194, 195
    food 21, 22
    greed 19, 71-6, 80, 84, 143, 169, 233
    guilt, satisfaction of 94-105, 233
    homicide 3
    honor and glory 25-6, 52-3, 53-4, 77-8, 106-26, 189, 207
    imposition of will and power 3, 19, 54
    oppression, freedom from 246, 252, 260
    political 17, 18, 25, 70-105
    of rebellion 252
    revenge 35, 37, 38, 41-55 *passim*, 116, 169, 233
    ritualistic *See* myth and ritual
    strategy and tactics, indication of 18-19
    territorial *See above* economic, political
    wife stealing 25, 27
Goethe, Johann Wolfgang von 145
gold 87-8, 236
Goodman, P. 38
Grant, Ulysses S. 156, 158
Gray, J. Glenn 89, 103, 161, 234-5

Great Britain 193, 195, 196
  Crimean war 6
  and Egypt 187
  France and Russia, alliance 194, 196
  and India 9, 200
  military forces 246
  Revolutionary War 149
  World War I 172, 177, 178, 179, 183-7 *passim*, 190, 191, 200-1, 211-12
  See also England; World War I; World War II
Greece 170, 198
greed (as goal) 19, 71-6, 80, 84, 143, 169, 233
Grey, Sir Edward 184, 185-6, 190, 195, 200
Gribeauval, Jean baptiste de 151-2
Guatemala 249
guerrilla warfare xiv, 243-60
  leaders 249-50
Guiana 209
Guibert, Jacques 152
  Essai général de tactique 153-4
guilt (and punishment) 94-105, 233
  relationship changed by Christianity 130
Gulf War xiii-xiv, 246, 255
Gustavus Adolphus, King 147, 149, 211

Hackett, General Sir John 163, 164-5
Haeften, Hans von 181
Haiti 217
Hammurabi 91-2
Hannibal 210
Hanoi 247
Harlow, H. 15-16
Hart, Basil H. Liddell *See* Liddell Hart, Basil H.
Hebrews 69
  chaos myth abandoned and Exodus mythologized 67-8
  sexual taboos 30
  warfare 66, 92
  concept of guilt and punishment 96, 97-8, 100, 101
  new concept of repentance 128-30
Hegel, Georg Wilhelm Friedrich 145
Henry IV, King 86
Henry V (Shakespeare) 102

Hinduism:
  Bhagavad Gita 118-21
  Code of Manu 91
  concept of guilt and punishment 96
  Mahabharata 108-9, 112-16 *passim*, 125, 138
  Vedic tales 65, 67, 68, 90
Hiroshima 221
Hitler, Adolf 143, 162, 187, 196-7
Ho Chi Minh 244, 254
Hobbes, Thomas 71
Hocart, Arthur 20
Holland 204
Homer: *Iliad* 108-12 *passim*, 115, 116-18, 121, 122, 123, 125, 126, 208-9
honor and glory 25-6, 52-3, 53-4, 77-8, 106-26, 189, 207
  martyred death in holy war 142
Hood, Robin 245
Horney, Karen 71-2, 84, 102
horticultural societies 4, 72, 77
  children 44-5, 47-52 *passim*, 79, 229
  and destruction of chaos 55-65
  and shift from hunting and gathering 46-8, 51, 53-4
  warfare 21-69
  See also myth and ritual; primitive people
Hottentots 56-7
Hsun Tzu 70
Hume, David 150
Hungary 187, 217
  See also Austria-Hungary
hunting and gathering tribes 20-1, 22, 46, 61, 73-4
  children 47, 48, 229
  See also primitive people

Ibo 43
Iliad (Homer) 108-12 *passim*, 115, 116-18, 121, 122, 123, 125, 126, 208-9, 256
India (ancient) 90, 91, 96, 124
  Bhagavad Gita 118-21
  Mahabharata 108-9, 112-16 *passim*, 125, 138
  Vedic tales 65, 67, 68, 90
India (modern) 9, 200, 251, 254
Indians, North American 251, 256
Indochina 217

INDEX

Indonesia 217
instinct, theory or warmaking as 1, 3-4
IRA 245
Iran 255
Iraq 243, 247
Ireland:
    internal conflict 243, 245, 249, 251
    potato famine 253
Isabella of Castile, Queen 210
Islam 140-1, 247, 254
    Jihad (holy war) 140
    The Song of Roland 136-9
    warrior code 124, 214, 217
Israel (ancient) 129, 130
    See also Hebrews
Israeli-Arab conflicts 187, 214, 217
Italy 168, 177, 187
    Renaissance 3
Iwo Jima 158

Jagow, Gottlieb 177, 186
James, Jesse 245-6, 256
Janowitz, Morris 106, 124
Japan 187
    Russo-Japanese war 196
    warrior code 123, 124
    World War II 158, 221
Jaurès, Jean 193
Jena, battle of 145
Jews:
    persecution of 141, 143
    See also Hebrews
Jivaro 29, 32
Joffre, Marshal Joseph 162
John of Patmos, St 134-5
Johnson, Lyndon 2, 201
Jomini, Baron Henri 156
Juenger, Ernest 235
Jurua 209

Kahn, Hermann 219, 220-1, 223-5
Kant, Immanuel 151
    Perpetual Peace 167-8
Kashmir 217
Khrushchev, Nikita 197
King Philip's war 104-5, 143
Kiwai 30
Klein, Melanie 215
Kluck, Alexander von 163

Korean war 12, 187, 212, 217, 255
Kuechler, General von 163
Kurds xiv, 251
Kursk 158
Kuwait 247

Lamb, Roger 149
"Lament of Ur" 99
Langer, Susanne K. 55
Laos 271
Le Loi 245
LeBlanc, Nicolas 152
Lee, Robert E. 156
Leibnitz, Baron Gottfried von 146
Lenin, Nikolai 197
Leonardo da Vinci 146
Libya 255
Lichnowsky, Prince Karl Max 177, 184
Liddell Hart, Basil H. 157, 210
Livy 71, 92
Lloyd George, David 185
Lorenz, Konrad 3-4
Louis IX, King 85
Louis XIV, King 144, 151
Luther, Martin 142
Luxembourg 181

McCarthy, Joseph 143
MacDonald, Captain Charles 7, 8
M'Gauran, Edward 149
McNaughton, John 193
Mahabharata 108-9, 112-16 *passim*, 125, 138
    Bhagavad Gita 118-21
Mahler, Gustav 165
Manning, Frederick: *Her Privates We* 159
Mao Tse-Tung 244, 260
Maring 30, 31-2, 54
Marlborough, Duke of 24, 28, 163
Marshall, S.L.A. 11, 12, 212
Martí, José 245
Martindale, Don 20
Marxism, Asian 254
Mather, Increase 104-5
Matthias, Emperor 85
Maurice of Nassau 147
Merchant, Carolyn 226-7
Mesnil-Durand, François 152
Mesopotamia 65, 91, 95-6, 99, 100

Michael, St 135, 136, 137
Middle East 243
"military-industrial complex" 192
military training and discipline 4, 7, 11-12, 17, 23
  citizen militia 193
  officer elite and peasant army 5, 77, 147-8, 154
  See also honor and glory; strategy and tactics; warrior; weapons
Mills, James 87
Moltke, Helmuth von 177, 179, 180-1, 190, 199
Mongolia 217
Mont St Michel 136
Montagnards 251
Morocco 217
Münzer, Thomas 131
music 19, 165-6
  dance and song of primitive people 26, 29, 30, 32, 36-7, 73
  Eskimo's songs 46
Muskie, Edmund 229
Muslims See Islam
Mussolini, Benito 187
My Lai 34-8 passim, 248
myth and ritual:
  chaos myth 55-65
  in Christianity 130, 133, 134, 135, 136
  The Song of Roland 136-9
  death of parent avenged 49, 50, 53
  guilt, trial and punishment 96-8, 104, 130, 233
  historicizing of 68-9
  monarch, perception of 90-4, 96-7, 99-100
  of mourning death 38, 239
  peasant-based societies 76, 77, 85, 233, 236
  ritual killing (sacrifice) 54, 56, 60
  taboos and purification rites 26, 27, 30-1, 32, 33, 36, 37, 39, 40, 213, 232
  warfare 17, 18, 19, 21-65 passim, 73, 74, 126, 145, 213, 235-6
  of city-states 65-9
  guerrilla-type 246
  origin of, hypothesis 34
  revenge as motive 35, 37, 38, 41-55 passim

  See also religion

Nagasaki 221
Napoleon (and Napoleonic wars) 93, 145, 152-7 passim, 163, 164, 165, 210
Nasserism 254
Neolithic people 20-6, 34, 35, 50, 54, 69, 213, 235-6
  See also primitive people
Newman, Randy 208
Nicaragua 247, 255
Nicholas II, Czar: World War I 8, 85, 172-6 passim, 178, 180, 183, 190, 199
Nicolson, Arthur 184
Nietzsche, Friedrich 242
Nixon, Richard 201
nuclear armament and warfare 157, 192, 217-25, 240-1, 243

objectives See goals and objectives
Ojibway 24, 28
Oman, Sir Charles 107
O'Neil, Thomas (Tip) 208
oppression, freedom from (as goal) 246, 252, 260
Orokaiva 30-1
Ortega y Gasset, José 145
Ovid 226
Owen, Wilfred 144

Paléologue, Maurice 172, 182-3
Palestine (ancient) 66, 89, 93, 97, 101
Palestine (modern) 217, 247
Papago Indians 31, 33, 58, 59, 60
Pascal, Blaise 146
Paton, Margery 210
peasant-based societies 4, 26
  children 79-85, 94-5, 202
  family-structure 79-86
  goods and power 74-81, 84
  government, tactics of 252
  monarch, perception of 90-4, 96-7, 99-100
  peasant rebellions 98-9, 100-1
  religious myths 90-4, 96-100
  ruling elite 75-8, 82-7, 90-4, 96-100, 190-1

social structure of hierarchic castes 76, 78-82 *passim*, 99
undermining factors 253
warfare 5, 70, 76, 77, 82, 85, 86, 89-90, 92, 93, 147-8, 154
   as divine chastisement 99-101, 104-5
   failure in 92-3, 97-8, 100, 102, 103
   women 79-80, 82, 83
Perls, Fritz 9, 12, 38, 71, 95, 215
Peru 248
Philhelene 131
Plains Indians 24, 25, 32
Plato: *Crito* 96
Pliny 226
PLO 247
Poincaré, Raymond 172, 182
Poland 217
political goal 17, 18, 25, 70-105
potato famine 253
Pourtalès, Count Friedrich von 175-6
power (as goal) 3, 19, 54
powerlessness:
   feeling threatened 189-207, 233
   tactics against 246
prestige *See* honor and glory
primitive people 20-65
   and chaos myth 55-65
   dance and song 26, 29, 30, 32, 36-7, 73
   decoration of the body 26, 30, 73, 74
   food and eating 21, 22, 26, 30, 31, 61, 72, 73
   killing 27-31, 38, 42, 43, 49
   sacrifice 54, 56, 60
   purification rites 26, 27, 30-1, 36, 37, 39, 40
   taboos 26-7, 30-1, 31-2, 33, 61, 213, 232
   warfare 3, 20-54, 61, 209, 235-6
      revenge as motive 35, 37, 38, 41-54
      strategy and tactics 22, 23-4, 25, 27-28, 106
   See also horticultural societies; hunting and gathering tribes; Neolithic people
propaganda 8, 17, 89-93, 244, 256
Prussia 3, 5, 8, 144-5, 147, 151, 162
   See also Frederick the Great
Puritans 104-5, 142-3

racism 251-2
"Rambo" films 256-9
Rauschning, Hermann 196-7
Reagan, Ronald xiii, 255
Reich, Wilhelm 12
religion:
   as divine propaganda 89-93, 252
   modern ideologies 254
   and monarchy 90-4
   peasant-based societies 77, 81, 90-4, 96-100 *passim*
   public trial and punishment a divine ritual 96-8, 104
   war as divine chastisement for social guilt 99-101, 104-5
   See also Christianity; Hebrews; *Iliad*; Islam; *Mahabharata*; myth and ritual
revenge (as goal) 35, 37, 38, 41-55 *passim*, 116, 169, 233
Revere, Paul 250
Revolutionary War 149
Richer, Jean 146
ritual *See* myth and ritual
Romanovs 85, 86
Romans 130, 251
   army 192
   historicized mythology 68
   warfare 69, 210
      failure 92
      and guilt 93, 97-8
      and myth 68
      and religion 66, 132
Roosevelt, Franklin 197
Roosevelt, Theodore 197-8
Roy, Jules 251-2
Rumania 170, 177
Ruskin, John 88
Russia:
   Austria and France, alliance 151
   Austria, Prussia and Russia, French war on 144-5
   England and France, alliance 194, 196
   World War I 8, 85, 168, 172-87 *passim*, 190, 192, 199
   See also U.S.S.R.
Russo-Japanese war 196

Saddam Hussein xiii
Salzberger, Marina 213

INDEX

Saxe, Marshal Maurice de 152
Sazanov, Sergei 172, 173-4, 175, 178, 183, 190, 200
Schlieffen, Count Alfred von 180, 196
Schmoller, Gustav 196
Schubert, Franz 165-6
Schwarzkopf, General Norman 247
Scotland 253
self-image *See* honor and glory
Seneca 226
Serbia: World War I 170-4 *passim*, 176, 177-8, 179, 181-2, 183, 184
Seven Years War 151
sexual patterns and taboos 26, 27, 30-1, 32, 33, 39, 73, 74, 75, 213, 232
Shaka 29
Shakespeare, William: *Henry V* 102
Shasta 209
Shi'ites xiv
Sioux 24
slavery 25
Socrates 96
Somme, Battle of the 158
Song of Roland 136-9, 141
South America 243
Spain 146
Spenser, Edmund 226
Springsteen, Bruce 167
Stalingrad 158
Stallone, Sylvester 256-8
strategy and tactics:
    feudal or aristocratic societies 106-7
    and goals 18-19, 24-5
    passivity and indirection 210-11
    primitive peoples 22-8 *passim*, 106
    sixteenth-eighteenth centuries 146-55
    nineteenth century 156-7, 162
    twentieth century 157, 158, 160, 162, 164
        See also nuclear armament and warfare
Sumeria 96
Sun Tzu 206, 210
Sweden 147, 193
Switzerland 146, 193
Szápáry 173, 174

Tacitus 23, 70
tactics *See* strategy and tactics
Talleyrand 154
Tapuya 209
Tartaglia, Nicolo 146
Tauler, Johannes 131
technological warfare 6, 17, 18, 19, 54, 144-231, 240-1
Teilhard de Chardin, Pierre 121-2, 125
terrorism 243, 244, 245, 246-7, 248-9
Thatcher, Margaret xiii, 229
Tibet 217
Tillich, Paul 127
Timor 29-30
Tisza, István 171-2, 189, 200
Tito, Josep 249-50
Toch, Hans 188, 189-90, 198
trial and punishment 96-8, 104, 233
Trubetzkoi, Prince 173
Truman Doctrine 198
Turkey 174, 198
Turney-High, H.H. 23, 24
Turpin, Archbishop 141

Underhill, John 143
uniforms *See* decoration and dress
United States:
    Civil War 156, 158, 244, 248
    fear of Communism and military might 143, 187, 192, 193, 194, 197-8, 218-23 *passim*
    guerrilla warfare 247
    Indians, attitude toward 104-5, 142-3
    Korean war 12, 187, 212, 217
    military forces 246, 255
    police terrorism 249
    Revolutionary War 149
    Vietnam war 2, 6, 34-40 *passim*, 162, 187, 217, 248
    See also World War I; World War II
urbanization 253
U.S.S.R.:
    fear of capitalism and military might 143, 187, 192, 193, 194, 197-8, 218-23 *passim*
    guerrilla warfare 247
    invasions of Czechoslovakia and Hungary 187
    military forces 246, 255
    nationalistic violence 243, 254
    World War II 158, 216

Vedic tales 65, 67, 68, 90

Vietnam war 2, 6, 34-40 *passim*, 162, 187, 217, 244-5, 248, 256
Villars, Duc de 211
Virgil: *Aeneid* 69, 138
visual effects 6, 19, 148-9, 159
 See also decoration and dress
Voltaire 150

Wagner, Richard 165, 166
warfare:
 basic modes 17
 as community experience 38, 101, 102-3, 105
 definition 1-2
 description 19
 elimination of, difficulty 12
 enemy 246, 254-9
warrior 123-6, 214, 217, 236
 feudal or aristocratic 3, 5, 107-8
 godlike attributes in myths 68, 69
 ideal warrior, characteristics 121
 Iliad and *Mahabharata* 108-23, 125, 126, 138, 208-9
 primitive 23-30, 37, 39, 54
 and soldier, difference 23
 See also honor and glory
weapons:
 personified as enemy 255
 primitive people 20-1, 22, 23
 sixteenth and seventeenth centuries 146, 147
 eighteenth and nineteenth centuries 151, 152, 154, 156
 twentieth century 156-60 *passim*, 192, 218, 219
 nuclear 157, 192, 217-23, 240-1
Wellington, Duke of 211
Westmoreland, General William 213
Will, George F. xiv
William II, Kaiser 175-81 *passim*, 184, 190, 199
Wilson, Sir Henry 185
Winter, S.G., Jr. 221, 222

women:
 burned as witches 225
 "correct" attitude to 244-5
 and nature, identification with 225-7
 in peasant-based societies 79-80, 82, 83
 in primitive societies 25, 26-7, 30-4 *passim*, 73, 74, 209
 in public workforce 229
 warfare xiv-xv, 25, 27, 30-4 *passim*, 208-18 *passim*, 222-3, 240-1
 See also children
World War I 7, 8, 105, 158, 166, 168-87, 192
 bonding between classes 211-12
 leading figures 199-201
 motivation 168-87, 189-90
 myth of 145
 officer class 191, 212
 pace of advance 163
 peace 196
 reality of 159, 160-1
 statistics 4, 168
 trenches 162
 weaponry 157, 159-60
 women 217
World War II 8, 39, 103, 124-5, 143, 162, 221, 245
 bombing 247
 firepower 160
 impact on troops 158
 killing in 11-12
 pace of advance 163
 statistics 4
 women 216-17

Yacef, Saadi 250
Yanomamo 25, 30, 55-6, 60, 61, 62
Ypres, third battle of 158

Zen Buddhism 123
Zimmerman, Alfred 177
Zulus 29, 60